D1153070

GUIDE TO PROJECT MANAGEMENT

OTHER ECONOMIST BOOKS

Guide to Analysing Companies
Guide to Business Modelling
Guide to Business Planning
Guide to Economic Indicators
Guide to the European Union
Guide to Financial Markets
Guide to Investment Strategy
Guide to Management Ideas
Guide to Organisation Design
Numbers Guide
Style Guide

Brands and Branding
Business Consulting
Business Miscellany
Business Strategy
China's Stockmarket
Dealing with Financial Risk
Economics
Emerging Markets
The Future of Technology
Headhunters and How to Use Them
Mapping the Markets
The City
Wall Street

Essential Director
Essential Economics
Essential Investment
Essential Negotiation

Pocket World in Figures

GUIDE TO PROJECT MANAGEMENT

Achieving lasting benefit through
effective change

Paul Roberts

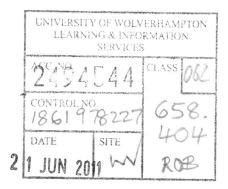

THE ECONOMIST IN ASSOCIATION WITH
PROFILE BOOKS LTD

Published by Profile Books Ltd
3A Exmouth House, Pine Street, London EC1R 0JH
www.profilebooks.com

Typeset in EcoType by MacGuru Ltd
info@macguru.org.uk

Printed in Great Britain by
Clays, Bungay, Suffolk

A CIP catalogue record for this book is available
from the British Library

ISBN 978 1 86197 822 6

The paper this book is printed on is certified by the © 1996 Forest Stewardship Council A.C. (FSC). It is ancient-forest friendly. The printer holds FSC chain of custody SGS-COC-2061

FSC
Mixed Sources
Product group from well-managed
forests and other controlled sources

Cert no. SGS-COC-2061
www.fsc.org
© 1996 Forest Stewardship Council

To Sarah, Matthew and Ruby, with love

Contents

Acknowledgements

I would like to thank my Fifthday business partner, Roger Middleton, who directed and developed our organisation during the time I devoted to writing this book. Thanks also to Stephen Brough at Profile Books for offering sound advice and for editing the text, and to Penny Williams for identifying and making essential changes as the book neared completion. Lastly, I would like to convey my thanks to the many clients of Fifthday who have shown their enthusiasm for this book and helped me better understand the practical challenges which must be overcome in order to implement an effective project management environment.

Introduction

Many businesses do not change when they need to, nor do they change when they have to. If they did, many fewer would fail. But, like people, they only change when they want to.

If a change in the way an organisation achieves successful project outcomes is to be considered, it should be seen as a culture change, involving adjustments in mindset, values and behaviour; it may involve abandoning norms and sacred cows.

Managing projects cannot be separated from managing the whole business. Effective management of "business as usual" delivers evolutionary improvements. Good project management brings about step changes in performance. If projects are to deliver profitable outcomes, then it is as crucial to look outside traditional project environment as it is to look inside. Yet project management is too often considered a discipline that applies only to those called project managers. It is delegated to people who struggle against sometimes impossible odds to deliver a successful outcome. Experience demonstrates that a project requires the collaboration of many stakeholders, including those who commission and finance it, those who will use the end product and those who build it. It takes a whole organisation to make a project a success.

If an organisation is serious about improving the way it manages projects, it will have an opportunity to improve the way it manages its business.

This book explains not just the principles and techniques of project management, but also why it is interconnected with managing a business. Packaging a piece of work and calling it a project does not protect the business from the consequences of its failing. Just as a business can benefit from a well-managed project, so can it be damaged if it fails. There is much to learn from projects that have failed to meet expectations:

■ **The Hubble Space Telescope.** Launched in 1990, NASA's extraordinary project promised to bring pictures of the universe of a clarity never seen before. Despite overcoming enormous technical challenges, the malfunction of a measuring device used during the polishing of the primary mirror rendered every image blurred. NASA suffered huge and adverse publicity as a result, and had to wait three further years before the necessary corrections could be made and its reputation could be reinstated.

- **License application mitigation project.** The Washington State Department of Licensing initiated a five-year, $42m project to computerise the state's vehicle registration and license renewal processes. The budget ballooned, the requirements were drastically changed during the course of the project, and even if it had finished, the outcome would have been obsolete by the time it was completed. After seven years, and when approximately $40m had been spent, the project was cancelled.
- **The Scottish Parliament.** This cost more than ten times the budget for the building. Arguably, the money could have been invested elsewhere and given the taxpayer a better return.
- **The Channel Tunnel.** This is a magnificent technical achievement that did not generate sufficient customer interest to secure its financial future. The project overcame the most extraordinary hurdles, yet was it commissioned because it could be or because it should have been?
- **Kansai International Airport.** Opened on an artificial island off the city of Osaka in Japan in 1994, this extraordinary project was plagued by speculation that planners badly underestimated how much the island would sink, and whether it would do so evenly as the site settled. Six years after opening, the airport's operator was driven to invest in flood protection measures, partly funded by higher landing charges which resulted in a huge drop in traffic. So, although the project overcame many tremendous challenges (including surviving the Kobe earthquake), the operator is still heavily in debt, and in many people's minds, Kansai will be remembered as the "sinking" airport.

These organisations suffered because they failed to recognise how project management could affect their business.

This book aims to help organisations manage the possibility that their projects and businesses may suffer for lack of effective governance. As the saying goes, "A little risk management saves a lot of fan cleaning ..."

1- The components of effective project management

For any new form of management to be accepted, it must be sold to those who do not yet believe in it. Until an organisation has had time to get used to the new way of working, apathy and cynicism towards its introduction are likely. It is common for the promoters of change to be subject to some friendly fire because not everyone will think as positively about project management as they do.

Project management has much to do with identifying and managing the risks a project may face. It can be unsettling for those who are used to solving problems once they have arisen rather than working in advance to prevent the problem arising. This is the essential difference between risk management and "issue" management and is central to the introduction of a project-based culture. Many people may be impressed by the hero who charges in to solve problems, but arguably those who studiously identify things that could go wrong and do a great job of avoiding the need to call in support deserve greater praise and assistance. These two extremes of character can be seen not only in individuals, but also in organisations. There are issue-managing and risk-managing organisations. The former encourage and reward heroics in managing current problems and challenges. The latter praise those who seek in advance to mitigate the likelihood or impact of those problems and challenges. Project management is more effective in an environment that supports the management of risks because this gives the organisation greater control over its fortunes.

This is not the only challenge that promoters of change face. Effective project management, like any form of governance, brings with it a necessary element of administration needed to control the project. This too will be challenged by those who object to the introduction of a new way of working, procedures, routines and regulations. Care should be taken that the administrative measures are not stifling and are light enough to ensure that the right decisions are made by the right people at the right time, and that the value of them is generally understood.

Sooner or later (probably sooner), the cost of introducing a new form of management will be questioned and a budget will be needed if the benefits are to be enjoyed. Senior managers have a great many priorities on which to spend scarce resources so the money being spent on embedding project management must be promoted as an investment with a planned, measurable return. In other words, embedding the principles of project management within an organisation should be managed as a project in itself. This will help mitigate some of the challenges identified above.

Any attempt to alter opinions or working practices will face difficulties. If the approach being described here is considered along the lines of changing a culture, the following risks identified by John Kotter in his book *Leading Change* will be those to be mitigated:

- there is no sense of urgency;
- a powerful, guiding coalition is not adequately created;
- the programme lacks clear vision;
- the vision is poorly communicated;
- essential change is prevented by a will to protect the status quo;
- short-term wins are not systematically planned or delivered;
- victory is declared too soon;
- changes are not anchored in the organisation's culture.

Later chapters consider these risks, especially how a case may be made to introduce effective project management. But throughout the life of a project it is important to remind those involved in and affected by it of the value that effective project management can bring, both in increasing the chances of the project being successful and the organisation benefiting, and in reducing the chances of its failing and the business being damaged.

Selling the benefits

Project management must address issues that matter and that people want to solve. It is essential to ask questions before presenting solutions. What are the problems that the individual or organisation faces? Where do their priorities lie? Where could the greatest gains be achieved for the least investment?

For example, if there is a concern that too much project work is duplicated, it could be suggested that effective project management encourages everyone to work to a plan. But what is the benefit of a plan? It helps to explain that once people are clear about their own and each other's responsibilities, there is likely to be a reduction in rework and duplication. In seeking a form of words persuasive enough to overcome the objections of others, it is often illuminating to ask "So what?" in order to expose the heart of the benefit and to make it clear how the changes the project will bring will make their lives better.

Not every benefit will carry the same weight with every stakeholder. Some, such as the project's end users, will be encouraged to hear that effective project management "provides for the definition, design, implementation and control of quality, thereby reducing the risk of a poor outcome". Others, such as those with commercial responsibilities, will be more interested in knowing that it "requires the justification for the initiative to be regularly reappraised, thereby managing the risk of making a poor investment". Arguments should be tailored to meet the interests of different stakeholders.

It can help to have a list of the benefits to refer to when facing objections to the introduction of project management, or simply to articulate how it will make everyone's lives more ordered. Effective project management allows an organisation to:

- involve the right people at the right time for the right reasons to ensure that the best quality decisions are made;
- encourage customers and suppliers to participate so that the result is mutually beneficial;
- focus on the milestones of the endeavour to encourage a greater and common understanding of what will be delivered;
- reappraise the justification for the initiative regularly, thereby reducing the risk of making a poor investment;
- demonstrate how resources can be used as effectively as possible, thereby allowing their efficient use across the organisation;
- emphasise the risks the project faces so that the likelihood of their occurring and their impact can be managed;
- agree on the definition, design, implementation and control of quality, so reducing the risk of a poor outcome;
- minimise the dangers of unmanaged "change";
- be clear about who does what, thus reducing duplication of effort and removing the potential for "responsibility without authority";
- manage unforeseen problems sensibly and practically.

What are a project's characteristics?

A project has several characteristics that set it apart from an organisation's "business as usual". Business as usual can be characterised as:

- requiring activities to be carried out repeatedly and/or regularly;

- employing resources of similar skill-sets;
- being constrained by annual, cycle-driven deadlines or budgets.

An organisation's typical business-as-usual activities may include:

- delivering its products and/or services to its customers;
- maintaining its financial affairs;
- managing its people;
- keeping its systems and processes running from day to day.

Business as usual is what departments do to maintain the performance of the organisation. If it can be established that a project differs from this, it can be shown why projects need and deserve a tailored form of management. There are several things that differentiate a project from business as usual:

- **A project produces a "defined deliverable".** A project is a vehicle for delivering change. It provides the governance by which an organisation can move from one steady-state to another, from A to B. One result of a project is a "defined deliverable", something which, by its use, enables the new steady-state to operate effectively. So this deliverable must be of sufficient quality to serve the purpose demanded of it.
- **A project has a defined end date.** There are many examples of projects whose deadlines are revised time and time again. For example, the European Fighter Jet has had several delivery dates set and missed. This may be because the defined deliverable was not defined as well as it should have been. A project should have a target end date otherwise it will lose focus, probably go over budget and delay the business from benefiting from its investment. Furthermore, since a project is temporary, any delay in its completion means that those working on it cannot be released for other tasks.
- **A project has a defined budget.** This will extend for the life of the project, in contrast to a departmental budget, which will cover the financial year.
- **A project uses a wide range of resources.** A project will need to benefit from the capabilities, knowledge, skills and experience of people from a wide range of backgrounds from within and, possibly, outside the organisation. However, a business-as-usual

department is, almost by definition, characterised by a narrower range of knowledge and skills.

◪ **People will be involved in peaks and troughs during the project.** Whereas a department is likely to have roughly the same number of people working in it throughout the financial year, a project will use a variety of people at different times in its life. For instance, the people specifying what the project must achieve will probably be most heavily involved at the beginning and at the end, whereas those developing the end product may be most involved during the middle phase.

◪ **A project has a life cycle.** Philip Larkin, a 20th-century English poet, once described the structure of a novel as having "a beginning, a muddle and an end", and many projects feel as though they are in a constant muddle. A project needs attention every day to reduce the risk of disorder and confusion, but it also needs direction from senior managers to ensure that it starts and stops according to plan. So the beginning is intended to create governance suitable for the project's management, and the end is to make sure that the project has an outcome that meets expectations.

Business as usual may share some of the hallmarks of a project. For instance, every month management reports will be produced to assist the company's decision-making. These reports are defined deliverables, but their creation is a repeatable, low-risk activity that does no more than maintain the steady-state of business. Similarly, business as usual requires a defined budget. However, it is usually calculated in order to maintain or improve performance during the coming year.

A project is intended to deliver a step change. Such changes may transform processes, performance or culture. In seeking to improve something, a project is moving firmly into a territory where expectations are less easy to predict or manage. It must produce something that, perhaps, has not been produced before, at least not in the same circumstances. There will be expectations about when the project will be completed, how much it will cost and what it will deliver. Articulating a clear and commonly held understanding of these variables is what makes each project both unique and risky.

Risk is a feature of projects. That so many fail is often because the risk of failure has been managed inadequately. Common reasons for failure include:

- inadequacy of the plan;
- absence of a plan;
- poor monitoring or control;
- unmanaged change;
- inadequate communication;
- constrained budgetary provision;
- poor management of expectations.

If uncorrected, such failures will lead to any one or combination of the following:

- missed deadlines;
- exceeded budgets;
- substandard quality.

Time, cost and quality are the three criteria by which failure is most commonly measured. But what about success? Can a project be judged a success if it delivers:

- on time;
- to budget;
- to specification?

These may be measures of successful project management, but they are not adequate measures of a successful project. A project may result in a fit-for-purpose outcome, on time and on budget, and may have excited those who were involved, but did it make a positive difference? If it failed in this respect, what was the point of the investment? A successful project is best characterised by the change it delivers.

How can projects deliver change?

Projects are undertaken to produce benefits and add value. The outcome should result in benefits that outweigh the investment. Later chapters will consider how to describe and quantify benefits, but first it is important to understand how the comparison of benefits and costs can help to define the scope of the project.

Figure 1.1 illustrates a company's plan to develop operating procedures that its offices will be required to implement to gain savings from consistent and improved working practices. There are clear dependencies. For example, none of the implementations can happen until the operating procedures have been developed.

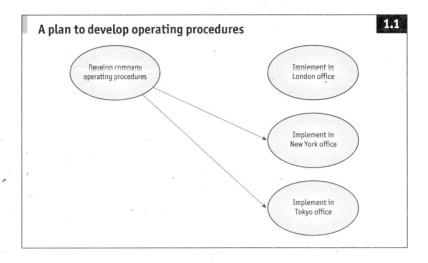

A plan to develop operating procedures `1.1`

Develop company operating procedures

Implement in London office

Implement in New York office

Implement in Tokyo office

How many projects are needed to deliver this outcome? It could be four, one for each area of work. Or it could be two, one to develop the procedures and one to implement them in the offices. Or perhaps there would be economies from treating the whole endeavour as one project.

The decision is made easier when taking into account the value that must result. None of the implementations can take place if the operating procedures are not developed. But would the initiative be viable if it was not implemented in the Tokyo office? This is not clear. The critical question is whether the exclusion of Tokyo would so significantly reduce the benefits of the initiative that the investment could no longer be justified.

In any project there will be a point at which the investment being made is outweighed by the expected return on that investment. In this way, a project and a commercial business are no different. The question about how many projects there are can be addressed by taking a commercial perspective, as illustrated in Figure 1.2 overleaf.

The development work on the left-hand side of Figure 1.2 will contribute to the costs of the project, while the implementation activities, although requiring some investment, will principally contribute to the generation of value. Whether the investment can be justified depends on knowing what value each implementation will generate. One may be insufficient, two may be enough and perhaps the third would be needed to make the case indisputable. Therefore, all four areas of work should fall under the same governance to ensure that the intended positive difference between

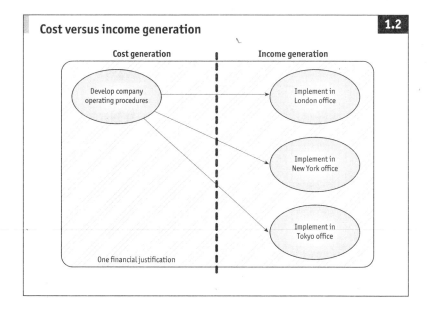

Cost versus income generation 1.2

Cost generation | Income generation

Develop company operating procedures

Implement in London office

Implement in New York office

Implement in Tokyo office

One financial justification

costs and benefits is protected. This balance, with cost on one side and income (or benefit) on the other, is the foundation of any individual project. It answers the crucial question, why do we want to undertake this project?

What is a project?

Every characteristic described so far has helped to describe the nature of projects, but what is a project? Many definitions exist, including the following:

- a unique set of events with a main goal and defined objectives and agreed plans for achieving that goal;
- an activity with a specified beginning and end date that is intended to meet stated objectives;
- a temporary effort undertaken to create a unique product or service;
- any organised campaign to change/improve something.

However, none of these properly consider a project in the wider sense that it delivers the outcome, including the benefits that justify it.

A project is better defined succinctly as a temporary management environment created to deliver a specified outcome according to a defined business justification:

- **A temporary management environment** A project can be thought of as a commercial company intended to last for a defined period. It will share many of the characteristics of a business, being composed of people, objectives, plans and controls. It is the governance that knits them together and provides the order and structure that maximises the probability of success. The management environment needs to stay in place no longer than it takes to implement the specified outcome.
- **Created to deliver a specified outcome.** This is the goal, objective, product, service or situation referred to in some of the other definitions. The desired result must be defined in terms of timescale, cost and quality.
- **According to a defined business justification.** This is why the temporary management environment has been created. It is not simply to produce a result; that result must benefit the organisation.

What is project management?

Project management is doing what it takes to make sure that all those with an interest in the project always have the same clear answers to the following questions:

- **Who needs to be involved in managing a project?** There may be many people who have an interest in the project for a wide variety of reasons. These are the project's stakeholders. While the project may benefit from their views and opinions, not all of them need to be involved in managing it. So it is necessary to establish clearly the roles, responsibilities and reporting arrangements of those specifically charged with directing and managing a project from start to completion.
- **What must a project deliver?** A way of describing an outcome is to talk of it in terms of a deliverable. So the project must deliver a defined outcome such as the company operating procedures described in Figure 1.1 on page 9. However, there will also be deliverables needed along the way, all of which must be articulated sufficiently well in advance to increase the likelihood of achieving the intended result. Examples may include a project

plan, a feasibility study report, a business case, a requirements specification, a marketing report or a piece of machinery.

▰ **When must it deliver?** It is clearly necessary to identify a date for the end of the project, but there will be additional milestones that must be achieved throughout its life such as those identified above. Each must have its own completion date.

▰ **How much must be invested?** How much will the project cost? The many projects that exceed their budgets are salutary evidence that costs must remain in focus throughout a project's life.

▰ **Why is this project necessary?** If this question cannot be answered authoritatively and persuasively, it is doubtful that the project is justifiable.

Each of these five questions must be answered, and the answers must be genuinely understood and agreed by a project's authorities not merely at the beginning but also throughout a project's life. Furthermore, they must be clearly documented as part of the governance of the project.

But what about the environment outside the project? John Donne, an English poet and preacher who died in 1631, wrote, "No man is an island, entire of itself." The same is true of projects; they exist in a world in which they must compete with the demands of business as usual and the benefits other projects are proposing. Therefore, the wider organisation must support the concept of project management, not just a single project.

The components of effective project management

For a project to thrive, it must exist within surroundings that are congenial to its commissioning, management, funding, specification, building, testing and delivery. Projects launched in the wrong environment rarely succeed. The characteristics of a project-focused environment are illustrated in Figure 1.3.

The extent to which any of the components in Figure 1.3 already exist is a measure of an organisation's maturity in project management. It follows that there will be not only different levels of competence in different organisations, but also a path from one level of maturity to the next which will depend very much on the culture and needs of the organisation.

Project sponsors and owners

If projects are to thrive, they need people who will promote them actively. The business case described earlier is the sales pitch. The document itself

Characteristics of a project-focused environment **1.3**

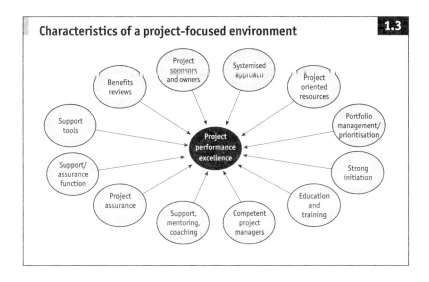

will not sell the merits of the project, or make decisions about when and whether the project should start or stop. This is the role of its sponsors, and those charged with delivering a beneficial result. However, the discipline of project management also requires sponsorship. Given that not everyone will be instantly persuaded of the merits of this way of working, enough senior and authoritative individuals in the organisation must be prepared to endorse the approach and maintain its influence and value.

A systemised approach

This is a defined and clearly articulated approach to project management. Sometimes it is called a methodology and is often a document that describes the processes, responsibilities and deliverables involved in the approach. Methods can be wildly misunderstood. They can be considered too expensive, too bureaucratic or too restrictive. It is important that the value of a particular systemised approach is properly considered before it is either backed or dispensed with.

A methodology is a support for management, not a substitute for it. It is only useful when applied. No value will come from an operating manual nobody uses.

A systemised approach usually includes:

- an overview to articulate the methodology sufficiently well to describe its scope and demonstrate how the parts hold together;

- a list of project roles and responsibilities to outline the expectations placed on the key stakeholders;
- procedures describing the steps people must take to make the project a success;
- a list of results describing what the procedures must produce;
- templates to outline the look and feel of the most common deliverables;
- examples that provide guidance on what a completed template might look like;
- hints and tips to serve as a body of reference for answers to questions that are likely to come up.

Most companies would use a book like this or an industry-standard project management methodology as the starting point for creating their own tailored approach. There are plenty of methodologies that focus on information technology (IT) projects. Surprisingly, there are few off-the-shelf pure project management methodologies available. A leading example of a pure project management approach is PRINCE.*

PRINCE (an acronym derived from Projects IN Controlled Environments) recognises projects as endeavours that may take place in a variety of environments, both technical and non-technical. It was originally developed in the 1980s by the UK's Central Computer and Telecommunications Agency (CCTA) as standard for IT project management. However, it was quickly recognised as an approach that could be tailored to the needs of almost any project. Its wide use identified improvements and changes that were incorporated in PRINCE2,† which was released in 1996 and is used in more than 50 countries.

Whichever method an organisation chooses, it must satisfy important criteria. It should be:

- successfully used elsewhere;
- robust, internally consistent and free of evident fault;
- clear enough to be sold and communicated to others, readily and easily understandable;

---

* PRINCE® is a Registered Trade Mark and a Registered Community Trade Mark of the Office of Government Commerce, and is Registered in the US Patent and Trademark Office.

† PRINCE2™ is a Trade Mark of the Office of Government Commerce.

- viable – it must be able to promise real value in return for the investment made in it;
- scaleable – as it must serve a range of projects that vary in size, complexity and risk;
- relevant – because it should cover the wide discipline of project management. There are many methodologies that focus on a limited technical approach to project management that may be relevant only to those technical projects.

Project oriented resources
Any organisation may have within it a project manager or two. Whether the wider organisation is literate in the language of project management is another matter, yet the whole organisation's structure has a part to play in making project management effective. If the organisation structure is unsupportive, projects are more likely to fail.

Portfolio management and prioritisation
Few organisations will undertake only one project. It is common to have a portfolio of projects that have to be identified, selected, prioritised, commissioned and initiated. This usually results in a number of projects competing for attention for a variety of reasons, including:

- mandatory or legal imperatives;
- commercial opportunities;
- cost-reduction opportunities;
- learning and developmental opportunities.

However, in their enthusiasm to deliver everything, many organisations' efforts lead to new problems such as:

- shortage of funds;
- conflict between projects;
- demanding or unrealistic timescales;
- increases in risk;
- failure to deliver business as usual.

To combat these problems it is best to prioritise projects using several criteria to rank initiatives and then to back only those that are most deserving and rewarding.

Strong initiation

Projects need the best start in life if they are to thrive. Initiation is a specific project management phase within which a project's management environment is created. During this phase, the merits of the project are further scrutinised to confirm its viability so that, if worthy, it may be planned within agreed expectations of time, cost and quality. The project management team, including the project manager, may then guide it towards its various measures of success. Without a robust and reliable initiation process, projects are unlikely to succeed.

Education and training

Each person in a project needs to know something of the project's management environment and the wider organisation that nurtures it. If a culture of effective project management is to be encouraged, the language used in managing projects must be clearly understood and commonly applied by all those involved.

Training will help to bring about the desired culture change but, like each of the other components listed here, it will be of little value on its own. At best, training will provide people with the skills and knowledge to do things better or differently. Training may motivate people, but the investment in it will be worth little if the principles and techniques it promoted are not applied in the workplace.

Competent project managers

For a project to be successfully delivered it requires competent project managers. They must understand project management and have appropriate project experience. It is not good enough that they are competent specialists with knowledge of IT, or pharmaceuticals, or engineering. Their position in the project may be enhanced if they are literate in the nature of the initiative, but they are employed as a project manager to manage the time, cost and quality expectations of the project's stakeholders. Project managers are like the hub of a wheel, holding the spokes together so that motion can be achieved. But they are not the only, or indeed most important, people involved in the project. There will be others such as the project's sponsors and owners who will have considerable influence.

Project management is a specific discipline deserving investment; organisations involved in a significant amount of project work would do well to recognise that.

Support, mentoring and coaching

The extent to which an organisation offers support, mentoring and coaching is a good measure of its commitment to project management. For individuals and organisations to learn and grow in competence, it is essential that investment is made in their development.

However, this does not mean that companies should necessarily invest in yet more training. The turnaround of an organisation so often depends on the gradual embedding of preferred practice in real projects. The investment made in training, education and recruitment will be worthwhile only when people work and learn together.

This can be achieved in many ways, including the following:

- **Post-training coaching events.** A cost-effective way of ensuring that the lessons of a course become embedded in a person's way of working soon after receiving the training.
- **Working lunch refreshers.** It is helpful to refresh knowledge and skills with support in specific topics of interest.
- **Skills forums.** An ideal way to share experience, improve the systemised approach and raise everyone's standards. However, without proper ownership and control, forums can quickly become worthless.
- **Newsletters.** A helpful way of describing the ever-changing context within which the projects sit to an audience that would otherwise look mostly inwards.
- **Road-shows.** Like newsletters, these aim to maintain an interest in the relevance of project management. They invite participation but require investment. However, in mature project management cultures it is not unusual for two or more road-shows to be scheduled throughout the year.
- **Intranet sites** (web-based sites available to a restricted, usually internal, audience). Common today, intranets provide a means of storing and making accessible the organisation's systemised approach so that it is not just available to anyone deemed to need it, but also represents the most current, single version of the truth (svot).
- **Buddying.** This works best when it is requested rather than enforced. Individuals are assigned a buddy with whom they can learn more about themselves and project management. This has huge advantages in that it is an organic, self-regulating approach, becoming only as large a mechanism as it needs to

be; if people find little value in it, they will cease to participate. It allows participants to share experience, ask for advice in an unthreatening, informal environment and grow as managers and leaders.

Project assurance

This is a mechanism by which projects may be checked against a series of criteria to ascertain both the effectiveness of their management and their continued potential to deliver the intended benefit. Assurance does not automatically mean audit. Indeed, the use of the word "audit" can make people fearful which in turn may make it difficult to uncover problems and their causes. A range of assurance measures can be used to give an organisation greater confidence in managing projects. The purpose in all cases is to review the project (not the project manager) with the aim of increasing the likelihood of a successful result. The following are forms of project assurance:

- **Project management health check.** The project is reviewed (perhaps by invitation) by project management experts from elsewhere in the organisation, often drawing on the use of buddies. The outcome will be a report identifying areas of strength that could be promoted to other people and actions that need to be taken. There may or may not be a need for an external party to check progress following the report.
- **Project management internal audit.** The project is reviewed formally, perhaps as a result of an alert or some evidence of a failing. It is likely that the audit will be conducted by someone who is impartial and competent to identify opportunities for improvement and propose solutions for the project management team to implement. Progress is tracked by the reviewer.
- **Project management external audit.** This is similar to an internal audit but is conducted by an external party to specific terms of reference. As with any formal audit, there will be a requirement to attend to any areas of concern within a defined timetable, after which some sanctions may be applied.

Although an audit can sometimes be an uncomfortable experience, project assurance should be seen as a natural and supportive part of the discipline of project management because it seeks to improve processes, people and projects.

Support/assurance function

A support/assurance function (SAF) is often called a project or programme office. Indeed, naming conventions are merely one area in which there is a huge opportunity for alternatives. Most mature, project-focused organisations have some form of project support and/or assurance function. Its scope, objectives and way of working will be as unique as the project(s) it seeks to support. Many will offer a combination of support and assurance to an audience potentially composed of the most junior and senior extremes of management. The services it offers may be equally diverse, ranging from administrative support to the development and maintenance of an organisation's approach to project management. Where it is placed in the organisation will depend on its brief; it may support one project, a portfolio of projects, or a company-wide programme (which will be described later).

Support tools

There are a great many project support tools on the market, most of them software-based. Most provide helpful but limited support in developing and maintaining a plan. However, during recent years, the features they include have become more sophisticated. There is now software that will capture progress information and share the resulting analysis in appropriate formats with the rest of the organisation.

Despite these advances, project tools remain limited by the data they contain, the people who operate them and the organisation's capacity to absorb them into its working practices. Because of the complex nature of their installation, organisations can be reluctant to implement software tools that may have to satisfy the needs of many stakeholders and can affect working practices. Expectations of the value they can deliver compared with the operational risk of their installation should be carefully considered.

Benefits reviews

As the purpose of a project is to deliver a transformation that injects value to the organisation, it is surprising how few organisations conduct post-project reviews to assess the success of their projects.

At best, a completed project will have succeeded in producing a deliverable of acceptable quality, on time and to budget. But these are not measures of true project success; all they determine is that the project finished. The organisation deserves evidence that the promised return on investment has been achieved.

In this respect, the mark of a mature project management culture is that it contains a benefits realisation phase in its project management life cycle, and conducts a benefits review during or at the end of this phase. Yet even when the benefits realisation phase is part of the systemised approach, the benefits review does not always take place automatically. Although many organisations recognise that benefits need time to accrue after a project is complete, a much smaller proportion actually measure them to confirm that they outweighed the investment made. This is strange, given that the point of a project is to deliver measurable value. However, it is understandable. Benefits are notoriously difficult to quantify. For instance, how can a commercial value be placed on increased customer satisfaction or improved morale? If a benefit cannot be valued, it is almost impossible to determine how much should be spent on delivering it. Benefits must be quantified at the outset and measured at the end of the benefits realisation phase if an organisation is to judge whether or not it made a worthwhile investment in the project.

2 Conceiving projects

Where do projects come from? Are they part of a master plan or a response to a challenge or a problem? Most organisations' projects are a combination of both. Some companies prefer a selection of projects that suits their strategy; others prefer a mix that responds to their immediate operational needs; and many fall in between. In all cases, the lowest common denominator is a list of projects.

As the list lengthens, the implications for the way a company controls its projects grow. For instance, its structure may have to change in order to

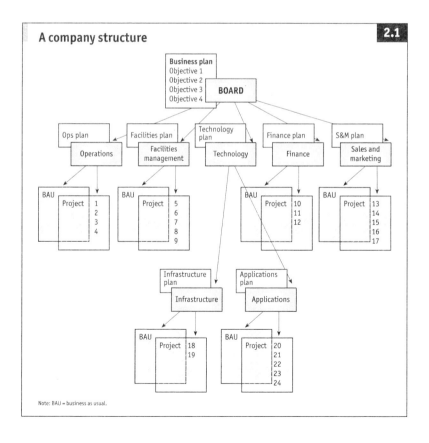

A company structure 2.1

Note: BAU = business as usual.

accommodate managing resources across several projects or it may have to become more flexible about setting priorities.

There are several ways of meeting the challenge of identifying projects.

Project identification by department

Figure 2.1 on the previous page is an example of a company structure. The board oversees five directorates: operations; facilities management; technology; finance; sales and marketing. Technology is subdivided into infrastructure and applications.

How a company identifies projects usually depends on its structure. In the example, the annual business plan starts with the board and cascades through the departments. Each layer of management looks at the plan from its own perspective, identifying activity for which it will be responsible and which will help achieve the board's objectives. This is likely to be a combination of business as usual and a portfolio of several projects. The desired outcome is that by the time the plan has percolated through every layer of management, everyone knows what part they have to play in it.

Each department has a portfolio of projects to deliver, funded from a proportion of the annual budget. As the budget holder, the head of each department is often given ownership of those projects. However, their role will not be easy; as well as carrying out business as usual, they have a portfolio of projects which depend on resources and deliverables from other departments.

This traditional approach to identifying projects is spectacularly inefficient and demonstrates the importance of managing projects differently. Figure 2.2 shows that there are many interdependencies between the projects. For example, Projects 2, 8, 17, 18 and 22 must all be delivered successfully to meet Objective 2 in the business plan. However, successfully delivering those projects may require joint activity and sharing resources with other departments.

The structure is inadequate because it was designed to deliver business as usual, not change. The longer projects stay within departments, the greater is the challenge in co-ordinating them. A specific management approach is needed if the projects are to meet Objective 2.

A classic response is to create a portfolio management governance, which is empowered to oversee every project. This can work, but it may be costly and deliver little value beyond the tactical co-ordination of different activities and use of resources.

There is an alternative. The company could identify the projects

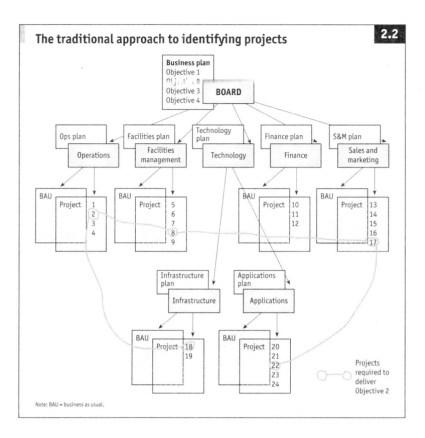

The traditional approach to identifying projects 2.2

Note: BAU = business as usual.

necessary to deliver Objective 2 and assign each its own management team. This way, identifying the portfolio of projects is separated from the constraints of the organisation's structure.

Project identification by business objective

Figure 2.3 overleaf illustrates a radically different way to identify projects.

Projects are not allocated to departments but identified independently after analysis of the business plan's objectives. They are distinguished by their ability to help achieve an objective, and there are fewer of them because they are not multiplied by the number of departments involved in delivering them.

This will have a significant impact on the way the business operates. For any company that delivers much of its business or internal change through projects, the benefits will be significant, not least from avoiding

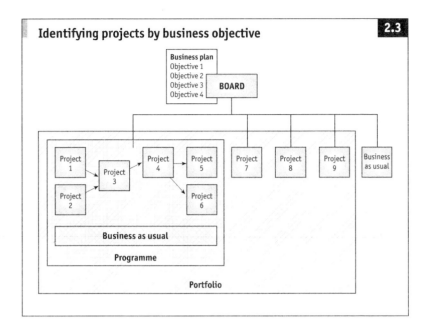

Identifying projects by business objective `2.3`

inefficiencies generated by the passing of a project from one department to another. But there will be a cultural and procedural cost. It is possible to implement this approach only if an organisation is prepared to adopt the basic principles outlined in this guide. Figures 2.2 and 2.3 show the fundamental differences between an organisation that achieves change through departmental activity and one that does it through projects.

This is not to say that the departmental approach cannot be made to work. It may well be the point from which the cultural change begins. But it does not provide effective governance for projects to thrive and deliver successful outcomes. If an organisation is serious about adopting a project-focused approach, it should make sure its projects are based as directly as possible on its business objectives, not on a blinkered departmental vision. Only then is it possible to have faith that the outcome of a project will contribute directly to the strategy.

Before understanding how to derive a project from a company's business plan, it is necessary to know what is meant by a portfolio and a programme.

A portfolio

A portfolio was described earlier as a list of projects. An organisation may have one or many portfolios characterised by a common budget or a common department.

The purpose of creating a portfolio of projects is to increase the likelihood that they will succeed and to reduce the risks of failure arising from undertaking them in a complex and volatile environment. So it is better to define a portfolio as a group of projects gathered into a governable unit to facilitate their effective co-ordination and success.

Unlike a project and a programme, it is likely that the portfolio will never end. As projects are completed new ones take their place, so when judging the success of a portfolio that has no fixed outcome it is necessary to look for a steady stream of signals that:

- projects are being delivered on time;
- projects are being delivered on budget;
- projects are being delivered to specification;
- projects are enabling business benefits to be realised;
- the plan is regularly updated and approved by the business sponsors;
- the portfolio is aligned to the business plan;
- the portfolio frequently contributes to the achievement of business objectives.

These benchmarks apply to projects that fall within a common budget or department. It is possible to conceive a portfolio of projects specifically pulled together to deliver a particular business objective. In other words, a greater degree of intelligence has been applied to the creation of this kind of portfolio because it has an end target in mind. This is a programme.

A programme

A programme is a vehicle for progressing, co-ordinating and implementing an organisation's strategy, specifically by linking an often complex combination of business-as-usual activity and new projects all focused on the delivery of a defined objective. It is not business as usual because a programme seeks to deliver something different.

However, the term is often misused. For many people, a programme is simply a large project. A large project and a programme have similarities. They both:

- seek to deliver a beneficial outcome;
- deserve a special form of management structure.

But the shared characteristics go further than this. Some of the differences are shown in Table 2.1.

Table 2.1 **Differences between a project and a programme**

Project	*Programme*
has relatively few sponsors	has many sponsors
will be a contained disaster if it fails	may be a corporate disaster if it fails
is focused on a deliverable	is focused on a business objective
will deliver benefit after completion	will deliver benefit in phases
has a short- to medium-term lifespan	has a long-term lifespan
has variable risk	is always high risk
has a focused scope	has a wide scope
excludes business-as-usual activity	includes business-as-usual activity

For example, a project may have been identified to deliver a new sales management computer system. It conforms to the characteristics of a project:

- There will be a limited number of sponsors, probably extending little further than the sales manager.
- If the project fails to deliver the new system, the company can fall back on what it has used previously.
- It must deliver an implemented sales management computer system and trained sales staff.
- When the sales force has used the system for some time, the project costs will be recouped through extra or higher-value sales arising from slicker management of leads.
- Implementation may be reasonably expected within a year of the project being planned.
- The risks will be managed mainly within the sales and IT departments.
- The scope can be contained within clear organisational, budgetary, time and geographic boundaries.
- business-as-usual activity should remain largely unaffected by the project (until it is completed).

Compare this project with a programme through which a manufacturer and distributor of potato snacks seeks to enter a new foreign market. The programme will have these characteristics:

- There will be several sponsors, coming from operations, commercial management, distribution, sales, marketing and manufacturing. Virtually no part of the company will remain untouched by this endeavour.
- Failure in the new foreign market could be corporate disaster. At the very least, the sponsoring director might be asked to resign.
- The programme must deliver a series of co-ordinated outcomes which together bring about the business objective of succeeding in the foreign market. Such outcomes may themselves be managed as projects integral to the programme. This series of co-ordinated outcomes has an important implication for the economic justification of the individual projects that fall within the programme. Where a stand-alone project should be commercially justifiable, one that falls within a programme may not be on its own. Some projects within a programme may only exist to enable future projects to be undertaken. If the subsequent projects are shelved, the earlier projects may deliver little or no benefit. The business case for every project in the programme must be considered together if the programme's overall justification is to be properly understood. For instance, the programme in this example may contain a project to produce new packaging for the foreign market. On its own, it would generate no benefits. It is only justifiable as an enabler for benefit-generating projects elsewhere in the programme.
- To minimise the risk of failure, the programme may be designed to deliver benefit in phases, for instance by focusing first on one country in which demand is considered sufficient to outweigh the costs.
- The programme may have a long life, especially if it is split into phases. Conversely, if it is dropped, it may not last as long as anticipated.
- With any programme risk is inevitable. Not only is the company taking a calculated risk with a significant investment, but it is also running the risk that its existing business may be compromised during the programme's lifetime.
- Virtually every part of the business will be engaged in or affected by the programme.

◤ A defining characteristic of a programme, compared with a project, is that its management team must take responsibility not just for the change in activity within its scope but also for business as usual continuing successfully. At least until the first phase has delivered some commercial benefit, the programme will be funded by business as usual, whose resources will be involved in the programme. Furthermore, the company will need everyone to adapt to the demands and challenges of the new business environment the programme will deliver.

In any portfolio there may or may not be technical, strategic or commercial dependencies between the projects – it has not been constructed with them in mind. Instead, the grouping of projects is characterised by their being funded from a common budget or being overseen by a defined part of the organisation. A programme, however, is a portfolio of technically, strategically and/or commercially interlinked projects where the dependencies must be identified and managed if an objective in the business plan is to be met. Furthermore, the nature of programmes suggests that there will often be a degree of business-as-usual management required from within the programme to prepare the business for a new way of working.

Understanding these concepts is essential if projects are to be conceived and managed effectively. Project identification is not only about forming a list of projects; it is also about understanding them sufficiently well to place them in a suitable management environment, which is independent of the underlying organisation structure and which will enable them to thrive.

So although the need for a project may be raised from within one part of an organisation, it is not always the case that the eventual project must be managed, funded and resourced from the same place.

When are projects identified?

The need for a project can arise at any time, but many are identified during the annual planning cycle because the organisation is focusing on what it would like to achieve during the coming year. Yet both the organisation and the outside world will change during that year so a contingency budget should be created for initiatives approved outside the planning cycle.

When a project is identified, three things will apply:

- unless this is the first time the organisation has identified projects, it is likely that there will be a portfolio of projects that are under way, having been commissioned during the previous year, into which the new project may be slotted;
- the project's selection, prioritisation and commissioning should be managed, not left to the whim of budget-holders;
- some basic information must be known about each potential project if informed decisions are to be made about its future.

Most organisations have a pro forma to be used to outline a potential project. This is not only to make sure that subsequent debate is informed, but also formally to place the idea of the project in the organisation's roster of work. Thus the project does not emerge from chaos but is the product of a considered and cost-controlled process.

The pro forma is often called a project outline (see Table 2.2 for a typical example). This simple document seeks to record the answers to the most important questions at this early stage before the project is commissioned.

Table 2.2 **A typical project outline**

Sponsor	The name of the person who has driven the initiative thus far.
Title	The name of the potential project. If the initiative is confidential, use a code name.
Objective	What is the purpose of the potential project? What problem or opportunity is it seeking to address?
Benefits	What benefits may be expected from the project, should it take place? Over what period is the return on investment expected?
Scope	Are there any specific inclusions or exclusions of note?
Key products	What will the project deliver?
Timescale	How long may the project take? Are there any important dates?
Investment	What investment will be necessary and over what period?
Investment needed for the next stage	What investment is necessary for the next stage of the project?
Planning assumptions	What assumptions had to be made when identifying key products, timescales, budgets and benefits?
Risks	What may cause the project to fail? What mitigations may there be for each risk identified?

If the senior managers think there is sufficient merit in the idea mapped out in the project outline and supported by their analysis, there is a chance of it becoming a real project.

There is a greater chance that those debating the merits of one potential project compared with another can do so when the features of each, no matter how scant, are clearly and commonly understood. Project outlines also make it possible to consider how the right projects may be selected, prioritised and commissioned for the vision to be achieved.

The way in which many organisations choose to achieve their vision is to put in place a combination of business-as-usual and change initiatives to deliver step-by-step improvements and value along the way. Once a year, those organisations develop their business plans, the result of which is usually a combination of old and new initiatives that will help achieve the business strategy.

For the most part, the once-a-year effort will focus on the initiatives the board want to deliver and will incorporate a combination of business as usual and change. At this level of the organisation, change is often best described in terms of programmes. Senior managers know that governance is needed to implement the delivery of something significant or new. But although programmes are designed with the innate governance to enable their control, they are still made up of interdependent projects. Add these to the other, smaller improvements that a company needs to make during the year and the organisation may have a large portfolio of initiatives that demands and deserves some form of overarching continuous governance.

Continuity is at the heart of the argument for a form of management of business change. Projects are being identified all the time, so there is a significant risk that initiatives can be identified and initiated that have little or no reference to the business plan, its sponsors or the organisation's vision for the future.

In recognising that a relationship exists between a project and the business plan, it should be possible to confirm that the list of projects being proposed or undertaken will substantially deliver the company's change agenda. So if an organisation wishes to know its true destination, it should look to the portfolio of projects it has chosen to invest in by design, by instinct or by mistake.

An organisation needs a clear line of sight between the business plan and its portfolio of projects, and assurance that the projects it undertakes will deliver the change it desires. Three steps can help to establish and maintain this line of sight. They are as easy to remember as ABC:

- **Articulating** – describing the business plan so it helps to identify projects.
- **Balancing** – making sure that the proposed portfolio of projects is constructed to deliver across a range of measures.
- **Commissioning** – sponsoring those projects that will make sure the organisation delivers the change component of the business plan.

Articulating

There are many guidelines about what should be in a business plan. Each organisation will probably have something that it uses year after year. As a result, each example will vary in its ability to describe effectively how the company's targets can be met.

Whatever the format of the business plan, a common starting point is needed. It should be possible to express the business plan as a series of statements that both summarise the content and help to identify projects. The following list, which took no more than an hour to compile, is a summary of a real organisation's wordy business plan. The company will:

- retain its most important clients;
- win new clients;
- secure recurring revenues rather than one-off fees;
- further its alliance partnerships;
- deliver increased revenue;
- deliver increased margins;
- become number one in its marketplace;
- undertake short-term, high-yield projects;
- deliver a wider range of products;
- reduce its implementation timescales;
- reduce its implementation costs;
- deliver minimum maintenance products;
- engage in fixed-price or shared-risk initiatives;
- prioritise and justify every initiative it undertakes;
- have market-leading product quality and testing processes;
- use cutting-edge product implementation processes;
- manage its projects using repeatable, proven principles and techniques;
- use new and innovative technologies;
- provide opportunities to help retain experienced staff;

◪ apply lessons learned from experience;
◪ attract and develop junior staff;
◪ increase the gap between itself and its competitors.

This may seem a random set of statements drawn from a document. It may be true that the business plan lacks focus or may fail across a range of success criteria. So before identifying projects that can contribute to its success, the business plan should be balanced.

Balancing

The statements above can be categorised in groups (see Table 2.3).

Table 2.3 **Grouping business plan statements**

What will commercial success look like?	*How will clients judge success?*
The company will:	*The company will:*
• retain its most important clients	• deliver a wider range of products
• bring in new clients	• reduce its implementation timescales
• secure recurring revenues rather than one-off fees	• reduce its implementation costs
• further its alliance partnerships	• deliver minimum maintenance products
• deliver increased revenue	• engage in fixed-price or shared-risk initiatives
• deliver increased margins	
• become number one in its marketplace	
• undertake short-term, high-yield projects	
Which processes must be excellent?	*How will we show we have learned and grown?*
The company will:	*The company will:*
• prioritise and justify every initiative	• use new and/or innovative technologies
• have market-leading product quality and testing processes	• provide opportunities to help retain experienced staff
• use cutting-edge product implementation processes	• apply lessons learned from experience
• manage its projects using repeatable, proven principles and techniques	• attract and develop junior staff
	• increase the gap between itself and its competitors

This is a simple and early example of a business plan expressed as a balanced score card of measures, a technique developed by Robert Kaplan and David Norton to describe what strategic success could look like. An organisation's targets and measures are described in four balanced quadrants: commercial, customer, process and learning. When combined they provide a consistent and sound means of describing how to reach and measure success. This helps to identify programmes and portfolios of projects the organisation must undertake if it is to be successful.

The thinking behind the balanced score card is that commercial success can come from selling customers what they want, but the processes needed to deliver the products and services they buy must be sleek and effective, and they get that way by using people and intellectual capital in which there is continuous investment. The investment comes from prior commercial success, so the approach looks circular.

Because the quadrants are linked by this logic, the list of statements must be checked for consistency. Engaging in fixed-price or shared-risk initiatives may not permit increased margins; developing junior staff may be a challenge while using new and innovative technologies that may create redundancies. Some objectives may be beyond the organisation's control; the most important clients may not buy the wider range of products. An organisation must ask itself: "Which would matter most: client engagement or product leadership?" If the statements are inconsistent, so may be the business plan from which they were derived and the portfolio of projects that stem from it.

Table 2.3 is not complete, however. There are no measures. If these statements are to be used to confirm the portfolio's contribution to the business plan, each must be quantified. Table 2.4 overleaf contains examples from each quadrant.

Despite this further analysis, it is still not possible to identify projects that will help to achieve these targets. Not every target will rely solely on a project or series of projects. Some will depend on increased or improved productivity such as reducing implementation timescales. Others may require increased vigilance but not a change of behaviour, for example securing recurring revenues rather than one-off fees. Some targets may be achieved by a combination of projects and business as usual; some projects already under way or under consideration might make a limited contribution to the achievement of one or more targets. However, there may be targets that can be achieved specifically as a result of a project or programme of projects. For instance, if a company wishes to implement its own project management method based on an industry-recognised standard, this may need to be commissioned as a single project.

Table 2.4 **Revised business plan statements**

What will commercial success look like?	*How will clients judge success?*
• secure recurring revenues rather than one-off fees	• reduce its implementation timescales
Revised:	*Revised:*
• During the coming year, the company will secure $500,000 worth of recurring revenues from clients that have always previously made one-off payments	• During the forthcoming year, the company will deliver three implementations of its standard product in seven weeks rather than nine
Which processes must be excellent?	*How will we show we have learned and grown?*
• manage its projects using repeatable, proven principles and techniques	• provide opportunities to help retain experienced staff
Revised:	*Revised:*
• During the coming year, the company will implement its own project management method based on an industry-recognised standard	• The company will reduce the turnover of staff with more than ten years' experience by 20%
• During the coming year, the company will deliver two projects using the new method	

So it is possible to derive some projects from the business plan. But an organisation moving towards a project-focused approach must be sure that other projects already under way or proposed without reference to the business plan are likely to contribute to its strategy. The organisation must assure itself that it has a portfolio of proposed and actual projects that is aligned to its vision.

This is done by challenging, not least because work on the existing portfolio has commenced. While it may seem sensible to abandon one project in favour of another, money has already been invested and it is a commercial decision to write off an investment, not an intellectual one.

However, this argument is helpful in understanding why time was taken to create a balanced set of strategic measures. The main motivation of many organisations will be to achieve the measures in the commercial quadrant, but projects and business-as-usual activity will be needed to deliver across the balanced score card if ultimate commercial success is to be achieved.

A technique that can help achieve this involves three ingredients:

- the business plan expressed as success criteria;
- the existing project portfolio;
- any newly proposed projects.

By comparing the existing portfolio and proposed projects with the list of targets, it is possible to determine the fit. If the relevant information is available, it is a relatively simple exercise. Ask whether each existing or proposed project's contribution to achieving each measure in turn is direct, indirect, partial or absent (see Table 2.5).

Table 2.5 **Project contribution to strategy**

Strategic imperative	Project 1	Project 2	Project 3
Will this project contribute to the company securing $500,000 worth of recurring revenues in the coming year from clients that have always previously made one-off payments?	Direct	Indirect	Absent
Will this project contribute to the company delivering three implementations during the coming year of its standard product in seven weeks rather than nine?	Absent	Absent	Absent
Will this project contribute to the company implementing its own project management method based on an industry-recognised standard during the coming year?	Indirect	Absent	Absent
Will this project contribute to the company delivering two projects in the coming year using the new project management method?	Absent	Absent	Absent
Will this project contribute to company reducing its turnover of staff of more than 10 years' experience by 20% during the coming year?	Absent	Direct	Absent

Several significant conclusions can be drawn from this simple example:

- No projects are contributing to the company delivering speedier implementations. Customers will not be pleased.
- Even if the company develops a new project management approach (of which there is little evidence), no projects will use it.

◪ Project 3 is making no contribution to the company's strategic aims. Why is it being funded?

The power of this technique extrapolated across every strategic imperative and all existing and proposed projects is enormous. Here are some questions that can help in deciding which projects should be pursued:

◪ Are there projects contributing directly to achieving specific strategic imperatives, making them more likely to be met?
◪ Which strategic imperatives are unsupported by projects and so run the risk of being missed?
◪ Which projects are not contributing to any strategic imperative?
◪ Do the projects identified above give cause to reconsider whether all strategic imperatives have been identified?
◪ Is there a balanced portfolio of projects contributing across the four quadrants?
◪ Is the organisation focusing on one of the four quadrants at the expense of the others?
◪ Is the organisation more concerned about measurements than objectives?
◪ Is the organisation conducting projects because it wants to, not because it needs to?

Managers should ask themselves such questions. If direct, indirect, partial and absent are each given a value, it is possible to develop some information to aid the debate about which projects should be undertaken, which should not and where the business plan appears to be unsupported.

Figures 2.4–2.7 show examples of such data expressed in a way to encourage focused debate. In Figure 2.4, the height of each bar is less important than their relative heights in indicating a balanced portfolio. Figure 2.5 shows the portfolio's contribution to achieving a single strategic objective. Figure 2.6 (see page 38) shows the strategic value of an individual project. It is often valuable to add depth and substance when making a business case. Figure 2.7 (see page 38) shows how much each project will contribute to a specific quadrant.

However, this is not the only way of considering the relative contribution of a proposed or actual project. So far the analysis has not compared each project's potential risk and reward so the proposed portfolio has not been balanced.

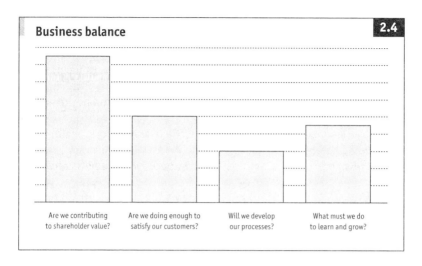

Business balance `2.4`

- Are we contributing to shareholder value?
- Are we doing enough to satisfy our customers?
- Will we develop our processes?
- What must we do to learn and grow?

Every project carries a risk for every reward. For example, a new market opportunity might suggest attractive rewards but there may be operational risks in pursuing it. Almost every decision a business makes comes from weighing the potential reward against the risk. Since projects are a vehicle for delivering business change, each will bear a risk and reward profile that must be considered both independently and in the light of every other potential or actual project. The organisation will probably not be able to afford every project it wishes to undertake. The portfolio needs thinning.

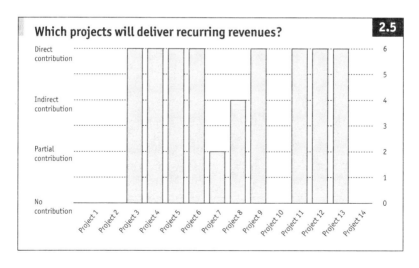

Which projects will deliver recurring revenues? `2.5`

The portfolio's contribution to achieving a single strategic objective

2.6

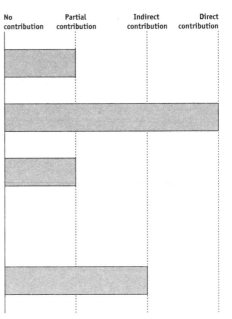

| | No contribution | Partial contribution | Indirect contribution | Direct contribution |

Will this project contribute to the company securing £500,000 worth of recurring revenues during the coming year from clients that have always previously paid one-off payments?

Will this project contribute to the company delivering three implementations during the coming year of its standard product in seven weeks rather than nine weeks?

Will this project contribute to the company implementing its own project management method based upon an industry-recognised standard during the coming year?

Will this project contribute to the company delivering two projects in the coming year using the new project management method?

Will this project contribute to the company's reduction in the turnover of staff of more than 10 years' experience by 20% during the coming year?

Which projects will shareholders find most attractive?

2.7

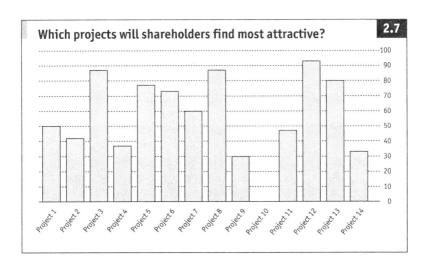

Risk and reward (or benefits) management is discussed in Chapter 5; however, little detail about a project may be known in its early life. Many questions will need to be answered, but few can be pursued until fuller funding is made available. In the absence of being able to undertake a detailed analysis of the benefits and risks that any project may promise, the organisation can obtain the high-level information it needs by recording each project against a series of measures, some focused on rewards and some on risks (see Table 2.6). Each statement is answered "yes" or "no".

Table 2.6 **Rewards and risks of a project**

Rewards	*Risks*
• This project is strategically imperative.	• The project will present significant technical challenge.
• This is a regulatory or legally mandated project.	• The project will require significant procedural change.
• There is potential for long-term value creation.	• The project will require significant organisational change.
• Perceived expected financial benefits are high.	• Implementation costs are expected to be high.
• Expected value to customers is high.	• The project cannot be implemented quickly.
• Expected value to employees is high.	• There is little appetite and/or capacity for this proposal.
• This project includes a "wow" factor.	• There will be significant impact on business as usual.

Each statement with a "yes" is given a score of 1. Once each project has been measured against these statements, it is possible to assess the overall balance of risk and reward inherent in the portfolio. The matrix on which the projects will appear is shown in Figure 2.8 overleaf.

- **Empty vessels.** These can be pursued easily but will not deliver much reward. They may appear attractive because of their relative ease of implementation, but if they fail to deliver much reward, they will tie up resources that could have been invested elsewhere.
- **Money pit.** Projects that are high in risk and low in reward may appear unpalatable, but they may be necessary. Like empty vessels, they deserve debate to avoid the danger of their being discounted merely because of their risk profile.

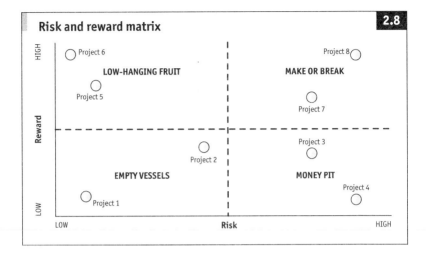

Risk and reward matrix   **2.8**

- **Low-hanging fruit.** These are preferable to empty vessels. Not only are they relatively low-risk projects, but they also appear to promise high rewards.
- **Make or break.** Projects in this category will be the ones people in the organisation know about already. They will be controversial and challenging and may divide opinion. They will make or break the portfolio, the department or even the entire business. If any projects in the portfolio deserve further and full examination of their costs and benefits, these do.

Such analysis will make it much easier for senior managers to debate the merits of projects that are under consideration. The information itself may be simply expressed, but the discussion it generates will be valuable and should avoid the tacit acceptance of a portfolio of projects that may be flawed.

Commissioning

Once a potential project has been sufficiently described in outline, and its priority, risk and value have been assessed, it may be commissioned. This involves making financial provision for:

- the first stage;
- the whole project.

Both figures may be derived from the project outline, and although they may be based on some big assumptions, they are currently all that the organisation has on which to make projections. The first stage will require funding to explore more fully the nature of the initiative so that, among many other things, a better expression of the budget it will need can be gained. Meanwhile, the high figure in the project outline will have to serve as a guide. Under no circumstances should the budget for the whole project be given to the project management team. Funds should be provided in stages to maintain control of the emerging project.

As identified earlier, the management of the conception of a project and its subsequent governance cannot be provided adequately by the business-as-usual structure. Projects, portfolios and programmes cannot thrive in silos, so those who are to participate in project management at any level must understand and act according to a commonly agreed set of responsibilities.

3 Project roles and responsibilities

When considering the organisation of a project it is helpful to look at the structure of the company itself. A project's organisational structure should contain layers of authority that allow people at different levels to use their particular skills, knowledge and experience to take the right decisions at the right time. In the same way that the organisation's structure will (or should) have been designed to meet its particular needs, so should the organisational structure of the project be tailored to meet its objective. It must also offer a means by which the expectations of those involved or who have an interest in the project may be met.

Who should be involved in managing a project?

The people brought together to commission, manage, fund, specify, build, test, use and benefit from a project's outcome must together have the skills, knowledge, experience and personal attributes necessary to carry out the project successfully, no matter how demanding the circumstances become.

There needs to be general agreement on who:

- defines what is required;
- provides the budget;
- directs the people involved in the project;
- authorises changes;
- manages the day-to-day work.

Projects are a means to create value or achieve desired change and should not exist independently from the business that commissions them. Once its business plan has been developed, the company needs a management team to oversee the whole portfolio of projects. During the year it should:

- identify further opportunities;
- commission projects;
- prioritise resources;
- secure funding;
- realise benefits.

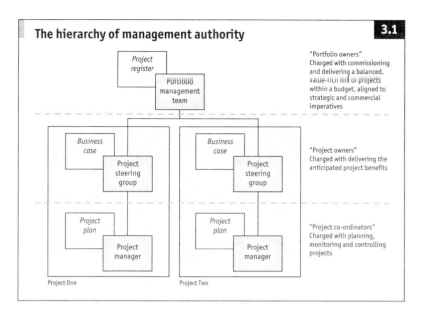

The hierarchy of management authority 3.1

Project register

Portfolio management team

"Portfolio owners" Charged with commissioning and delivering a balanced, value-rich mix of projects within a budget, aligned to strategic and commercial imperatives

Business case

Project steering group

Business case

Project steering group

"Project owners" Charged with delivering the anticipated project benefits

Project plan

Project manager

Project plan

Project manager

"Project co-ordinators" Charged with planning, monitoring and controlling projects

Project One   Project Two

This team is called the portfolio management team and it has a separate role from that of the project steering groups (the various bodies to which the ownership of individual projects is delegated). In turn, the project steering groups have different responsibilities from the project manager, who plans, monitors and controls a project. However, all three must do their jobs well if an organisation's projects are to succeed. This hierarchy of management authority is shown in Figure 3.1.

The portfolio management team

Typically, at the beginning of a financial year, the portfolio management team will be put in charge of a range of projects, including those identified in the business plan and possibly others that have run over from the previous year. This mix of projects is known as the portfolio, which, in common with the wider business, has to flex and change throughout the year. As it does so, the portfolio management team is responsible for commissioning and delivering a value-adding mix of projects within a budget, aligned with the imperatives set out by the business.

The team will normally meet every month to:

- identify candidate projects (from the business plan or elsewhere);
- commission business cases;

- apportion resources across the portfolio;
- identify suitable project steering groups;
- delegate ownership of projects to project steering groups;
- prioritise projects in the portfolio;
- manage situations where benefits may be at risk.

Given the wide interest in the assorted projects, the portfolio management team may be large, increasing the risk that it will fail to operate effectively. Therefore, it is sensible to construct the team according to specific criteria:

- Do all participants carry the authority needed to make any decision required of them?
- Have participants been drawn from all areas from which decisions will be needed, including sales/marketing, operations, technology, facilities/property, legal, human resources?
- Are participants likely to remain committed to their responsibilities for the whole year?

At the end of the year, it should be possible to judge the team's success by looking at the extent to which:

- the mix of projects has helped to achieve defined business objectives as planned;
- commercial and strategic targets have been met;
- the projects within the portfolio have been delivered on time and within budget;
- the projects have produced results of acceptable quality;
- the portfolio has been administered efficiently.

Project steering group

The project steering group is accountable for the success of its project. It is responsible for making sure that the expectations set out in the business case for the project are met. If the project is seen as a small business, the steering group is its board of directors. It will commission the project plan from the project manager and, assuming it is agreed, will authorise the start of the project. It will also authorise any significant changes to the plan that are outside the project manager's authority. It secures and assigns resources. As the project manager will have only limited authority, the project steering group adjudicates on any conflicts within the project and resolves problems between the project and third parties, internal departments or other projects. It is given its authority by the portfolio management team once the financial and other resources have been allocated.

A project steering group should be made up of people who;

- are committed to a successful project outcome;
- are authorised to make decisions;
- can provide or source resources;
- are experts in their fields.

They should be chosen for a combination of experience and authority appropriate to the project.

As well as getting together at important decision-making points, most project steering groups prefer regular, scheduled meetings at which the project manager can report on the present status of the project and forecast how things are likely to proceed. Typically, this might be every month. If they need to meet more regularly, this may be an indication that their (and the project manager's) authority is not clearly defined and that the project is at risk of being managed by committee.

The project steering group should not be allowed to become a committee. It should be made up of people who are both senior enough to make decisions and expert enough in their field to add essential knowledge, skill and experience. This may suggest that it could, or should, be open to any senior individual with an interest in the project. However, the fewer people involved in the project steering group, the easier it is to make decisions. Even so, a balance has to be struck between an autocrat driving the project and a cast of thousands.

Since the project will necessarily become a shared endeavour, it will need to involve many different, sometimes antagonistic, interests. Chief among these will be the customer of the deliverable to be produced by the project, the developers who will build it and those who will fund it. The project steering group will be required to make tough choices, and it is important that its decisions are sufficiently balanced across these different perspectives. The project will suffer if one person's view always takes precedence.

These perspectives can be brought to bear on many important decisions throughout the project. It will be seen how the interests of the funders, the customers and the developers must be accommodated to ensure that effective decisions are made about changes to the project or when making judgments about the satisfactory completion of deliverables.

The interests of these three parties should be represented at an authoritative level, but these people will be part of a group and will need leadership. Consequently, the project steering group is usually chaired by a project sponsor, who is responsible for delivering the commercial benefits outlined in the business case. The project sponsor is likely to have been the driving force since the project was conceived. The project sponsor's role on the project steering group is outlined below.

The project sponsor's role and responsibilities

Role
- promote the project's commercial imperatives;
- assume ownership of the project on behalf of the portfolio management team;
- seek to deliver a viable outcome.

Principal responsibilities
- take ownership of the business case from the portfolio management team and make sure it is maintained;
- brief the portfolio management team about project progress, alerting them if benefit escalation conditions have been met;
- authorise the start of the project;
- authorise the plan and agree expenditure;
- resolve any priority or resource conflicts through arbitration with those on the project steering group who represent the customer and the developer;
- organise and chair project steering group meetings;
- set escalation conditions for time and costs and ensure that the project manager provides suitable notification;
- authorise action if significant budget or timescale variances are forecast;
- authorise the closure of the project after agreement with other members of the project steering group;
- report the realisation of benefits to the portfolio management team in accordance with the agreed timetable.

The importance of balance in a project steering group and of a focused, authoritative project sponsor was demonstrated during the implementation of a new computer system for use by Britain's general practitioners (GPs), when some lax commercial and time management practices were observed. This was particularly evident during the user acceptance testing phase of the project. Faced with their new computer system for the first time, many GPs (the project's customers) asked the IT contractor for functions that were not in the specification. The contractor incorporated the changes and the GPs eventually received an improved system that met their needs. In the absence of authoritative commercial control, nobody asked if the changes should be allowed and the project's timescale and budget were exceeded because its organisational structure was missing this important view.

This is just one of a set of problems that arise from a poorly constructed project steering group. If there is a risk of it having too many members, separate out those who are there to provide opinions but who are not authorised to make decisions about the project. If these people represent teams or departments that will be customers of the project's deliverable, create a separate user forum through which they can express their views. Select one of them to chair the user forum and arbitrate where conflict arises. This person should sit on the project steering group to relay the forum's views and provide a single point of contact to determine the requirements the project's deliverable must satisfy and confirm they have been met at the end.

The same applies to the developers. If there are several suppliers involved, select one to lead and join the project steering group to convey their views about the design of the project's deliverable, making sure it meets any particular standards.

Sometimes the project may involve a customer from outside the organisation, for instance where a bespoke piece of machinery is being developed for an external paying client. In this case, it would be ideal for both the customer and the supplier to join the project steering group. Sometimes, however, issues such as commercial confidentiality will prevent customers and suppliers working as closely together as would be desirable. In these cases, the customer and the supplier should have their own project steering groups, in essence creating two interdependent projects where one would have been ideal.

Overall, the project steering group's performance can be judged against the extent to which:

- the business case is maintained, is always accessible and illustrates the difference between the company's total effort or investment in the project compared with the income or benefit from it;
- the project produces a value-adding outcome as identified in the business case;

- it has identified and empowered a single project manager to plan, co-ordinate and control the project;
- it has been able to set and apply escalation conditions for the project manager;
- it has been able to provide sufficient resources of the necessary quality to allow the plan to be fulfilled.

For examples of variations in a project's organisational structure see Chapter 4.

Project manager

The project manager co-ordinates the project on behalf of the project steering group and makes sure that it produces the required deliverables to the identified standard of quality, on time and within budget. To do this, the project manager develops an approved plan and then makes sure that all the milestones are achieved.

Commonly, a project manager's success is measured by whether the results required have been delivered on time, on budget and to the required standard of quality, but often changes are agreed during a project that may increase the costs or the time span needed to complete it. It would clearly be wrong to judge the project manager according to the original budget and timescale; it is better to measure how well the project manager has managed the changes and the expectations of those with a stake in the project.

Criteria for judging a project manager should include the extent to which:

- there is an authorised plan that shows progress to date and forecasts for time, cost and quality;
- escalation conditions for time and cost have been agreed with the project steering group and are being applied;
- there is a record demonstrating that changes to scope, timescale, cost and benefits have been approved by those with authority to do so;
- there is a record of risks to the project, together with mitigation plans and actions;
- the project steering group is kept regularly and sufficiently informed through progress reports and forecasts.

Some organisations assign several project managers to the same project, thinking this will lessen the risk. On the contrary, this means work is

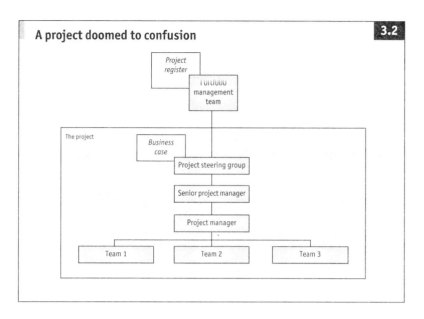

A project doomed to confusion 3.2

duplicated, gaps go unnoticed, leadership is unclear and communication becomes confused. The risk of the project failing is increased. The project in Figure 3.2 is doomed to confusion.

The project steering group is responsible for delivering a viable outcome, but who is responsible for developing the project plan? From whom would they expect progress reports? What are the implications of splitting authority between two project managers?

There should be one project manager who plans, monitors and controls the project. This person should have sufficient experience and personal authority to remove the need to duplicate this pivotal role. Selecting a suitable project manager will depend on factors such as:

- the value of the project;
- its timescale;
- the risks;
- how critical it is;
- who is available.

The more demanding a project, the more its project manager should be experienced and competent, so it is helpful to grade them (see Table 3.1 on page 51):

- PM1 – a project or team leader who would be expected to manage a team within a project, reporting to a project manager.
- PM2 – a project manager who would be expected to manage a project with minimum supervision.
- PM3 – a senior project manager who would be able to manage several projects at once and would readily help to develop the organisation's approach to project management.

The list is not definitive and will vary between organisations, but it can be used as a guide when organising the pool of a project's workers, recruiting new project workers or identifying and selecting people suitable for a specific project.

Is the project organisation structure suitable?

Having designed or inherited a project organisation, it is sensible to identify where the in-built risks may lie. Questions to ask include the following:

- Is there a clear separation of project ownership from its day-to-day management?
- Is there a clearly identified single project manager?
- Has each role been assigned to people with sufficient authority to undertake every responsibility allocated to them?
- Does the project organisation contain the authority within itself to make the decisions necessary to its continued progress?
- Are all three key perspectives (commercial, customer and developer) represented at the project steering group?
- Have the client's aspirations been accommodated?
- Have all responsibilities identified as necessary to the project been assigned to individuals?
- Do all individuals know their responsibilities and are they comfortable with them?
- Has the organisation structure sensibly accommodated its most important stakeholders?

The importance of a suitable project organisation structure as a foundation for its success should not be underestimated. Nevertheless, despite the principles, success depends ultimately on how effectively that structure works in a real company.

Table 3.1 **Project manager grades**

Skills	Knowledge	Experience	Character	Responsibilities
PM1 – project or team leader				
Project administration	Company business	Application of company approach to project management	Organised	Assist in project planning
Time, resource and quality planning	Company organisation structure	Demonstration of skills	Able to motivate others	Maintain the project change/issues/risk logs
Delegation	Company products and services	Management of people	Problem identification and analysis	Maintain project metrics, including time cost and quality tracking
Project control	Company approach to project management	Delegation of work	Communicative	Monitor and report progress against plan, identifying variances where relevant
People management	Planning and control techniques	Participation in at least one project environment	Confident	Assist in effective communications with internal and external stakeholders
Communications	Risk management techniques			
	Project tools			

Skills	Knowledge	Experience	Character	Responsibilities
PM2 – project manager				
Project administration	Company business	Application of company approach to project management	Organised	*Develop, and seek approval for, the project initiation documentation*
Time, resource and quality planning	Company organisation structure	Demonstration of skills	*Self-motivated*	*Maintain the project plan within identified constraints*
Delegation	Company products/services	Management of people	Able to motivate others	*Manage project changes/ risks/issues*
Project control	*Company financial environment*	*Management in a matrix environment*	Problem solving	Identify and delegate work packets to project teams
Negotiation	Company approach to project management	Delegation of work	Communicative	*Motivate and co-ordinate the project team and other personnel involved in the project*
Conflict management/ avoidance	*Industry-recognised project management methods*	*Managed at least two three- to six-month projects from start to finish*	*Influential/persuasive*	Monitor, report and control progress against plan, escalating when outside of agreed tolerances
People management	Planning and control techniques	*Induction of new project personnel*	Confident	*Maintain effective communications and expectations with stakeholders (internal or external) and propose*

Skills	Knowledge	Experience	Character	Responsibilities
Induction	Risk management techniques		Professional	Maintain project metrics, including time, cost, quality and benefits tracking
Communications	Project tools		Delivery focused	Maintain the business case to allow project steering group assessment of continued project viability
				Implement and operate effective change management
				Develop, and seek approval for, the project closure documentation
PM3 – senior project manager				
Project administration	Company business	Application and development of company approach to project management	Organised	Develop, and seek approval for, the project initiation documentation
Time, resource and quality planning	Company organisation structure and personnel	Demonstration of skills	Self-motivated	Maintain the project plan within identified constraints

Skills	Knowledge	Experience	Character	Responsibilities
Delegation	Company products/services	Management of people	Able to motivate others	Manage project changes/risks/issues
Project control	Company financial environment	Management in a matrix environment	Problem solving	Identify and delegate work packets to project teams
Negotiation	Company approach to project management	Delegation of work	Creative	Motivate and co-ordinate the project team and other personnel involved in the project
Conflict management/avoidance	Industry-recognised project management methods	Managed at least *three* three- to six-month projects from start to finish	Communicative	Monitor, report and control progress against plan, escalating when outside of agreed tolerances
People management	Planning and control techniques	*Managed at least two concurrent projects*	Inspirational	Maintain effective communications and expectations with stakeholders (internal or external) and propose solutions to resolve conflicts
Interviewing	Risk management techniques	*Facing clients*	Influential/persuasive	Maintain project metrics, including time, cost, quality and benefits tracking

Skills	Knowledge	Experience	Character	Responsibilities
Selection and recruitment	*Project and portfolio tools*	*Working with suppliers*	Confident	*Maintain business case to allow project steering group assessment of continued project viability*
Induction		*Interviewing potential project personnel*	Professional	Implement and operate effective change management
Communications		*Selection and recruitment of new project personnel*	Delivery focused	*Develop, and seek approval for, the project closure documentation*
Client, account and supplier management		Induction of new project personnel		*Participate in the interviewing, selection and coaching of project practitioners*
Consultancy				*Promote the benefits of the company approach to project management*
Sales			–	*Participate in the development of the company approach to project management*

Note: Differences between levels are shown in italics.

55

4 Project organisation and resource management

Whose project is it?

Many people, all with differing expectations of success, will have a stake in a project so it is important to identify and manage their varied expectations. When a project begins, a pool of individuals (or groups) will have an interest in it, either because they will be affected by it or because they may affect the project itself. The project's organisation structure can be developed by identifying those in the pool who can contribute best to its effective management and, ultimately, its success. The following techniques are helpful in selecting who should be part of a project's organisational structure.

The stakeholder map

Drawing up a stakeholder map is a quick and simple way of identifying everybody who may affect, or be affected by, the project (see Figure 4.1).

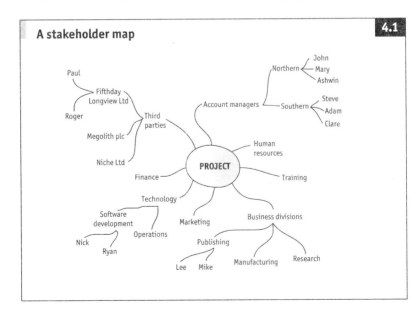

A stakeholder map

4.1

From the project at the centre, lines are extended to the stakeholder groups, subgroups and individuals. For instance, the technology department may be large and contain many people who will not have an interest in the project, so it has been split into software development and operations. The individuals in software development have been identified, one of whom may be the department head who has skills especially useful for this project.

Each line is extended until it can be discounted or named individuals are identified. They may become candidates for the project's management team, but should be assessed further.

The stakeholder matrix

The next stage is to identify which stakeholders are critical to the project's success. A simple matrix can help (see Figure 4.2).

This matrix positions stakeholders in terms of their "power" and "support", measures that help to determine who should participate in managing the project. Power is not just the authority derived from a person's job but also includes knowledge and expertise. Support indicates the degree to which someone will back the project. Both may change, so although the matrix is relevant when drawn up, it is likely to become out of date soon after.

When the individuals identified in the stakeholder map are placed on the matrix the degree to which the project has effective and authoritative sponsorship will quickly become apparent. The top half of the matrix

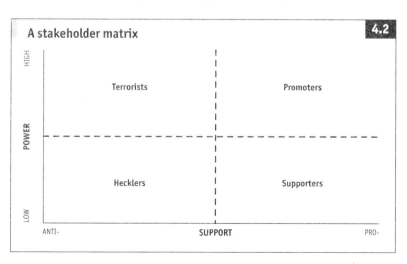

A stakeholder matrix — Figure 4.2

reveals possible candidates for the project steering group. It would be instinctive to focus on those who are promoters, but any terrorists may best be managed by inviting them to participate in the project. Then their concerns can be addressed more effectively and they may be more inclined to see its benefits and move from the left side of the matrix to the right.

If there is nobody in the top half of the matrix, the project is unlikely to secure the sponsorship it needs. Those who have commissioned it must ask themselves whether their project has the necessary backing.

With little power or influence, the hecklers and supporters in the lower half of the matrix are unlikely to be a source of authority for the project. However, this pool will supply some of the team members who will participate in, but not manage, the project.

This dynamic view can change as individuals fall from or rise to power. Moreover, supporters and hecklers can form groups that gain power and influence as their size increases. This may not affect the structure of the project organisation directly, but it is sensible to revisit the matrix regularly.

For example, a project customer who is dissatisfied with the deliverable received may be relatively powerless, but if hecklers unite into a terrorist group and withdraw their support, they can affect a project's commercial benefits being realised.

Developing a project management structure

Creating a project's organisational structure can be difficult. The following examples are based on fundamental principles but propose very different structures appropriate for the different projects.

Development and implementation of a computer system

Many business projects contain a significant technology component that needs careful consideration based on expert opinion. Few projects, however, are "technology only". In most cases, a business person's behaviour will have to adapt if the full benefit of the change is to be realised. Consequently, the organisation structure should not be designed around the premise that any project involving technology is a technology project; it will be a shared endeavour between the technology, user and commercial stakeholders, all of whom should be represented in the project organisation structure.

In this example, a senior executive is sponsoring the project. A case has been made for new technology to be introduced in the hope that it will reduce operating costs in the administration department. The company's internal technology department will source, tailor and implement the computer system.

The senior executive should be the project sponsor and the administration department's manager should be a member of the project steering group, authorising the specification and acceptance of the system his team will have to use. The administration department manager will also be sufficiently senior to provide users to test and help implement the system.

The systems development manager will also serve on the project steering group to advise on the choice of supplier, confirm the suitability of the selected software and provide the technical resources needed to develop the system.

Given the skills, knowledge and experience required, the project manager could come from any team provided that the individual has the ability to plan, monitor and control time, cost and quality. Some knowledge of the project is always advisable, however, especially if the manager can draw on previous similar experience. With this in mind, the project sponsor could choose the candidate from:

- the administration department;
- the technology department;
- a specialist project management agency or department.

There is merit and risk in each choice. By picking a member of the administration team, the sponsor would sensibly place control of the budget and time imperatives in the hands of someone other than the project's suppliers. So the project manager would be known to the sponsor and should be motivated to achieve the organisation's aims. This does not necessarily mean, however, that the individual will have the requisite project management experience.

A member of the technology team may have carried out similar projects many times before and most of his work may have been project based. Even so, although the IT component of the project will be significant, it is more than just about the development and installation of software. There will be training and induction activities, user tests to be planned and conducted, and issues arising from the working practice changes required from the administration department.

If all else fails, the candidate may be sourced from a specialised project management resource provider. The person may have little experience

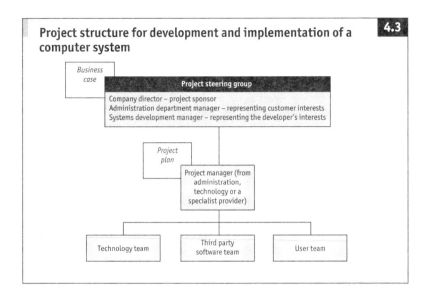

Project structure for development and implementation of a computer system `4.3`

of software development projects, but can draw on the competencies of colleagues to deliver the desired outcome on time and to budget.

In any of the three possible outcomes, the team is unaffected by where the project manager comes from. A structure for discussion is illustrated in Figure 4.3.

An office move

A company wants to move a team of 100 people from one building to another. The team manager has secured funding for the move, which involves participation from the technology department (which will uninstall, move and reinstall computers and printers) and the facilities department (which will prepare the new office and crate and move possessions).

The project has a champion, the team manager, who will have had to justify the move in commercial terms and so is a candidate to become the project sponsor in the project steering group. The same person may also have specified and approved the layout of the new office and will approve its suitability before the team starts to use it, which means he also represents the customer's views. Therefore, he will be responsible for not only the financial viability of the move but also the fitness for purpose of the new office, two aspects of the project that may conflict.

Two people may be able to represent the developers of the solution the

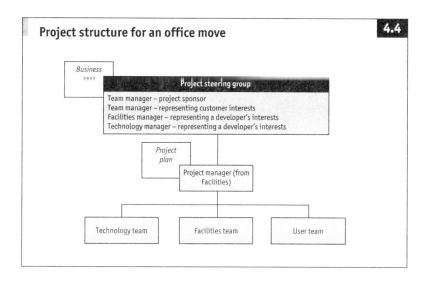

Project structure for an office move — 4.4

project is to deliver. One may come from the technology department and authorise the provision of technical resources and the most appropriate strategy for delivering a suitable technology service. The other may come from the facilities department and authorise the use of suppliers to make the move and make sure it meets approved standards. Both would be the most senior people in the project to deal with technical issues that could not be resolved by anyone else.

As in the first example, there are several potential sources for the project manager:

- the team that is moving;
- the facilities department;
- the technology department;
- a specialist project management agency or department.

The strongest case may be to identify a project manager from the facilities department because its members will have carried out such projects many times and have a wealth of experience. Their work will have been project based, so they may well have the necessary project management skills. A possible structure for this project is illustrated in Figure 4.4.

A conference
A company regularly holds public conferences. Delegates are invited

to hear speakers on a range of topics for which they are charged a fee. Although the commissioning and running of a conference has the characteristics of a classic project, not every conference requires a separate project steering group because managing conferences is business as usual for those involved.

There is, however, a particular risk to be addressed. Conference managers are expected to deliver a successful conference. Yet success means different things to different people. To the sales manager, it may mean making a profit. For the head of editorial, however, who decides the conference's content and speakers, success may mean a positive response from the delegates. Meanwhile, to the conference department manager, success may mean having accurate marketing materials, effective booking mechanisms and seeing everyone turn up on the day to hear speakers in the advertised order.

The risk is that with these different measures of success, the conference manager will be unable to secure an important go or no-go decision should the number of delegates be low. Should it fall to the conference manager to negotiate with a sales manager who wishes to cancel the event and the head of editorial who wants it to continue?

A single, carefully selected project steering group may be able to oversee all conference projects, providing the various conference managers with a single, consolidated source of authority, resource provision and decision-making capability to which they can turn. A possible structure for this project is illustrated in Figure 4.5.

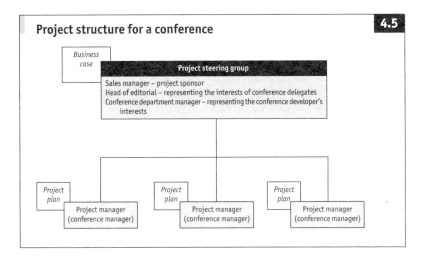

Project structure for a conference 4.5

A *time management solution*

An organisation wants to implement a process for recording the time spent by its employees on planned and unplanned activity. A computer system will facilitate this, but employees will be significantly affected because they will be penalised for failing to complete timesheets on time, and will be restricted from undertaking any activity for which a timesheet code does not exist.

The project has been sponsored by the head of operations who wishes to increase productivity through more focused, planned work. The developers will be members of the technology department, but there will also be a small but significant emphasis on the legal matters involved, so human resources will have to ensure that regulations are complied with.

The project is likely to touch every part of the organisation, not only because most people will have to complete a timesheet at the end of each week, but also because the management information arising from the computer system will be used by many departments in a variety of ways.

The project steering group has a clear project sponsor, the head of operations, while members of the human resources and technology departments will represent the interests of the solution developers. Given the potentially large number of users of the solution, however, there is a good case for forming a user forum. This may include anyone who

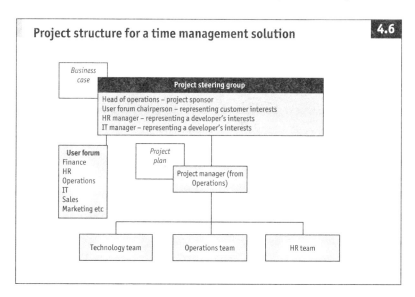

Project structure for a time management solution 4.6

has an interest in the fitness for purpose of the products of the solution – that is, the computer system, the management information it produces or the way it may affect working practices. The project sponsor should identify someone to chair the user forum who can arbitrate on all matters it discusses and present a single consolidated view of requirements.

Although a significant technology component is envisaged, manual procedures could in theory achieve the same end, so the sponsor may wish to select someone from the operations department to manage this project. The project organisation structure could look like Figure 4.6 on page 63.

Resource pool management

A project is a management environment with the internal authority to make the right decisions at the right time, but as it also affects the organisation itself, it is important that an organisation examines how it provides resources to projects at the same time as carrying on its usual business.

A common complaint is that a combination of projects and business as usual pulls too many people in too many directions. Priorities are unclear; all the stops are pulled out for a priority project until something happens to compromise the operation of the rest of the business. At that point the project (much to the chagrin of its management team) is pushed to one side. Organisations with a strong emphasis on operational excellence often consider projects to be of secondary importance, which is understandable because business as usual funds projects, but this can be dangerous as it may affect their ability to change in order to prosper, or survive.

A resource pool is a group of people within a single management structure, usually with common skills. Effective resource pool management helps to balance the competing demands of the people who are responsible for business as usual at the same time as releasing enough of them to deliver a portfolio of value-focused projects.

Imagine installing a fish tank to be stocked with a wide variety of tropical fish. The fish come from a specialist supplier who has many pools, each containing a different species. So an assortment is chosen subject to the supplier having enough fish of each type to meet the demand and the customer having enough money to pay for them.

The same is true of projects. The management team responsible for staffing a new project requests resources from a wide variety of internal and, possibly, external sources. In this way, they obtain the mix of skills, knowledge, experience and character they believe will serve the project well. This creates a further responsibility for the people who manage the pools from which the resources have been picked. Just as the specialist supplier of fish has to manage the quantity and health of fish in each pool, so too must someone in the project-focused organisation take responsibility for managing the people who may be needed to work on projects. A project manager charged with finding a specialist team leader for a particular phase of a project may feel aggrieved if the one remaining expert has been promised to another project. This would be doubly frustrating if the only alternative on offer was one of three market analysts of which the company has a surfeit. Resource pool management is needed to ensure that both business as usual and projects have enough people of the quality they need at the right time.

Resource pool management can be carried out according to free market or regulated principles.

The free market

Figure 4.7 illustrates a free market. Having been given authority to deliver a successful outcome, the project management teams attempt to secure the resources they need from a variety of sources, both internal and external. External sources such as third-party resource suppliers may require a bigger investment, but the project management team has authority to deliver a commercially viable outcome. As long as the project's benefits outweigh its costs, they can argue in favour of employing external resources.

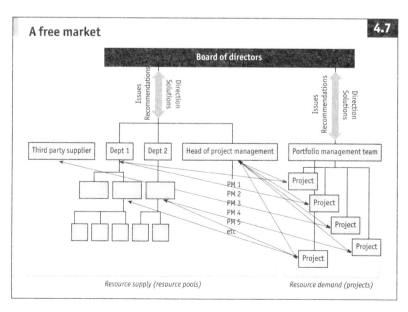

A free market 4.7

Resource supply (resource pools)   Resource demand (projects)

Internal suppliers such as those in Department 1 and Department 2 can work in much the same way as an external provider, with one significant exception. Although they are resource pools, many of these internal departments must also carry out business as usual successfully, so most department managers are charged with managing the supply of resources to projects and business as usual.

Things become more complicated when a project makes a demand on the resource pools that other projects are also making demands upon. It is better for the organisation if such competition can be regulated.

The regulated market

This structure differs in two important ways from the free market model (see Figure 4.8):

- ■ The supply and demand relationships between project and resource pool managers have been replaced with a single resource management function.
- ■ The resolution of problems arising from shortages or oversupply of resources no longer rests with the resource pool managers but with the resource management function.

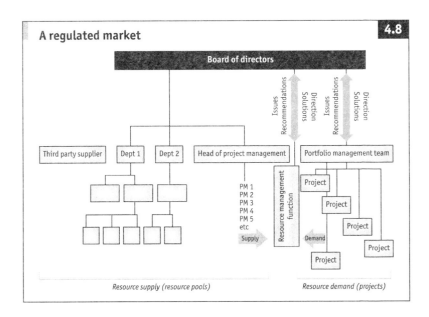

4.8

A regulated market

Resource supply (resource pools)   *Resource demand (projects)*

Having a resource management function does not remove the need for the resource pool managers to nurture their teams. Nor does it mean that they should not plan for future project and business-as-usual demands. It can, however, add these considerable benefits:

- forward planning of resource numbers so that cross-department recruitment campaigns can be managed;
- increased negotiating power with third-party resource providers;
- improved arbitration where resource conflicts arise;
- skills management (using skills profiles for selection rather than availability alone);
- decreases in the incidence of potentially available resources being reserved for the personal use of their department (resource pool) managers.

To make this happen, the resource management function must:

- plan and maintain forecasts for company-wide resource demands based on regularly gathered project resource plans;
- plan and maintain forecasts for company-wide resource supply based on regularly gathered department resource plans;
- match resource demand from potential and existing projects with the potential and existing supply available from internal and external resource pools;
- identify, report and respond to resource supply and demand trends;
- plan, co-ordinate and support recruitment campaigns across the organisation.

At the end of a year, it should be possible to judge the function's success by measuring:

- to what extent resource utilisation has been maximised;
- the availability of a current, company-wide resource plan;
- whether, at any time, all projects have a forecast of resource demand and all departments have a forecast of resource supply.

Matrix management

Both models recognise that projects are usually neither owned by, nor contained within, a single department. They are shared endeavours that draw on the skills, knowledge and experience of a variety of stakeholders whose expectations differ. Projects cut across the departmental divides, creating a matrix. Managing resources through both line and project structures is called matrix management. When used effectively, it allows organisations to deliver better business as usual and projects simultaneously. Without it, projects often suffer because business as usual takes priority.

In both the free and regulated models there is also a head of project management who plays a key role in a matrix management environment.

Head of project management

The head of project management is principally a resource pool manager responsible for managing a team of project managers to satisfy the demands of project steering groups as they seek candidates for emerging projects. This person will manage the longer-term needs of the department by recruiting, developing and retaining the best project managers required to maintain a healthy pool of personnel.

The head of project management should be an experienced person who can contribute to the continued development and application of the organisation's approach to project management. Even so, if the resource pool is small, this may not be a full-time role and could be performed by a project manager in addition to existing duties.

The head of project management should not become involved in business-as-usual or project matters other than those for which he already has specific responsibilities. Matters arising within individual projects should be managed by those involved in them. The head of project management is, however, expected to prevent or manage anything related to the efficiency, supply or quality of project management personnel.

The person given this role may also sit on a project steering group, or possibly serve as a member of the portfolio management team.

To ensure consistency, impartiality, balance and integration of services with other stakeholders, the provision of project support and assurance to project managers (such as health checks, quality reviews, administrative support, and so on) is best provided from outside this resource pool.

The head of project management's specific responsibilities are to:

- supply project managers to project steering groups when given a demand forecast;
- manage the pool of resources effectively within the agreed headcount;

- make sure the project managers in the pool apply the company's approach to project management;
- prevent and resolve issues regarding the efficacy, supply or quality of project managers;
- recruit, retain/release, develop and reward the pool of project managers according to their performance;
- provide personal mentoring and support to project managers;
- provide training and education for the company's approach to project management.

The head of project management should be authorised to:

- recruit and release project managers to satisfy current and forecast demand effectively;
- conduct annual appraisals and to recommend rewards/penalties.

At the end of a year, the head of project management's performance should be assessed by:

- the extent to which demand for project managers has been met;
- how regularly the resource plan for project managers has been maintained;
- the extent to which project managers have achieved their targets.

This demanding role requires appropriate managerial ability and experience in project management.

5 Planning: risks and rewards

There is only one time when it is possible to state the cost and end date of a project with certainty: when it is complete. No matter how well supported it is, every assertion until then is an estimate. Even if a customer or supplier wishes to fix a price or the deadline is "of the essence", too much can change for anyone to treat the budget or timescale as anything more than a target. A target and a plan, however, are two very different things. A target is an objective or a goal. A plan should describe how that goal will be met.

Targets such as dates and budgetary figures are easy to set, and because they are, in the desire to meet them a project can become driven by urgency and economy rather than pragmatism and balance. All too often, projects fail because a target was mistaken for a plan.

In cultures where there is an urgency to see results, the benefits of planning are often forgotten until it is too late. In many instances plans are not produced because it is thought there is not enough time to think ahead. A former colleague of the author once ruminated that his organisation never appeared to have the time to plan, yet it always found enough time to do the project twice.

In organisations where projects are small or familiar, there is sometimes a feeling that there is no need to plan. The risk of the absence of a plan is not thought to be great enough to warrant creating one. But this does not recognise the high likelihood of change. Even small or simple projects or those similar to some undertaken previously can be affected by change. The time given to drawing up a plan is time used to understand how different the world is since a similar project was undertaken and how much more it may change during the life cycle of the next.

For many people, including some project managers, planning is either too difficult, too unpleasant or both. Not everyone has a natural aptitude for planning, nor does everyone enjoy it. But project managers must understand the importance and benefits of a plan if they are to fulfil their role competently.

A plan has many benefits. It can confirm whether or not the identified targets are achievable, and if they are not, the plan can provide the evidence for further debate. A plan can be used to express a clear and commonly understood approach to the project. It can help to identify its risks and to establish the factors on which success will depend.

A Monty Python sketch, "The 100 yards for people with no sense of direction" (in *Silly Olympiad*), in which the competitors run off in different directions, illustrates the way in which many projects are conducted. Time is invested in creating a plan, yet when approval is granted to move from initiation into the delivery stage, the plan is abandoned and chaos ensues. A plan has the added advantage of providing a means for keeping a project on track. In short, a well constructed plan is essential.

The principles of planning
Planning and control
Just what should be planned? How much detail should a plan contain? How long should an average task take? How many stages should a project have? It would be helpful if there were some simple rules of thumb for answering such questions. However, every plan will be different in terms of its detail, the amount of risk it carries, or the way it has been structured. The best way to proceed is to plan what you wish to control. For example, if a manager asks for project progress reports to be provided at agreed intervals, the plan must have identified clear milestones that are delivered at the same frequency otherwise one report will change very little from the previous one.

Refining the plan
How long would it take to landscape a particular site? Perhaps three months would be sufficient. But there are many unknowns: no budget has been suggested; there is no design; the risks of the project have not been considered; and the potential for changes to the specification have not been taken into account. So it would be natural to compose a list (probably a long one) of assumptions and caveats that could be read alongside the estimate. Effectively, they would be guesses in place of facts. Many assumptions are made early in a project because the facts have not yet been revealed. But planning does not take place only at the beginning of the project. It is a continual process of refinement by which guesses are gradually replaced by facts.

Breaking a project into stages
Even before a project has been planned, it is not unusual for some people to wish to set the completion date or budget. This creates a challenge for project managers looking into the uncertain future; and the further into

the future they look, the more uncertain it becomes. This is why professional project managers divide their projects into stages.

A project manager will develop two plans: one that covers the whole project, and a much more detailed one that focuses on the next stage only. The first, the project plan, will carry a greater level of risk because it looks further into the future. The stage plan will carry less risk as it covers a shorter, more predictable, planning horizon. Each stage is used as a vehicle to deliver some of the intended deliverables and to increase confidence in the project plan. At the end of each stage, the project manager is able to return to the project steering group with an increasingly reliable project plan.

As well as helping to refine early estimates as the project progresses, breaking the project into stages:

- enables progress to be tracked and measured, providing assurance to the project's stakeholders; and
- allows the justification of the project to be reconsidered, making sure that it continues only if it remains viable.

Building in contingency

Although it may seem sensible to refine the estimates of cost and time required to complete a project as it progresses, some sponsors will wish to fix them as soon as possible so that budgets can be set and people can allocate sufficient time for their role in the project when it is needed. Despite the caveats that may accompany the plan, the targets become fixed in people's minds and the assumptions are forgotten. Even if the emerging plan suggests that the original targets were inappropriate or unachievable, they are now so embedded in the organisation's psyche that to challenge them can look like failure.

It makes sense, therefore, to add a contingency element to early estimates. Contingency is an estimated amount of time or money, carefully calculated when a project is being planned, to address identified risks and the potential amount of change the project may encounter. As each stage is passed, it should be possible to reduce the contingency element, accounting for what has been learned during the project's progress so far and the reduced risk that should remain ahead. Thus the contingency element is carefully assessed and is not a slush fund to be used for bailing out the project.

If the project manager can produce a set of contingency figures based on an audited risk analysis, the project steering group can be confident that the amount of contingency being requested is reasonable. The group may also wish to retain control of the contingency budget. In this way, the project manager can draw on the fund only with the project steering group's approval and only to mitigate a risk for which the contingency was originally identified.

Having a clear and auditable approach to developing a contingency fund has a further benefit. In making public the amount and how it is broken down, there is less likelihood that each layer of management will add an additional percentage, which might take the total project budget to an unacceptable level.

Management by exception

At some time during a project something will go wrong or a change will be requested that may risk it missing its time and cost targets. Therefore, project managers should be given authority within specific parameters to carry out their jobs without having to seek approval for changes to costs or deadlines. Agreeing to manage by exception removes the confusion of who is authorised to take charge when problems or changes arise.

Management by exception requires the application of escalation conditions. Project steering groups provide their project managers with a degree of time and budgetary flexibility so that they can act on their own authority within pre-agreed constraints. For example, if the escalation conditions for time and cost have been set for plus or minus two weeks and plus or minus 5% respectively, the project steering group need not be involved in the daily management of the project as long as its forecast end date does not vary by more or less than two weeks and the forecast cost remains within plus or minus 5% of its target.

If at any time the project manager forecasts that the project will not be completed within the agreed escalation conditions, the problem must be taken to the project steering group for a decision on how to proceed.

Escalation conditions do not mean that the project steering group is allowing the project manager to overspend or deliver late. They simply provide the necessary flexibility while underlining the project steering group's ultimate authority if the project should veer too far off track.

A red, amber and green coding system is used to show how the project is progressing. Red denotes that it is outside of one or both of its escalation conditions for time and budget. Amber means that the project is off target but in the designated manager's control. Green means it is on target.

Management by exception can be used to separate any two levels of authority. It can be applied to the relationship between the project steering group and the project manager, the project manager and the project management team, and the project steering group and the portfolio management team. Although only time and cost have been described, the approach can be applied to any date or numeric driven target, such as quantified benefits. Although it may not be immediately apparent, quality is accounted for by the negative figures applied to time and cost. For instance, if a project is forecast to be completed early or under budget, it may suggest that something has been forgotten or removed from its scope and that the output will be substandard.

Management by exception is a technique used to control a project. However, like the other principles described above, it must be considered when planning:

- the benefits of a project;
- the mitigation of risks;
- the quality of the deliverables;
- timescales and costs.

Planning the benefits

The benefits of a project are notoriously difficult to articulate and quantify. However, to strike a balance between the benefits of the project and the investment needed to fund it, both must be considered on equal terms. This means they must be measured in hard currency which, although difficult, is always desirable if the investment is to be justified.

Common examples of (as yet) unquantified benefits include:

- contribution to strategic objectives;
- generation of efficiency improvements;
- provision of access to new customers;
- provision of access to new markets;
- reduction/removal of competitive pressure;
- improvement in customer satisfaction;
- compliance with regulatory imperatives.

Quantifying benefits

Most benefits of a project, including those above, can be quantified in financial terms. It is usually possible to use the "so what?" argument to assist in setting a value. If the benefits are not quantified, the debate with those from whom the project is seeking funding will become one in which emotion is used in place of evidence. Although not always the case, most of the benefits identified above can be quantified in terms of:

- an increase in revenues/profits;
- a reduction in overheads;
- mitigation of risk;
- enabling activity elsewhere that will deliver one of the above.

Table 5.1 shows the results of quantifying some specific benefits.

Table 5.1 **Quantifying benefits ($)**

	Year 0	Year 1	Year 2	Year 3	Year 4
Increased revenues	–	**5,000**	**60,000**	**60,000**	**70,000**
Increased customer satisfaction	–	5,000	10,000	10,000	10,000
Competitor removal	–	–	20,000	20,000	20,000
Customers from new market	–	–	30,000	30,000	40,000
Cost savings	–	**8,000**	**10,000**	**11,000**	**11,000**
Headcount savings	–	5,000	5,000	5,000	5,000
Removal of redundant IT kit	–	3,000	5,000	6,000	6,000
Total	–	**13,000**	**70,000**	**71,000**	**81,000**
Cumulative total	–	**13,000**	**83,000**	**154,000**	**235,000**

But are these benefits anything more than a guess? The future is uncertain and nothing is guaranteed. However, when the project has been completed and the business has waited patiently through the post-project period, those who funded it will want to measure the return on their investment and compare the benefits with the forecast benefits in the business case.

The benefits in the business case must be clearly expressed so they can be measured and quantified financially. For example, customer satisfaction can be measured both before and after the project through a survey. Consequently, the business case may say that "a 5% improvement in customer satisfaction between year 0 and year 1 is envisaged as a direct result of this project. In year 2, it will increase by a further 5% and remain stable during years 3 and 4". This is an unambiguous target. At the end of each year, a measure can be taken of customer satisfaction to see if the targets have been met. Even so, unless the increase in customer satisfaction translates into a financial return, the project's backers would be justified in transferring their sponsorship to one that does.

With this in mind, the increases in customer satisfaction could be related to an increase in revenue. More satisfied customers may spend extra on the organisation's products and services. Thus a 5% improvement may "lead to an increase in sales of $5,000 in year 1 and a further $5,000 in year 2, after which sales will stay at the level of this extra $10,000". These figures can be measured before and after the project to determine whether the forecast was well judged.

Even so, it is often difficult to know that the project in question was directly responsible for delivering the increase in customer satisfaction and revenue because, for example, there may be other projects with similar targets. Forecasts can always change, but at the very least, the business case must present a compelling argument supported by analysis for a judgment to be made on whether to proceed with the project.

Cost/benefit analysis

The benefits of a project should outweigh the costs; however, the point at which the costs are outweighed by the benefits may be some way in the future. How far is a question that a cost/benefit analysis can help to determine.

Table 5.2 **Cost/benefit analysis ($)**

	Year 0	Year 1	Year 2	Year 3	Year 4
Benefits	–	13,000	70,000	71,000	81,000
Costs	2,500	15,850	64,620	27,400	24,250
Net	–2,500	–2,850	5,380	43,600	56,700
Cumulative	–2,500	–5,350	30	43,630	100,380

This simple cost/benefit analysis compares the investment and the intended returns of a project over time. In Table 5.2, the cost/benefit analysis shows a healthy return being made on the investment. In year 2 the benefits outweigh the costs invested to date and "payback" is achieved. In years 3 and 4 the profits grow substantially.

What matters now is to consider whether those figures are realistic as initial forecasts are often too optimistic. They should also be compared with the cost/benefit figures for other projects under consideration.

Discounted cash flow

The figures used in Table 5.2 are straightforward and take no account of the time value of money. Money received in the future is worth less than money received today, which can be invested. If the interest rate is 6%, $1 today will be worth $1.06 in a year's time. To put it another way, getting $1 in a year's time is like getting $0.94 today. In other words, the value of the future return on a project must be discounted in the cost/benefit analysis. This approach to forecasting more realistic monetary values is called discounted cash flow.

Table 5.3 adds more detail so the discounted cash flow can be calculated.

Table 5.3 **Discounted cash flow ($)**

	Year 0	Year 1	Year 2	Year 3	Year 4
Benefits	–	13,000.00	70,000.00	71,000.00	81,000.00
Costs	2,500.00	15,850.00	64,620.00	27,400.00	24,250.00
Net	−2,500.00	−2,850.00	5,380.00	43,600.00	56,700.00
Cumulative	−2,500.00	−5,350.00	30.00	43,630.00	100,380.00
Discount factor	1.00	0.94	0.89	0.84	0.79
Discounted net	−2,500.00	−2,688.68	4,788.18	36,607.40	44,951.32
Net present value	−2,500.00	−5,188.68	−400.50	36,206.90	81,158.22

Note: Figures have been rounded.

The first four rows are identical to those used in the straightforward calculation in Table 5.2. The new rows allow the net figure to be discounted by a number of percentage points. The discount factor is the amount by which the net figure must be multiplied in order to discount it by a specified amount. It is calculated like this:

$$\frac{1}{(1+i)^n}$$

where "i" is the rate and "n" is the number of years hence. So assuming a rate of 6% and a forecast needed for year 2, the calculation would be:

$$\frac{1}{(1 + 0.06)^2} \quad \rightarrow \quad \frac{1}{(1.06)^2} \quad \rightarrow \quad \frac{1}{(1.1236)}$$

$$= 0.89$$

The net figure is multiplied by the discount factor to determine a more realistic value called the discounted net, a value which, when accumulated over time, provides what is called the net present value. Thus it could be said of the example in Table 5.3 that this project will yield a net present value of $36,206.90 in year 3. However, the point at which payback is achieved has been pushed one year further into the future, compared with the non-discounted example. This "extra" year for the investment to yield a return is an important consideration for the portfolio management team.

Internal rate of return
The internal rate of return is another measure used to compare one project with another. Calculating it is similar to working out the discounted cash flow, but in reverse. For example, the project yields $36,206.90 based on a discount factor of 6%. A discount factor of 200% would give a yield of −$1,237.41, a negative figure. Somewhere in between these negative and positive figures is a discount factor that would give a zero net present value, in this case, roughly 150%. This is the internal rate of return. Put another way, if all the money that was invested in this project had been borrowed, and the project broke even, the interest rate paid on that borrowed money would be the internal rate of return.

As a rule of thumb, the higher the internal rate of return the better. However, it fails to take into account the size of the project. One with a relatively low investment may have the same internal rate of return as one worth many times more.

Financial dependency network
Sometimes individual projects in a programme are not necessarily expected to show a "profit". What they must do, however, is show how they will use their funding efficiently so that the benefits identified at programme level may be realised (see Figure 5.1).

The business programme on the right shows a forecast cost of $4,028,750

Financial dependency network **5.1**

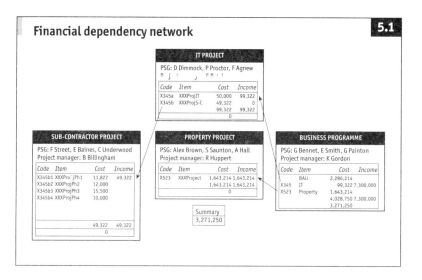

spread across a combination of business-as-usual activity and two projects (IT and property). For this investment, the programme forecasts income of $7,300,000. On balance, this suggests a "profit" of $3,271,250.

The IT and property projects are breaking even, as is the subcontractor project on the left. These projects are expected to deliver benefits that outweigh the investment being made in them, but these benefits are identified at programme level. Thus a different approach is needed to provide incentives for people involved in these sorts of projects. Rather than rewarding them when the benefits are achieved (which, in the case of a programme, might be in many years' time), it may be more effective to reward their ability to contain costs or produce quality deliverables on time. The programme must take care of the benefits management, not the projects themselves.

Planning for the unknown

Donald Rumsfeld, when US Defense Secretary, famously said:

> *Reports that say that something hasn't happened are always interesting to me because, as we know, there are known knowns; there are things we know we know. We also know there are known unknowns; that is to say we know there are some things we do not know. But there are also unknown unknowns – the ones we don't know we don't know.*

The Plain English Campaign commented: "We think we know what he means, but we don't know if we really know." Despite the complex way in which he expressed himself, what Rumsfeld said is relevant to project management:

- "There are known knowns." Rumsfeld was referring to things that have ceased to be risks because they have happened and thus it is not possible to prevent them. In projects, these are called "issues".
- "There are known unknowns." These are the risks that have been identified and which it may be possible to mitigate, that is, preventing a problem arising or reducing its effect if it does arise.
- "There are unknown unknowns." These are the risks that have not been identified or anticipated. They are the threats to a project's successful outcome that are not yet even known about.

Thus:

- a risk is something that may place the success of the project in jeopardy;
- an issue is a risk (known or unknown) that has happened;
- an assumption is a guess that, by virtue of being unknown, is a risk.

Risk management rather than issue management is essential to effective project management. Successful project managers seek to identify and mitigate risks, minimise the likelihood of issues occuring and reduce the number of assumptions made during the life of the project.

Any plan is a forecast. Risk management helps reduce uncertainty by using the steps in Figure 5.2.

Identify

Risks have different levels of detail. A high-level risk may be expressed as: "The use of new technology may create some unforeseen challenges during the project." This is non-specific, but early in the project's life cycle

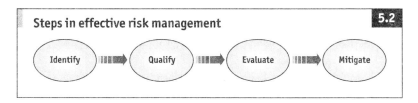

Steps in effective risk management | 5.2

Identify → Qualify → Evaluate → Mitigate

it may be sufficient to determine a "sense of riskiness", so some equally high-level mitigating action may be identified or an amount of contingency set aside.

These questions help not so much to identify specific risks but to establish the inherent riskiness in a project:

- Impact on business as usual
  - How long is the benefits realisation phase likely to last?
  - Will the project significantly affect the organisation's business-as-usual commitments, especially sales and operations?
  - Are any working practices expected to change as a result of the project?
  - Will roles and responsibilities change?
- Stability of requirements
  - What is the current burden of change within this business area?
  - What history is there of changing requirements in this business area?
  - Is this business area subject to external regulation?
- Governance
  - Will a systemised approach to the management of the project be applied?
  - Will a systemised approach to the development of any IT components be applied?
  - Will structured requirements-gathering and closure procedures be applied?
- People
  - How agreeable are senior executives to this project?
  - How dependable is the relationship between the developers and customers?
  - How long have those involved in the project worked for the organisation?
  - How well is the business understood by those working on the project?
  - What level of technical competence exists in the project team?
- Novelty
  - How new are any technological components of the project?
  - Has anything like this project been undertaken before?
- Complexity and size
  - How many customers or users are involved in the project?
  - How many suppliers will be needed?

- How many interdependencies will there be between this project and any others?
- How complex a technological change does this project represent?
- How long is the project likely to take?

As more becomes known about the project, the level at which risks are identified and articulated should become more detailed.

One or two people may have to create a high-level examination of a project's risk, but it is sensible to consult more widely when developing a more detailed risk register. This helps to make sure that specific risks are identified and are considered from an appropriate range of perspectives.

This calls for a risk workshop involving people from all parts of the project. No one should be excluded as the objective is to turn "unknown unknowns" into "known unknowns". Participants should be given a clear introduction and background from the project's sponsor. The project manager usually sets up the session, but if the project manager wishes to take part, an external, impartial organiser should be used.

The project manager should provide any relevant documents, including project management documents and reports on lessons learned from previous projects. It is helpful to highlight areas in which risks may be identified, such as:

- funding;
- timing;
- scope of requirements;
- customer expectations;
- supplier capabilities;
- roles and responsibilities;
- technology;
- methods;
- politics.

Participants write down as many risks as they think relevant on "reminder" notes. It is also helpful if they describe a mitigation, but this can be included later.

The way in which detailed risks are articulated matters a great deal. This note is neither helpful nor illuminating:

> **Risk**: No resources
> **Mitigation**: Tell management

A risk should be articulated as a combination of cause and effect like this:

> **Risk**: Key people from the legal team will be unavailable during the summer due to their engagement in other projects ... resulting in an inability to make critical purchase decisions.
> **Mitigation**: Secure the services of an external legal representative. Obtain portfolio management team authority to use legal team in precedence over other projects during the summer.

The underlined sentence shows the cause and its effect.

Many such notes should be produced during the risk workshop. When participants have had time to identify and articulate as many risks as they can, it should be possible to qualify them.

Qualify

It is important to rate and rank the risks to identify which most deserve the scarce resources available to the project.

The reason for writing the risks on reminder notes is to put them on a simple matrix like the one in Figure 5.3 overleaf.

This matrix rates each risk in terms of:

- likelihood – the probability that it will happen;
- impact – the effect on the project were it to happen.

The scales are not arbitrary because risks are positioned according to the scores in Table 5.4 overleaf.

Impact/likelihood matrix

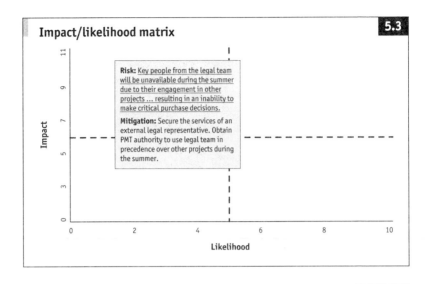

Table 5.4 **Impact/likelihood scores**

	Score	Risk
Impact	0	None, the risk has been fully mitigated
	3	Activity may be affected, but work can proceed to sign-off
	5	Deliverable may be compromised, but no effect on project completion
	7	Stage may be compromised, but completion is still achievable
	9	Project completion may be compromised
	11	Business or customer may suffer
Likelihood	0	The risk has passed
	2	Very low likelihood
	4	Low likelihood
	6	Even likelihood
	8	High likelihood
	10	A certainty

The impact list suggests some separation between the values, and the maximum value 11, which is outside the normal scale, suggests an effect on other projects, non-project activity or a client's interests.

Although the likelihood list appears to be no more than a sliding scale, it shows that issues can be identified, qualified and evaluated in the same way as risks. Risks and issues differ only in their likelihood. An issue has happened and scores 10 – a certainty.

Evaluate

Which is the more important, a risk or an issue? To those used to fixing problems, an issue is often more important because it is immediate and must be fixed; whereas those who are risk averse may wish to tackle a potential problem before it occurs. This argument, however, considers only whether it is a potential or actual problem. To properly understand the relative "value" of a risk or issue, it is necessary to assess its impact. When both the likelihood and the impact are considered it is easier to judge whether one specific risk or issue deserves more attention than another.

This is done by multiplying the two numbers to create a risk factor. A risk with a likelihood of 6 and an impact of 7 has a risk factor of 42; whereas an issue with the maximum likelihood of 10 (because it has happened) but an impact of 3 has a risk factor of 30. In this case, it may be more sensible to invest in mitigating the risk even though dealing with the issue seems more immediate.

It is simple to generate a risk factor to establish the relative value of the risk or issue. However, some organisations want to give each risk a financial value. The risk factor is considered in terms of financial exposure, multiplied by the likelihood expressed as a percentage (where 100% makes it an issue). For instance, a supplier who has agreed to a penalty clause may stand to lose $25,000 for late delivery. If the likelihood of this happening is 20%, the financially evaluated risk factor would be $5,000 (20% x $25,000).

Although the risk factor is now expressed in financial terms, it remains a useful way of comparing risks and helps determine whether the cost of mitigating a risk is proportionate. For instance, if it cost the supplier $10,000 to pay extra people to carry out some of the work and finish on time, this might be considered too expensive when compared with the relative $5,000 exposure. However, if the likelihood of a late delivery began to increase, the $10,000 may progressively become the more attractive option.

This approach is useful, but there is a danger that financial quantification will drive project personnel more towards analysis and further away from mitigation. In addition it can be difficult to know when to

Impact/likelihood numeric risk factors 5.4

			IMPACT		
0	**3**	**5**	**7**	**9**	**11**
2	6	10	14	18	22
4	12	20	28	36	44
6	18	30	42	54	66
8	24	40	56	72	88
10	30	50	70	90	110

(LIKELIHOOD is labelled vertically on the left-hand column: 2, 4, 6, 8, 10.)

stop quantifying the exposure. For example, the supplier at risk from the penalty clause may be exposed to more than the $25,000 charge. The sum could increase substantially through loss of reputation and other customers changing suppliers. The consequence is a risk matrix with no upper limit for financial impact, making it difficult to compare one risk with another, and almost impossible to cap the amount requested for mitigation.

A simple approach is usually the most effective. Not only is the numeric (non-financial) risk factor helpful in evaluating the relative worth of each risk and issue, but it also helps identify who should deal with it (see Figure 5.4).

A factor of 110 shows that an issue (which, by definition, has taken place) is affecting the business or a customer, so it must be referred to the portfolio management team for mitigation. Risks or issues with factors between 57 and 90 should be handled by the project steering group, and those with a factor between 21 and 56 should be dealt with by the project manager. Those scoring 20 or below should be assigned to team leaders.

This approach makes sure the right people hear about risks or issues for which they have authority to mitigate.

Mitigate

Mitigation is the process of making the likelihood or effect of a potential event less severe but, depending on the risk itself, there may be one or more mitigations available.

These are potential options: **S**hare; **E**ndure; **A**void; **L**essen.

Share

Risks are often shared. For example, the likelihood and/or effect of a washing machine failing may be sufficiently high to justify taking out a service contract. The risk is shared with the insurance company. Similarly, it is usual to share the risks and rewards of an initiative with a key supplier through penalty and reward clauses in contracts. For example, to mitigate the risk of a project going over budget, a customer might insist on compensation for every day by which the supplier exceeds a target completion date. However, sharing the risk does not always transfer the whole burden to someone else.

The project to redevelop London's Wembley stadium shows how mitigating one risk can sometimes have adverse consequences elsewhere. None of the initial tenders was sufficiently attractive to the Football Association (FA), but then an unsolicited tender proposed a more acceptable fixed-price contract. Knowing that a cost overrun was a major risk, the FA accepted the terms. However, the project ran late. The then chairman of Wembley said: "If we hadn't done that [agree the terms], Wembley would still be a shell and the FA would be bust." In this project a financial risk was shared but the risk of a poor-quality solution or late delivery was not, and it could be argued that it was increased because of the emphasis on a fixed budget.

Endure

As an assumption is a guess it is therefore a risk. It should be considered in terms of its likelihood and effect, but it may be decided that the project can live with – that is endure – the risk. For example, it might be assumed that everyone on the project will work an eight-hour day but decided that the project will live with the risk that some people may work fewer hours or be called to work on other projects.

Avoid

Some risks can be circumvented. For instance, a project may face a risk that proposed changes to a computer system may be delayed because of other technology priorities in the organization. This can be mitigated by using a manual alternative.

Lessen

It is possible to reduce the effect and/or likelihood of a risk. The specific mitigation may affect either the impact or the likelihood, or both, so it is important to know what the outcome should be. For instance, if the only person able to produce an important report is a novice employee, the likelihood of producing a poor-quality deliverable might be lessened by requiring their manager to set clear expectations at the outset. It might be further lessened by requiring the novice to produce a draft report at the halfway stage so that any quality concerns can be addressed. However, neither mitigation would reduce the effect of a poor report. To do that, the report's audience could be warned before publication to lower their expectations; something might still hit the fan, but not so much of it.

At the very least, the likelihood of a risk should be monitored to determine whether it is moving towards becoming an issue. For example, if there is a risk that time will run out before completion of user acceptance testing, the likelihood can be monitored by tracking the number of outstanding defects being recorded every day. If the number rises, so will the likelihood of the risk becoming an issue. If the number falls, the probability is lessening.

The risk register

It should now be possible to put all the information about a project's risks into a risk register to monitor and control them (see Table 5.5).

Table 5.5 **The risk register**

Risk	Likelihood	Impact	Factor	Mitigations	Cost
Pre-written, packaged software solution will not hold key sales data needed by marketing team, resulting in their inability to work effectively	10	3	30	**1** Continue to use existing sales and marketing system alongside new solution. ACTION: JP to advise sales team to prepare for parallel running. **2** Request a specific change from software supplier. ACTION: PT to obtain detailed quotation from supplier.	2 days per month to synchronise systems = $800 15 days' additional fees = $6,000

Risk	Likelihood	Impact	Factor	Mitigations	Cost
If the live date is missed, legal sanctions may be taken against our business, resulting in damage to reputation and other losses	2	11	22	**1** Identify this project as mandatory to make sure that it has priority over essential resources. ACTION: Sponsor to raise at next portfolio management team session. **2** Commence project early to allow for any slippage. ACTION: Sponsor to raise at next porfolio management team session.	Portfolio management team to consider effect on other projects Portfolio management team to consider effect on other projects
Based on supplier's past performance, delivery of equipment required for implementation will be delayed, resulting in delivery delay to client	6	9	54	**1** Identify an alternative supplier. ACTION: SS to ask Procurement for recommendation. **2** Instigate a penalty/ reward clause in the contract ACTION: JP to ask legal department for guidance.	$10,000 premium $5,000 reward provision

Risk	Likelihood	Impact	Factor	Mitigations	Cost
Key people from the legal department will be unavailable during the summer because of their engagement in other projects, resulting in an inability to make critical purchase decisions	6	9	54	1 Secure the services of an external legal representative. ACTION: Ask legal department for a recommendation. 2 Obtain portfolio management team's authority to use legal team in precedence over other projects during the summer. ACTION: Sponsor to raise at next portfolio management team session.	$1,500 premium
Total risk-based contingency budget					Maximum $23,300

In many of these examples, mitigation carries either a financial or a time cost, so each risk should be quantified financially to allow contingency funding to be provided for the preferred mitigation.

6 Planning: quality

A plan is a forecast. Many people think that a project forecast is expressed in terms of a completion date and a total budget, but neither can be predicted adequately until what the project has to deliver is known. Thus a forecast is better described as a probability assessment based on skill and experience of the time and resources required for the successful delivery of a specified end product.

The specified end product will not be produced by chance. It must be defined, planned, built, tested and accepted before it can be used for its intended purpose. This means that a successful outcome will mean different things to different people. The sponsor may consider as successful a project that delivers a low-cost, high-income-generating solution, whereas customers may expect it to provide something that works and is robust and reliable. For the developers, a successful project must deliver an outcome that is supportable since it may have to be maintained and managed over a long period.

When a project has been completed questions will be asked about its success. Posing them at the beginning of the project forces participants to identify success criteria, which might be:

- Does the new computer system process twice as many trades per day as the previous one?
- Does the new office provide each of the 350 staff with at least 36 square feet of desk space?
- Were all new staff recruited by the end of June?
- Have the new facilities been secured within their quoted budget?
- Have the new office operating procedures been made available to the Tokyo office as a priority?

These questions describe the quality of the project's intended outcome, but it is also essential to measure the quality of the project's output as it progresses. Only by having clearly defined and agreed measures is it possible to know whether a step in the project has been completed successfully.

Consequently, before creating a project time schedule or a resource plan, it is helpful to know what the project must deliver at periods in its lifetime and at its end. These are the project's milestones or "products".

If an activity fails to deliver or contribute significantly to the delivery of a product, it is reasonable to ask why time and effort were spent on it. This means it should be possible to show that all project activity contributes clearly to the delivery of specified products. Examples of products could include a:

- piece of tested software;
- marketing plan;
- test schedule;
- design document;
- "business case";
- presentation;
- conference;
- trained user.

Products result from activities; for example, training is the activity that delivers a "trained user" (the product). When planning a project that involves training, how long should be allowed and what is an appropriate investment? It is possible to answer such questions only when more is known about the product itself. The standard expected of the trained user must be defined. In the same way that success criteria have been described for the project, so is it possible to describe success at product level. In the example above, if the users have been trained to drive a car, these are some of the ways an examiner might judge their fitness to do so:

- Can they perform an emergency stop without stalling the engine?
- Can they reverse round a corner without hitting the kerb?
- Can they correctly identify and interpret road signs?
- Do they use their rear-view mirrors before every manoeuvre?

If time and cost were the only things worth planning, the roads would be full of drivers who had completed their training when their budgets and instructors' patience had run out. If the expectations of a project's products are clearly described:

- fewer activities will be forgotten;
- more activity will be focused on delivering the intended outcome;
- the suitability of estimates for timescale and cost will be improved;

- it will be possible to know when an activity has been "finished";
- expectations of a fit-for-purpose outcome will be commonly understood, thus reducing confusion and reworking.

The technique of product-based planning puts quality at the heart of planning, enabling the:

- products of the project to be clearly identified;
- products to be ordered into a reliable delivery sequence;
- quality of products to be described.

Product-based planning was first described as part of the PRINCE approach to project management (see page 14) and has become a widely practised, robust and reliable technique. It does not remove the need to plan a timescale and a budget, but it ensures that when developing the schedule and resource plan, they are based on a far better understanding of the intended outcome and approach.

Product-based planning produces the:

- product breakdown structure;
- product flow diagram;
- product description.

A simplified version of this valuable technique is described below. Details of enhancements can be found in the book *Managing Successful Projects with PRINCE2 (PRINCE Guidance).**

The product breakdown structure

This seeks to identify all products to be generated by the project to confirm the scope of what it is required to deliver.

It starts with the single product that the project is intended to deliver, which is the sum of a list of components. For example, a desktop computer comprises a screen, a keyboard, a mouse and a processing unit, which is itself the sum of smaller components, such as the hard drive, the motherboard, the power supply and the case.

Figure 6.1 overleaf shows a training course as a collection of component products. The training course is a "starter" product, but everyone's expectations of it may be different. To understand these better, break this high-

---

*   Office of Government Commerce, The Stationery Office Books, 2002.

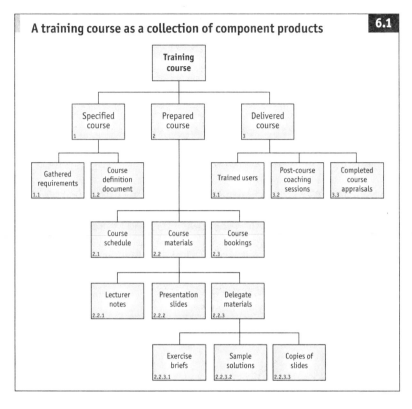

A training course as a collection of component products `6.1`

level, poorly defined product into ever smaller component parts until it has been expressed as the entire set of building blocks needed throughout the whole project.

Initially, the training course can be split into three smaller components: the specified course, the prepared course and the delivered course. It may be possible to estimate the development time and cost of each of the three products but there is unlikely to be enough information about them, so the specified course is decomposed into the gathered requirements and the course definition document. These are difficult to subdivide further, so this "root" stops there. The prepared course can be subdivided into many further products, each of which becomes redundant as those below it describe it better. For instance, there is no need to describe delegate materials – they are the sum of exercise briefs, sample solutions and copies of slides.

Planning should be a team effort, so it is wise to involve interested stakeholders in creating a product breakdown structure. A facilitator, usually the project manager, should lead the process. It can help to post reminder notes on a board as products are identified.

The facilitator should recap frequently what has been described so that everyone has a clear and common understanding. There are usually differences about products that should be in or out of scope. For instance, some may wish to include post-course coaching sessions (product 3.2) at which delegates meet the lecturer after the event; others may disagree. Each product identified will take time and money to develop and deliver, so a conclusion must be reached when the plan is created. If a product is to be excluded from the project but its development is still necessary to it, it remains on the product breakdown structure as an "external" product that must be accommodated in the plan eventually.

What began as a single deliverable is now much better defined as a list of component parts that together describe the scope of the project. The starter product has been decomposed into:

1.1	Gathered requirements
1.2	Course definition document
2.1	Course schedule
2.3	Course bookings
2.2.1	Lecturer notes
2.2.2	Presentation slides
2.2.3.1	Exercise briefs
2.2.3.2	Sample solutions
2.2.3.3	Copies of slides
3.1	Trained users
3.2	Post-course coaching sessions
3.3	Completed course appraisals

How detailed should a product-based plan be? The answer is the same regardless of whether the plan focuses on products or activities. As the plan will be used to delegate and control the delivery of products, the products that make up the end product should be subdivided only so far as the project manager can monitor their progress regularly and frequently. Project managers should ask themselves – and their project steering groups – how long they would be prepared to wait to discover whether a product had been completed or not. A good rule of thumb is 2–3 weeks.

Figure 6.2 overleaf shows some common errors in a product breakdown structure.

Some common errors in a product breakdown structure   6.2

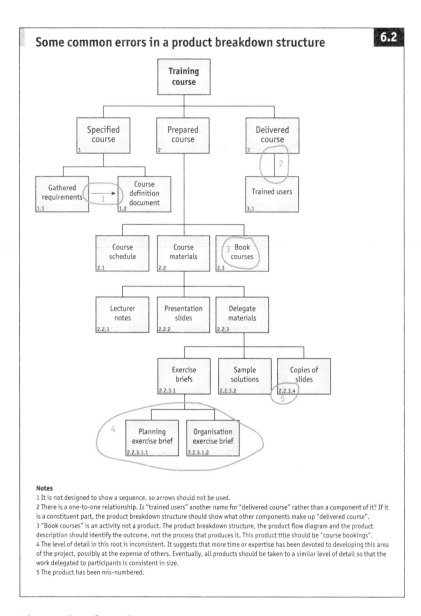

Notes

1 It is not designed to show a sequence, so arrows should not be used.

2 There is a one-to-one relationship. Is "trained users" another name for "delivered course" rather than a component of it? If it is a constituent part, the product breakdown structure should show what other components make up "delivered course".

3 "Book courses" is an activity not a product. The product breakdown structure, the product flow diagram and the product description should identify the outcome, not the process that produces it. This product title should be "course bookings".

4 The level of detail in this root is inconsistent. It suggests that more time or expertise has been devoted to developing this area of the project, possibly at the expense of others. Eventually, all products should be taken to a similar level of detail so that the work delegated to participants is consistent in size.

5 The product has been mis-numbered.

The product flow diagram

Once the product breakdown structure has been developed satisfactorily, it should be possible to produce a product flow diagram as illustrated in Figure 6.3 to show the sequence in which products must be developed.

Everyone involved will have an opinion on the best sequence and the process of creating a product flow diagram can help draw into the project a wide and varied range of expertise. It is sensible to involve the people who helped develop the product breakdown structure in drafting the product flow diagram. And it is desirable that senior managers take part as their views will be valuable. As everyone will be asked to estimate the time and investment needed to deliver each product, involving them early helps them to understand the project and the emerging approach.

Product flow diagram 6.3

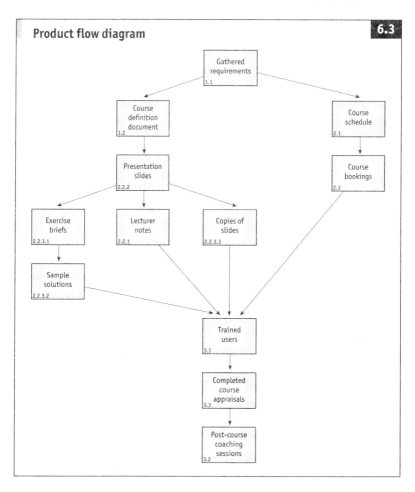

In constructing the product flow diagram the redundant, higher-level products should be removed and the remaining products should be placed in an order defined by their dependence. This can be time-consuming, but planning is a difficult and demanding process; it is better to identify the challenges and deal with them before it is too late or they become too costly to fix.

It is a good idea to use the same facilitator and to nominate a note-taker because products will be taking shape during this process and some of their characteristics will need recording.

At the outset, identify the start and end products, noting that there may be many products with no prior dependency. The sequence should flow from top to bottom and the remaining products should be positioned until most of them are on the board. To reduce misunderstandings, all products should retain the same names as on the product breakdown structure. The facilitator should regularly review how things stand and challenge them, and if appropriate change the order. It is important to allow debate, but the facilitator should not become so involved in the debate as to lose the chance to listen out for new products, which should be added to both the product breakdown structure and the product flow diagram. When all products are on the board, the arrows between them should be added, but only in pencil. It is normal for discussion to flare up again when the slightest change is made to the product flow diagram.

If the project is large or teams have already been formed, groups of products can be allocated to smaller teams. These teams may develop their own product flow diagrams, which are consolidated after debate. Alternatively, to improve the product flow diagram, they may work independently on the same products and then meet to identify and resolve differences.

Participants should not be allowed to express the plan in their own way on the product flow diagram. This can confuse others and introduce errors that will find their way into the time line and the resource plan. Every product should have at least one successor apart from the final one and at least one predecessor apart from the first ones.

A common mistake at this stage is to give the product flow diagram a timescale. This comes later in the planning process. Therefore, two products appearing next to each other (for example, presentation slides and course bookings) does not mean that they will be delivered at the same time. Indeed, the words "at the same time" should be avoided when discussing a product flow diagram. This allows the project to be discussed without preconceived and unsupported constraints, and matters relating

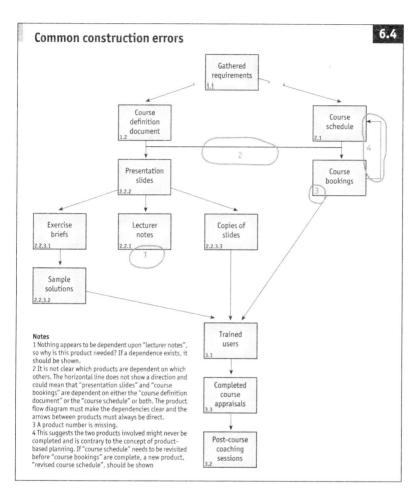

Common construction errors — 6.4

Notes

1 Nothing appears to be dependent upon "lecturer notes", so why is this product needed? If a dependence exists, it should be shown.

2 It is not clear which products are dependent on which others. The horizontal line does not show a direction and could mean that "presentation slides" and "course bookings" are dependent on either the "course definition document" or the "course schedule" or both. The product flow diagram must make the dependencies clear and the arrows between products must always be direct.

3 A product number is missing.

4 This suggests the two products involved might never be completed and is contrary to the concept of product-based planning. If "course schedule" needs to be revisited before "course bookings" are complete, a new product, "revised course schedule", should be shown

to quality can be articulated first so that time and cost expectations can be more effectively managed.

Some common construction errors are shown in Figure 6.4.

A robust plan means the same thing to everyone who reads it. Throughout the process so far, it is highly likely that questions will have been raised about each product and it is unlikely that everyone will have a clear and common understanding. The titles of the products are open to misinterpretation and do not fully describe their content, format and purpose.

The product description 6.5

Product title	Course definition document
Purpose	To ensure that the proposed course meets the client's needs such that approval may be granted for creation of the materials.
Composition	1. Introduction 2. Course duration 3. Course objectives 4. Instructional strategy 5. Prerequisites 6. Deliverables 7. Logistics 8. Timetable 9. Syllabus
Derivation	Course requirements
Format	A4 spiral-bound document, hardback and transparent cover bearing client's logo Colour
Audience	Customer sponsor
Quality criteria	1. Does it satisfy each item from the course requirements? 2. Is the volume of course content achievable within the timescale? 3. Has at least 30 minutes been devoted to risk management? 4. Is the course based around a case study? 5. Has a maximum number of delegates per course been stated?
Quality method	1. Quality review by supplier before presentation to client 2. Quality review by customer's internal quality review panel

The product description

It is often sensible to start the planning process with the product breakdown structure. The product flow diagram and the product descriptions are often developed together because the latter provides a definitive description of each product so that everyone has a clear and common understanding of it. While the product breakdown structure and the product flow diagram are being developed, the facilitator should challenge and capture the views of the participants on the character of each individual product through the product description (see Figure 6.5).

Title
This should be simple and clear.

Purpose
This section is not a repository for everything known about the product but a specific description of why it is needed, ideally in a single sentence.

If the purpose cannot be articulated, it is worth asking if the product is required at all.

Composition
This section should read like a table of contents. If the product is a document, the composition should list the section headings to appear in the end product. The content of each section can be expanded as this helps develop expectations of what the product will contain. Products are not always documents. "Trained user" is a product and its composition may be simply described as "a course delegate". Qualifying what standard that delegate must achieve comes later.

Derivation
This section is the equivalent of a list of sources. As well as listing the immediate preceding products needed from which to develop this product, it can also contain directions to any other materials or information necessary in its development. For example, the course definition document can only be developed once the course requirements have been completed. Additional information may be gleaned by interviewing a colleague who has had training elsewhere and is listed here to guide the person developing the course definition document to a further source of information. This section is also often used to list any standards to which the product developer should refer.

Format
This describes the physical characteristics of the product. In Figure 6.5 it is a document and its "look" has been described. If the product was "architectural plan", the format may be "A0 blueprint".

Audience
This important section lists the users of the product. It is important to know who they will be so that the next section can encompass their varying expectations.

Quality criteria
Because quality criteria define the characteristics of the product that would make it fit for its purpose, this list is the most important part of the product description. Just as the project has success criteria, so does each individual product and, in the same way, they are expressed as questions. If each question asked in this section were answered positively, the

product would be fit for its purpose and could be approved and signed off. The more sophisticated and elaborate the list of quality criteria, the greater the expectation of the quality of the end product.

This list not only confirms that the developed product is complete, but also steers the product developer towards getting it right first time. Knowing the audience and describing their expectations before development starts minimises the potential of developing a series of failed prototypes.

Creating a list of quality criteria can be helped by:

- arranging quality criteria in order of those who will use the product (the audience);
- asking everyone in the audience to prioritise the quality criteria relevant to them;
- checking all product quality criteria for consistency with project success criteria;
- asking whether the rest of the product description has been followed;
- expressing quality criteria as measurable and unambiguous questions to which "yes" or "no" are the only options;
- avoiding adjectives such as "effective", "clear" and "suitable" because each member of the audience will interpret them differently;
- checking the composition section and determining the quality criteria for each item listed. This will help if identifying quality criteria for the overall product is causing difficulties.

The number of quality criteria does not just indicate the product's prospective quality; it shows the quality of the product description itself.

Quality method

There are many ways of testing a product, including:

- examination;
- informal/formal review;
- inspection;
- demonstration.

In all cases, the product description is the yardstick against which the product itself is tested, and approval for the formal completion of the product can be sought only when the product is deemed fit for its purpose.

Quality method 6.6

Product title	Course definition document
Purpose	To ensure that the proposed course meets the client's needs such that approval may be granted for creation of the materials.
1	To provide a basis for change control
	To show how long the course will take to deliver
	To describe the objectives of the course
Composition	1. Introduction
	2. Course duration
	3. Course objectives
	4. Instructional strategy
	5. Prerequisites
	6. Deliverables
2	7. Something about logistics
	8. Timetable
	9. Syllabus
Derivation	Course requirements
Format	A4 spiral-bound document, hardback and transparent cover bearing client's logo
	Colour
Audience	Customer sponsor
Quality criteria	1. Does it satisfy each item from the course requirements?
	2. Is the volume of course content achievable within the timescale?
	3. Has at least 30 minutes been devoted to risk management?
	4. Is the course based around a case study?
	5. Has a maximum number of delegates per course been stated?
3	6. Is the document fit to be placed in front of a client?
	7. Is it long enough?
	8. How clear is the content?
Quality method	1. Quality review by supplier before presentation to client
4	2. Quality review by everyone else

Notes

1 There are multiple purposes listed, some of which duplicate what has rightly been included in the composition section.

2 This is unclear. The person charged with developing and delivering this product will need to know what is meant by this phrase.

3 These three examples are bad for different reasons. "Is the document fit to be placed in front of a client?" is subjective. The client's criteria need to be identified and written here instead. "Is it long enough?" is a closed question but begs the question "how long is long enough?". If the length of the document really matters, a better quality criterion would be: "Is the document less than ten pages long and more than five?" "How clear is the content?" is not a closed question, so any response will be a subjective judgment and of little value.

4 The product description has to answer the difficult questions as early in the project as possible. Proposing that a quality review will be carried out by everyone else suggests that either little thought has gone into deciding who should review the document, or that everyone really does need to review it. This will affect the number and fitness of the quality criteria.

There are many opportunities to introduce errors into a product description (see Figure 6.6).

Using product-based planning

Product-based planning is at the front end of the traditional planning process. It provides a means to articulate one of the three parts of a plan that is too often forgotten – quality – so that the time and cost components may be more reliably developed. The more that is known about the products of the project, the more robust the plan will be, so product descriptions should be developed as planning proceeds and greater clarity is gained.

It is highly desirable to involve the emerging project team in the planning process. It not only results in a better and more clearly defined outcome, but also promotes the involvement of senior stakeholders from whom approvals will be needed, and from team members who will be required to estimate the time and cost needed to deliver the project's products.

The people who have the task of delivering the project's products should be those who know them best. The project manager can never be an expert in every area of the project, so it makes sense for the product-based plan (particularly the product descriptions) to be developed in co-operation with the experts. The project manager should delegate creating some product descriptions to specific team members.

Having drawn up a product flow diagram, the team may be worried that a product description is needed for every product in it. However, in developing product descriptions, it makes sense to prioritise products that are critical, new or confusing, or all three. Producing proper product descriptions will lessen the risk of delivering something that is unfit and will need reworking.

Many organisations have a library of product-based plans and there is every reason to benefit from those drawn up for previous projects. This does not mean that a plan can be transferred from one project to another with a little tailoring, as all projects are unique. However, this is a great opportunity for the planners of the present to learn from planners of the past.

Another way of managing the potential number of product descriptions is to focus on the characteristics of the product that matter most. By shrinking the number of sections, it is possible to reduce the workload needed to create them. This can be achieved by replacing a number of product descriptions by a single table of product outlines (see Table 6.1).

Table 6.1 shows only five of the possible eight ways of characterising a product, but the loss of value arising from the absence of the remaining sections is balanced by creating an expression of quality that is more likely to be digested by the project steering group.

The product breakdown structure, the product flow diagram and the product descriptions will go through a number of changes, so maintaining robust control of the versions of the plan is important. New products

Table 6.1 **Product outlines**

Title	Audience	Purpose	Composition	Quality criteria
Gathered requirements	Developer	To capture the needs of the customer such that a solution may be described.	1 Introduction 2 Purpose of training 3 Scope 4 Audiences 5 Training needs 6 Logistical requirements: – timing – numbers – locations	1 Have all current project practitioners been included in an audience group? 2 Have training needs been prioritised? 3 Does the scope include all departments within the division? 4 Does the timing avoid bank holidays and the month of August? 5 Have locations been specified that enable all delegates to participate without incurring overnight accommodation costs?
Course definition document	Customer	To confirm that the intended course satisfies the customer's needs such that approval may be granted for the creation of materials.	1 Introduction 2 Course duration 3 Course objectives 4 Instructional strategy 5 Prerequisites 6 Deliverables 7 Logistics 8 Timetable 9 Syllabus	1 Does the document satisfy each item listed in the gathered requirements? 2 Is the volume of course content achievable within the allotted timescale? 3 Has at least 30 minutes been devoted to the study of risk management? 4 Is the course based on a case study? 5 Has a maximum number of delegates been stated?

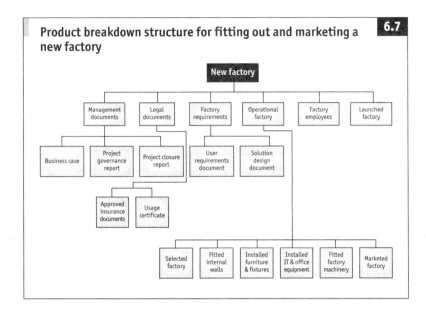

6.7

Product breakdown structure for fitting out and marketing a new factory

will be identified, existing products will be considered too detailed or too high-level, and some products will become redundant as knowledge improves and the plan is rationalised further. For instance, when developing a product flow diagram, there may be suggestions that the product breakdown structure has identified products that have not been fully broken down. Figure 6.7 shows the product breakdown structure for fitting out and marketing a new factory.

The product "factory employees" may be described as "paid employees, working in the factory", but placing it in the product flow diagram highlights a risk (see Figure 6.8).

The risk is that employees may be in place before the factory installations are completed and are being paid before they can do productive work. If factory employees really means "staff who have been offered a role with the company", the plan is missing the original outcome, "paid employees working in the factory", which remains an essential project milestone. Factory employees needs refining on the product breakdown structure, as shown in Figure 6.9 on page 108.

Figure 6.10 on page 109 shows the revised product flow diagram. The reconsideration of one product has changed the plan significantly.

The product flow diagram contains no timescale or budgetary information. This means a draft can be produced relatively swiftly and the basic plan

A risk highlighted by placing "factory employees" in the product flow diagram

6.8

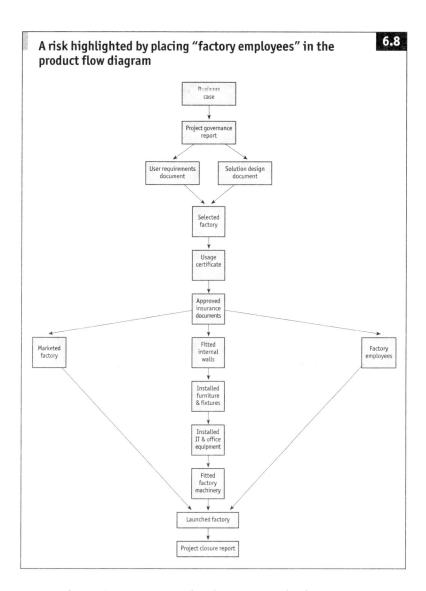

presented to senior managers so that they can consider the project's content without the usual pressure to debate time and cost. Until the products and their delivery sequence have been agreed, time and cost expectations will be largely unsupported by evidence and the product flow diagram describes the project without the need to commit too much advance resource.

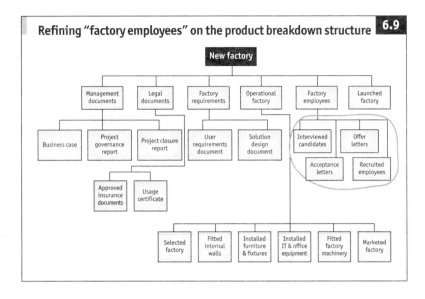

Refining "factory employees" on the product breakdown structure 6.9

If the timescale is brought up during discussion, the product flow diagram can accommodate it by dividing the project into stages against each of which a target date and budget may be placed. This should not mean that the date or investment has been promised, but this new expression begins to show how quality, cost and time expectations may need playing off against each other. Looking at Figure 6.11 (page 110), the project steering group will see what must be delivered to meet a deadline that, on reflection, may cause them to realise that compromises are necessary.

A means to an end

For a product-based approach to planning to succeed, there is no absolute requirement for each of the three parts of the technique to be applied. The technique is a means to an end. Ultimately, a plan will be more robust if it contains an expression of what the principal stakeholders will get for the time and money they invest in the project. However, all too often this is unclear, which is why a product-based approach is recommended.

The creation of a product breakdown structure, a product flow diagram and product descriptions means the plan is well under way. However, the inevitable questions remain: how long will it take to deliver these products and how much will it cost to complete the project? Now is the time to answer them.

Revised product flow diagram

6.10

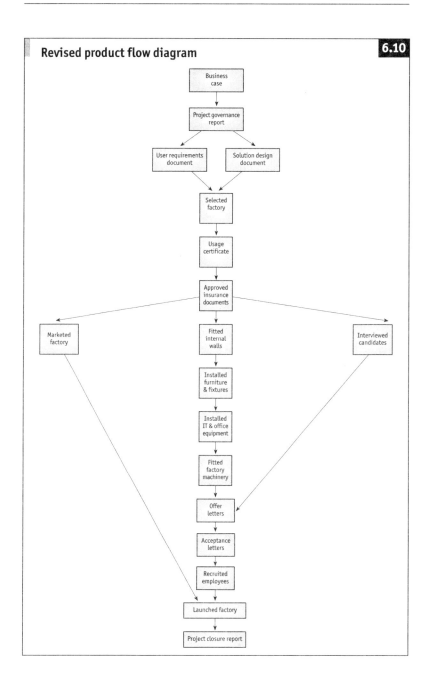

A product flow diagram with stages

6.11

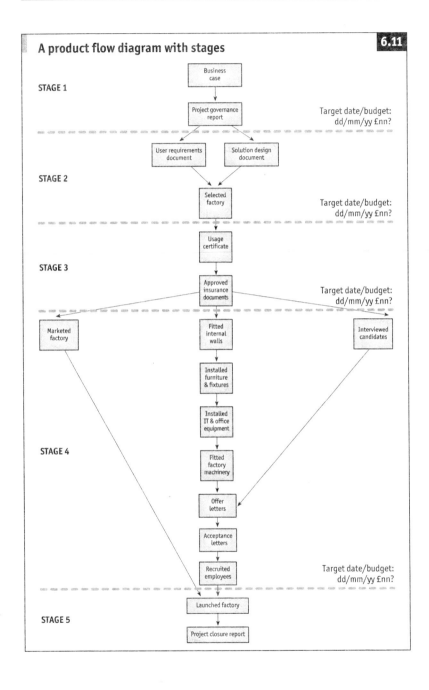

7 Planning: time and cost

The link between products and tasks

The importance of knowing what must be delivered cannot be under-estimated, but there comes a point when estimates of time and cost must be produced. To do this, you need to know what tasks will be necessary to deliver each product.

Many products begin life in draft form using the product description as a guide. Once the draft has been completed, it is usual for a review to take place. This is where one of the quality methods referred to in the product description will be employed. As the product is compared with the product description, reviewers identify errors, which they note and to which the developer must attend. Once the amendments have been made, it should be possible to submit the product for final approval.

The process can be summarised as:

- develop draft product;
- review product;
- amend product;
- approve product.

When drawing up a plan, it is helpful to know the relationship between products and tasks. Products are created as a result of the tasks above or any others considered essential. Therefore, a sequence of tasks must be performed to deliver each product on the product flow diagram. When imagining the list of things that must be done to complete the project, it is sensible to think of a sequence of products (the product flow diagram) in which each has a life cycle. The list will look like this:

Product 1
- Draft
- Review
- Amend
- Approve

Product 2
- Draft
- Review
- Amend
- Approve

and so on.

This important relationship will be revisited when the time schedule is developed. But before that something must be known of the techniques available to assist in estimating how long these products will take to develop and how much their development will cost.

Estimating techniques

An estimate is a probability assessment based on skill and experience of the time and resources required for the delivery of a specified product that has been considered at length during product-based planning. Knowing the product in greater detail makes estimating time and cost much easier. For example, how long is a piece of string (the product)? Once you know that the piece of string must be able to run twice around a package measuring 1m × 1m × 1m, leaving enough to form a double knot, the question can be answered.

Various techniques assist in estimating time and cost. They fall into two broad categories:

- Those that may be used without reference to any stored data or prior experience, for example:
  - top down and bottom up;
  - Delphi technique;
  - analogy.
- Those that require estimation data from previous projects, for example:
  - work distribution;
  - standard project/product.

Top down and bottom up

Top-down and bottom-up estimates are created at different points in a project's life cycle. A top-down estimate takes the whole project and applies an overall timescale and cost. It is created at the beginning of the project and breaks down time and cost across its stages, but it is unlikely to go into further detail because in the early days of the project, no further long-term detail will be available. Despite this, demands to know how long the project will take and how much it will cost will still be made and a response is necessary. Given the high-level nature of a top-down estimate, it is usual to add some contingency to allow for whatever risky assumptions have to be made. An example of a top-down estimate is shown in Figure 7.1.

Figure 7.1 contains expressions of time, cost and quality, but if the project steering group is to approve the plan, it will need something extra to give

A top-down estimate

		Stage 1	Stage 2	Stage 3	Stage 4	Stage 5
T O P D O W N	Time	8 weeks	8 weeks	10 weeks	15 weeks	15 weeks
	Cost	$20,000	$25,000	$45,000	$65,000	$5,000
	Quality	Feasibility study report	Needs analysis report	Design report	Developed solution	Tested, implemented solution

its members confidence that the first stage has at least been estimated to a lower level of detail (see Figure 7.2).

In Figure 7.2, the feasibility study report (the first product in this project) has been decomposed by a product breakdown structure into a set of smaller products so that a better estimate can be made of the time and cost they will consume in their development. When added together, these estimates should match the top-down estimates. If they do not, the project manager should provide the project steering group with refined top-down estimates and a formal request to amend the proposed budgets and timescales. This is bottom-up estimating, a technique supported by the product-based approach to identifying deliverables.

As each stage is completed, the process is repeated. As more becomes known about the project, the amount of contingency requested at each stage should be reduced and confidence in the overall estimate for the end of the project should increase.

A top-down and bottom-up estimate

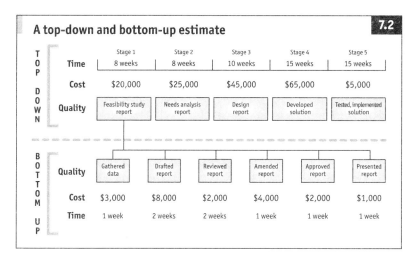

		Stage 1	Stage 2	Stage 3	Stage 4	Stage 5
T O P	Time	8 weeks	8 weeks	10 weeks	15 weeks	15 weeks
D O W N	Cost	$20,000	$25,000	$45,000	$65,000	$5,000
	Quality	Feasibility study report	Needs analysis report	Design report	Developed solution	Tested, implemented solution

B O T T O M U P	Quality	Gathered data	Drafted report	Reviewed report	Amended report	Approved report	Presented report
	Cost	$3,000	$8,000	$2,000	$4,000	$2,000	$1,000
	Time	1 week	2 weeks	2 weeks	1 week	1 week	1 week

Top-down and bottom-up estimating allows planning to take place at both project and stage levels, and helps overcome the challenge of the future becoming more uncertain the further ahead you look.

The Delphi technique

Named after the Oracle of Delphi, which the Greeks consulted before all major undertakings, this technique seeks to develop a consensus about an estimate through meetings, questionnaires and surveys. It was developed by the Rand Corporation in the late 1940s to forecast the impact of technology on warfare. Experts submitted their views on the likelihood, frequency and impact of potential attacks by the enemy. Other experts provided anonymous feedback and the process was repeated until a common view emerged.

Many projects have a considerable specialist aspect to them and project managers cannot be expected to be expert in every one. They can use the Delphi technique, carefully adapted, to obtain estimates in which they can have some faith.

Having used the experts to assist in creating product descriptions, the project manager asks them to state how much effort or budget would be needed to deliver these products. When the replies are received, feedback is obtained, usually anonymously. The experts are then encouraged to revise their earlier estimates in the light of these other views. During this process the range of the estimates should shrink as the experts home in on a figure they can all agree to. If complete agreement is impossible, average scores can be used to obtain what will still be a more reliable estimate than might otherwise have been produced.

This process takes time and should be reserved for areas in which the project manager has little expertise or where the range of initial estimates provided by experts is wide.

Analogy

Comparing the project, or aspects of it, with something similar is one way in which estimates can be developed. For example, a large computer organisation wanted to confirm that its software could handle 1m trades a day. This would have required more processor power than was available for demonstration. The company demonstrated that one processor could handle 100,000 trades a day and that two running in parallel could handle 200,000. It added three more processors and demonstrated that 500,000 trades were being handled. By doing this, potential customers accepted that by adding five more processors, 1m trades would be possible.

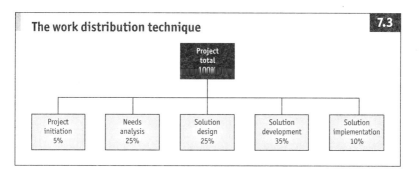

The work distribution technique 7.3

Similarly, physical and computer models are used to test different aspects of an aircraft's performance without having to construct a life-size version in advance.

Work distribution

Some types of project, such as the development of computer software or building new houses, are repeated within organisations. Much of the activity is repeated every time the project is undertaken so it would be foolish not to use past experience to improve estimates for the future. The work distribution technique relies on data gathered from previous, similar projects, which it apportions across the standard project life cycle to arrive at the proportions of effort or budget required by each stage (see Figure 7.3).

The success of such a model depends on the reliability of data from previous projects and the projects themselves being similar. However, if such data can be recorded (and improved over time), the model can be used quite flexibly. For instance, if a budget has been set aside, it is a straightforward task to apportion it across the different stages of a project

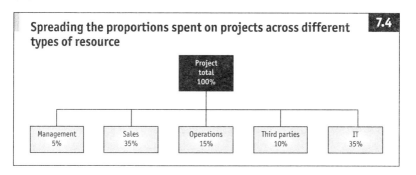

Spreading the proportions spent on projects across different types of resource 7.4

to get some sense of the amounts available for each. Alternatively, if the first stage has been completed and used a certain amount of the budget, the amounts likely for the future stages can be calculated.

Another method is to spread the proportions traditionally spent on projects across different types of resource (see Figure 7.4 on the previous page). Once again, this works best where the projects are similar and therefore the data are reliable.

Standard project/product

The standard project technique also depends on data from previous projects. In it a table is drawn up that applies two measures of the project so that an estimate for effort or cost can be calculated (see Figure 7.5).

This is similar to a rate card used by sales people to arrive at a price. In this case, the numbers (showing the effort in days needed to complete the exercise) have been refined over a period during which many standard projects have been repeatedly carried out. This produces a matrix that can be used to work out the effort required for future projects.

Figure 7.5 illustrates that this technique can be used not only for projects but for products as well. Many people who work on projects or business as usual do repeatable work that delivers essentially the same products every time which vary only in size or complexity. The table allows them to determine the effort needed on their next task simply by estimating its relative size and complexity. As long as both scales mean something measurable, the estimates can be extremely accurate.

For example, a department supporting computer users in a large organisation was responsible for moving people's desks and computer equipment to a new location and used a form of the table in Figure 7.5. For them, small in size meant that fewer than 10 users were to move,

Standard project/product technique 7.5

Size \ Complexity	Low	Medium	High
Small	1	2	4
Medium	3	5	9
Large	5	10	15

medium indicated between 10 and 19, and large referred to 20 and above. Low complexity meant that the users would be moving somewhere else on the same floor of the building, medium indicated that they would be moving to a different floor, and high meant a move to another building. Therefore, when someone wished to book a team move, an early estimate could be provided using the standard project technique.

Productivity

People are often called "human resources", but they are not robots and treating them like an inanimate resource underestimates the risk they pose to a project. These free-thinking, emotional, unpredictable human resources are, above all, different from each other. Rules of thumb when creating estimates about people's productivity include the following:

- **People will not be 100% productive.** The results of a recent survey were summarised as follows:

  > Flirting, gossiping and e-mailing friends is all in a day's work for office workers, it seems. A new survey suggests white-collar staff waste about 90 minutes of every day on non-work tasks. Workers spend 54 minutes a day gossiping, 16 minutes flirting, 14 minutes surfing the internet, nine minutes e-mailing family and friends and three minutes shopping online.

  Project managers, therefore, should allow for non-productive time if estimates are to be realistic. This is not to suggest that they should unquestioningly allow for some of the more dubious non-work practices identified in the survey, but they should take account of sickness, training and annual leave. This means that most organisations have a standard productivity rate, which can vary between 65% and 80%.

- **Productivity does not always increase when more people are allocated to a task.** Sometimes the reverse is true. Creating a document is often best left to one person; to assign an additional person may double the duration as they discuss it between them. The quality may well be improved, but that is only one outcome. If the target is economy, it is often preferable to identify the best person for the job and allow him to tackle it alone.

- **People have different productivity rates.** Choosing the best person for the job, or the fastest, may not always be possible. As people work at different rates, a person's experience and speed must be a factor when creating an estimate. A junior member of the team might take two days to deliver a specific product, whereas a more senior member could do the same work in half the time. When thinking about how long something will take to deliver, it is usual to think of ourselves. This "halo" effect assumes that everyone else is a good as we are. But everyone has a unique complement of skills, knowledge, experience and competencies, so an estimate should be tailored to the person who will actually deliver the product. A series of factors can be developed to account for different work rates. Alternatively, named individuals or skill sets should be identified before estimating the effort required to deliver each product.

▪ **Productivity increases are usually temporary.** Frederick Herzberg, an American psychologist, showed that even after increasing workers' salaries, the motivational and productivity improvement lasted for a relatively short time, after which they reverted to what he called the "Potter Line", a rate of productivity which, for them, was normal.

Here are some ways a project manager can increase the likelihood that estimates will be dependable:

▪ **Let people estimate their own work.** The halo effect can be used to the project's advantage. If someone estimates for themselves, they know best the speed at which they work and what else they have to do during the same period of time. There is an added advantage that once team members have estimated their own work, they have created a form of contract with the project which makes it difficult to suggest that the estimates are unreasonable or unachievable.

▪ **Make planning assumptions clear.** Once the planning assumptions are documented, they are available for questioning and challenge. In this way, the project management team can assure themselves that the estimates are based on reliable and robust planning conditions.

▪ **Agree product descriptions.** The product is intended to be the outcome that satisfies its intended audience. This target should be agreed before development begins, not only to increase the likelihood of a successful delivery, but also to ensure that both the delegator and the person being delegated to have the same product in mind. Once the outcome is agreed, any debate about timescale or budget is more rational.

- ◪ **Look at metrics from previous work.** If a team member suggests it will take ten days to complete a product when it took 20 to fulfil a similar objective, the project manager has useful evidence for improving the reliability of the estimate.
- ◪ **Negotiate penalty/reward clauses.** Estimates can be made to appear more reliable when penalties drive up the standard of performance and productivity, at least temporarily. Offering a reward can have a similar effect. Much depends on the person or team since everyone is motivated by something different.

Planning timescales and budgets

The product flow diagram is a necessary foundation for planning time and cost. Although it does not include a timescale, it does provide a clear delivery order for the products. Figure 7.6 shows a simple product flow diagram that can be used to produce a timescale and budget for the project.

Because effort has gone into developing the product flow diagram, the dependencies should be reliable. If they are not, the costs and timescales may be flawed.

The duration and costs of development for each product must be estimated. It is usual to create an estimating sheet containing most of the information on which the Gantt chart (see Figure 7.7 on page 122) and resource plan will be based. A sample estimating sheet might look like Table 7.1 overleaf.

The estimating sheet is product-based, but the tasks required to deliver

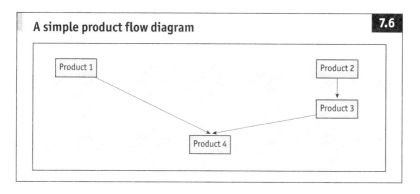

A simple product flow diagram 7.6

Table 7.1 **Sample estimating sheet**

Product	Tasks	Resources	Cost	Assumptions
Product 1	Develop	PR	0.8	PR took this long on previous project
	Review	ST/MW	0.5/0.5	Constrained to half-day as slot for teleconference is already booked
	Amend	PR	0.25	PR took this long on previous project
	Approve	PSG	0.1	Assuming PSG will approve via e-mail
Product 2	Develop	AK	0.5	Based on 0.1 per item x 4 items, plus contingency of 0.1
	Review	PR/MW	0.1/0.1	Estimate based on MW experience
	Amend	AK	0.25	Based on need to rework half original
	Approve	PSG	0.1	Assuming PSG will approve via e-mail
Product 3	Develop	PR	0.8	PR took this long on previous project
	Review	ST/MW	0.5/0.5	Constrained to half-day as slot for teleconference is already booked
	Amend	PR	0.25	Assuming quarter of product to be reworked, plus contingency
	Approve	PSG	0.1	Assuming PSG will approve via e-mail
Product 4	Develop	AK	0.8	AK estimate based on experience
		Train fare	$100	Costs to visit trade show
	Review	ST/MW	0.25/0.25	ST estimate based on experience
	Amend	AK	0.25	Assuming quarter of product to be reworked, plus contingency
	Approve	PSG	0.1	Assuming PSG will approve via e-mail

Note: Costs are in person-days when not monetary.

the products will be estimated. This is why they appear in the next column. The third column requires the project manager to suggest who should undertake the task. As the plan is not yet anywhere near complete, it is unlikely that the project steering group would allocate any people to the project other than the project manager. Therefore, the names or initials in the third column indicate the people the project manager wishes to secure. If names are not known, it may be sufficient to state what skill type is required, for instance, a junior analyst or a senior business specialist.

Human resources are not the only cost that must be identified. Although people may be the most significant investment, other costs attributed to the project must be included, such as travel, accommodation, materials and equipment. In a larger project, it is usual to have many human and non-human costs, so knowing the person or resource type and having some robust prior knowledge about the product (the product description) make it possible to estimate these costs.

In Table 7.1, the fourth column (identifying the planned costs) is a mixture of two expressions of cost: financial (the cost of going to the trade show) and effort (every other figure). Since the project steering group will want a set of financial figures, these two forms of expression will need to be combined into one single financial figure. This will happen soon when the resource plan is developed, but the non-financial effort figure is needed first because it will not be possible to calculate the duration without it.

Duration is a period of time, measured in hours or days. Effort is the time it would take a single, average person to complete the task if able to work at 100% productivity all the time, unfettered by any other work or distraction. Effort is measured in person-hours but people are rarely, if ever, able to sustain periods of any significance in which they can work at 100% productivity. Furthermore, many people are assigned multiple tasks, sometimes combining other project and business-as-usual work. Therefore, allowing for a productivity rate of 80%, the duration allocated for a four person-day task would need to be five days, provided that person has no other concurrent tasks.

Understanding effort in this way allows work to be spread across a number of people. For instance, four person-days do not necessarily need to be delivered by one person. They could be shared and, potentially, reduce the duration of the task.

The last column of the estimating sheet is where planning assumptions, which often remain in the project manager's head, are logged. The plan, of which the estimating sheet is a part, must be able to stand on its own without needing a project manager to present it. It must be self-contained so that anyone reading it has all the information they need.

Now there is sufficient information to create one of the most familiar depictions of a project plan, a Gantt chart. This describes the plan's duration and was developed by Henry L. Gantt in 1910. He produced many different charts which caused others to take an interest in what was a revolutionary way of communicating a message, but the type of chart commonly used today was refined in 1942. Figure 7.7 overleaf is an example based on the estimating sheet.

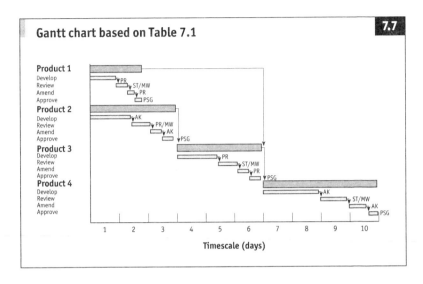

7.7

Gantt chart based on Table 7.1

Information from both the product flow diagram and the estimating sheet has been combined with the products and tasks shown on the Y axis. The human resources are shown next to the tasks, and the dependencies from the product flow diagram are shown by arrows linking the products (task dependencies are also shown to indicate the order in which they should take place). Even though it may have been a challenging exercise, the time taken to develop the product flow diagram will have been well spent. The dependencies shown in the Gantt chart are based on the skills, knowledge and experience of everyone who participated in the product-based planning workshops, rather than the instinctive view of the project manager.

The X axis represents information not present on the estimating sheet. The timescale or duration is estimated using the various information sources. They are:

- the product descriptions;
- knowledge of the people and other resource types to be employed;
- the effort intended for those resources;
- knowledge of estimating techniques and experience in using them.

Figure 7.8 shows how the duration of product 4 was determined.

From the estimating sheet, it is known that AK is required to devote 0.8 person-days to the development of product 4. Two days have been

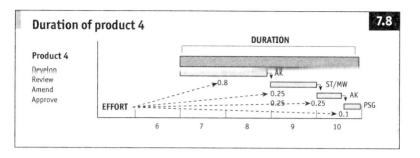

planned for the duration of this task to allow for AK's rate of productivity and any other tasks he may be undertaking. ST and MW are both asked to deliver a quarter of a day's effort during one day. Whether they are required to work in sequence or in parallel, they are not expected to exceed the quarter of a day's effort they will charge to the project's budget or to finish any later than at the end of day 9. The approval of the product, sought from the project steering group in the final task, requires a small investment of their time: 0.1 of a day's effort. Yet how sensible is it to provide them with half a day in which to complete the task? Members of the project steering group are busy people, so there is a risk that their signatures will not be forthcoming on the afternoon of day 10 unless the project manager has been particularly effective in alerting them in advance. With this risk in mind, it may be sensible to allow the project steering group more time, perhaps a week, in which to complete approval, no matter how small the effort.

The emerging plan contains an expression of quality, an illustration of the duration and an inference of what the costs may be. Now the budget needs to become more coherent so that everyone can see when the various financial commitments will be made.

There now is sufficient information from which to compile the resource plan, the third and final component of the forecast (see Table 7.2 overleaf).

This view is essential if the project manager is to have any hope of forecasting, monitoring and controlling the project's costs. It contains the person-day effort figures from the estimating sheet, but presented over time. These figures can be summarised in several ways. If an important event, such as the end of a financial month, falls at the end of day 5, the project manager would be able to show that the effort forecast during the current month is 5.5 person-days, and 2.0 in the next. Additionally, the figures can be summarised horizontally to give the project manager the total figure to be negotiated with the resource pool managers, who will

Table 7.2 **The resource plan**

	Day 1	Day 2	Day 3	Day 4	Day 5	Day 6	Day 7	Day 8	Day 9	Day 10	Total
PR	0.80	0.35		0.80		0.25					2.20
ST		0.50			0.50				0.25		1.25
MW		0.60			0.50				0.25		1.35
AK	0.50	0.50	0.25				0.80			0.25	2.30
PSG		0.10	0.10			0.10				0.10	0.40
Total	1.30	2.05	0.35	0.80	1.00	0.35	0.80		0.50	0.35	7.50

have to provide the people. For instance, AK is not required for 100% of the time, but he must devote 2.3 days in total for which the project must budget.

What this resource plan does not show is financial information; in particular, the $100 cost of visiting the trade show is missing, but so too is anything to indicate what the eventual cost of the project will be. To calculate this, a rate is needed for each of the various people who are working on the project which, when multiplied by the number of person-days, will cost their input (see Table 7.3).

Below each person's name is a rate; for instance, PR costs $300 per day and is needed for 2.2 person-days, giving a total investment in PR of $660. The whole cost of the project is $1,900, including the non-human costs shown beneath the total human element.

Many organisations split their resources into three main types:

- human revenue;
- non-human revenue;
- capital.

The first two have been identified already, but the capital costs, such as buying a building or a piece of computer hardware for the project, have not. Thus many organisations will express the budget in terms of revenue and capital.

The plan now shows what needs to be delivered, when and how much it will cost. This is the heart of what a good project plan should be. However, to determine whether this plan is achievable, the project manager needs to know that the resources he proposes employing are available, particularly if he has particular participants in mind. Without

Table 7.3 **Resource plan with financial information**

Human	Day 1	Day 2	Day 3	Day 4	Day 5	Day 6	Day 7	Day 8	Day 9	Day 10	Total
PR	0.80	0.35		0.80		0.25					2.20
$300/d	$240	$105		$240		$75					$660
ST		0.50			0.50				0.25		1.25
$200/d		$100			$100				$50		$250
MW		0.60			0.50				0.25		1.35
$200/d		$120			$100				$50		$270
AK	0.50	0.50	0.25				0.80			0.25	2.30
$200/d	$100	$100	$50				$160			$50	$460
PSG		0.10	0.10			0.10				0.10	0.40
$400/d		$40	$40			$40				$40	$160
Total human	1.30	2.05	0.35	0.80	1.00	0.35	0.80		0.50	0.35	7.50
	$340	$465	$90	$240	$200	$115	$160		$100	$90	$1,800
Non-human travel							$100				$100
Total	$340	$465	$90	$240	$200	$115	$260		$100	$90	$1,900

this, the plan is little better than an aspiration. The project manager must negotiate with the resource pool managers who nominally "own" these people to secure them for the period indicated by the project plan. It follows, therefore, that the resource pool managers also need a plan, showing which of their resources are engaged in what type of work, where, to what extent and for how long. An example is shown in Figure 7.9 overleaf.

Here two people, resources 1 and 2, are being used across five projects. The top half of the figure shows when each person is due to be engaged in each of the various projects; the bottom half shows the person-days commitment. On the basis of the timeline at the top, resource 2 appears to have two projects to work on during week 2, which, without knowledge of the relative effort needed for each, might be thought achievable. Indeed, without the bottom half of the plan, resource 2 might be encouraged by a resource pool manager to "do his best" to carry out projects 4 and 5 at the same time. The bottom half of the plan, however, shows that resource 2 is required to put in seven person-days' effort in five working days.

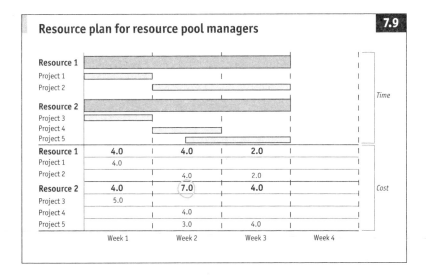

7.9

Resource plan for resource pool managers

	Week 1		Week 2		Week 3		Week 4	
Resource 1	4.0		4.0		2.0			
Project 1	4.0							
Project 2			4.0		2.0			
Resource 2	4.0		7.0		4.0			
Project 3	5.0							
Project 4			4.0					
Project 5			3.0		4.0			

Without overtime or lowering quality standards, this cannot be achieved. This message, together with everything else shown in Figure 7.9, needs to be made available to the project manager so he can see the effect on his own project plans.

Using the flexibility of the plan

Initially, most plans have a degree of flexibility. For instance, the duration or start and end dates of some tasks may be changed. So too might the number of people assigned to tasks, or the quality of the output might be negotiated. But any change made to one aspect of the plan usually has an effect elsewhere, so taking advantage of the potential flexibility in a plan is not always straightforward. The activity network illustrates this point.

This is a way of looking at the project's timeline to gauge the effect of moving tasks or products. For instance, Figure 7.10 is a summary of the Gantt chart in Figure 7.7 on page 122.

Product 1 is slightly different in character from the others. It can slip on the timescale for a limited period without affecting the end date of the project itself. If its end date moves beyond day 6, product 4 will be affected because it depends on product 1 and will slip by the same amount. However, until product 1 affects product 4, the flexibility for it to move may be helpful. The activity network identifies tasks and products where there is potential for movement and explicitly identifies those where there is none. It looks like the product flow diagram laid on its side (Figure 7.11).

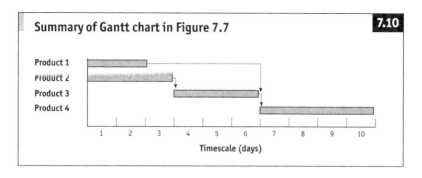

Summary of Gantt chart in Figure 7.7   **7.10**

Product 1

Product 2

Product 3

Product 4

Timescale (days)

Figure 7.11 describes some of the time-related characteristics of each product, with an example box identifying what is meant by the numbers:

- ☑ EST – earliest start time. The earliest point at which the task or product may commence.
- ☑ EFT – earliest finish time. The earliest point at which the task or product may be completed.
- ☑ LST – latest start time. The latest point at which the task or product may commence before it affects others.
- ☑ LFT – latest finish time. The latest point at which the task or product may be completed before it affects others.
- ☑ DUR – duration. The number of working days between the EST and the EFT, or the LST and LFT.
- ☑ FL – float. The difference between the EST and the LST or the EFT and the LFT. This is the amount by which the task or product may slip before it affects others.

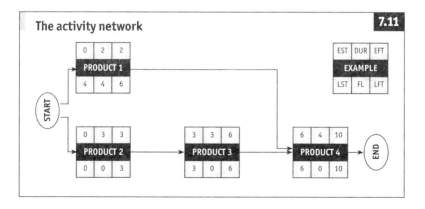

The activity network   **7.11**

In the example, product 1's capacity to slip is shown because it has a float of 4, but all the others have none. Because of their zero float, products 2, 3 and 4 are on the critical path; any slippage by any task or product on this path will result in an identical slippage in the project's end date.

A project may have more than one critical path and any of them might change during the course of the project as the float capacity is consumed by slipping tasks. Therefore, the critical path(s) is an area of risk in the project.

The fact that product 1 has some float may be helpful to the project manager. What would the effect be if product 1 were started later?

In Figure 7.12, product 1 has been allowed to start later with no effect on the project's end date. If managing the timescale and quality were the only things that mattered, this might be an acceptable change. However, since the project manager must also manage the budget, the effect of this change on the resource plan also needs to be determined. It may have been impaired already because PR is scheduled to develop both product 1 and product 3 at the same time.

As suspected, the effort planned for days 1 and 2 has shuffled across to days 4 and 5, and PR has become overcommitted on day 4. The likely consequence is that the project will slip, or the quality of product 1 will suffer as PR tries to keep within the deadline.

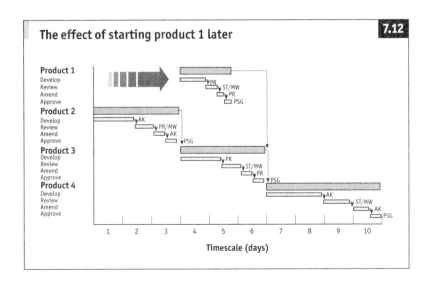

7.12

The effect of starting product 1 later

Table 7.4 **The effect on the resource plan of starting product 1 later**

	Day 1	Day 2	Day 3	Day 4	Day 5	Day 6	Day 7	Day 8	Day 9	Day 10	Total
PR				1.60	0.35	0.25					2.20
ST		0.50			0.50				0.25		1.25
MW		0.60			0.50				0.25		1.35
AK	0.50	0.50	0.25				0.80			0.25	2.30
PSG		0.10	0.10			0.10				0.10	0.40
Total	0.50	1.70	0.35	1.60	1.35	0.35	0.80		0.50	0.35	7.50

Resource levelling

Time, resource and quality are linked in the project plan, so change to one is likely to have an impact on another. Such challenges can arise at any time, but they come to light particularly when comparisons are made between what the resource pool managers are able to supply and what the project manager wants. This must be resolved through resource levelling.

The resource plan in Table 7.4 contains an example of a resourcing peak, which is circled. This is where the effort required from people exceeds their capacity to deliver it. Equally, there are examples of resourcing troughs, where people appear to be unproductive. Resource levelling aims to smooth the peaks and troughs so that resources are being used as effectively as possible. This is more easily done in a project where the resources have been assigned full-time, since the troughs are gaps in which people could be more productive rather than periods when they could be engaged in another project. This removes much of the need to negotiate with resource pool managers. However, because the opposite is true where the resources are assigned only for part-time engagements, it is significantly more difficult to level the resource plan.

Shifting tasks is one way of moving effort from one part of the plan to another and can work in a project's favour, for example where a peak is resolved by shifting the task with float to a point where a trough is filled. However, there are often more creative options available. These will be used not only at the end of the planning process, but also when the plan has been approved and is in operation. Further techniques to level and control the plan will be discussed in later chapters.

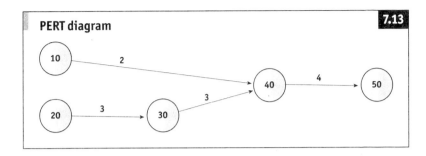

7.13

PERT diagram

Project evaluation and review technique

Another way to express the duration of the project is shown in the project evaluation and review technique (PERT) diagram. Developed during the 1950s by the US Department of Defence, it helps identify the critical path and establish the earliest and latest start and finish times, duration and floats. The product flow diagram for the example above would look like Figure 7.13.

The circles represent milestones and 10, 20, 30 and 40 are equivalent to products 1, 2, 3 and 4. They are numbered in tens so that additional milestones may be added if necessary. In this example, 50 represents the end of the project. The numbers in between are the duration of activities.

There are some important differences between this expression, the product flow diagram and the Gantt chart, as well as some limitations. For instance, the PERT diagram shows five milestones where the product flow diagram showed four. This is because the project evaluation and review technique requires each milestone circle to consume no time and require no resources. Therefore, the duration associated with each milestone is shown on the line that succeeds it. Thus the duration between milestone 40 and the end of the project, milestone 50, is four days. From a product-based perspective, milestone 50 might be questioned. What are its success criteria? Are they any different from those of milestone 40? If they are, might extra time be needed to achieve them?

This is not a technique to be used in addition to the approach described during this chapter, but as an alternative. Although it makes reference to milestones that may be considered "products", the emphasis on the quality definition of the products is far less. Furthermore, PERT is intentionally a means of representing a time schedule. It is rarely used to develop budgets.

Ready to go?

The planning process described here and in Chapter 6 has followed the sequence:

- Products
- Resources
- Effort
- Timescales

The creation of a project plan is a process that should begin with a reasonable understanding of what the project has to deliver: its products. It should then be possible to determine what resources will be needed and what effort and costs will be expected. Only then will it be possible to produce a timescale. This is a sensible approach to planning, yet all too often the process begins with a Gantt chart, with no reference to deliverables, quality or resources.

At the end of these steps, the plan will contain expressions of how expectations of quality, budget and durations are to be met. They will be consistent because the right amount of money to deliver the specified products in the proposed timescale will have been calculated. It may well be that the plan fails to meet expectations in one or more respects, but any change to one aspect of the plan usually has an impact on another, so the process should be reapplied to any changes. In this way, the plan is refined to a point at which it satisfies as many stakeholders' expectations as possible, ideally all of them.

The four words above spell PRET, which means "ready" in French. Only by covering these steps in this order is the plan ready to be submitted for approval.

8 Initiating projects

Except for the portfolio management team, which normally should be in place before the organisation undertakes a large number of projects, most of the project-specific roles emerge as a project gets under way. Some organisations would prefer that there were rules governing when

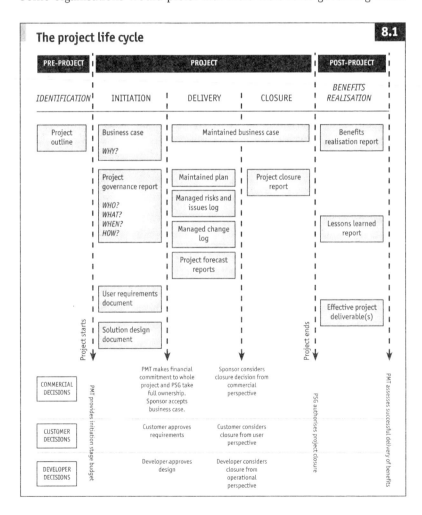

The project life cycle — 8.1

PRE-PROJECT	PROJECT			POST-PROJECT
IDENTIFICATION	INITIATION	DELIVERY	CLOSURE	*BENEFITS REALISATION*

Project outline

Business case — *WHY?* → Maintained business case → Benefits realisation report

Project governance report — *WHO? WHAT? WHEN? HOW?*

Maintained plan → Project closure report

Managed risks and issues log

Managed change log → Lessons learned report

Project forecast reports

User requirements document

Effective project deliverable(s)

Solution design document

Project starts

Project ends

PMT provides initiation stage budget

PSG authorises project closure

PMT assesses successful delivery of benefits

COMMERCIAL DECISIONS — PMT makes financial commitment to whole project and PSG take full ownership. Sponsor accepts business case. | Sponsor considers closure decision from commercial perspective

CUSTOMER DECISIONS — Customer approves requirements | Customer considers closure from user perspective

DEVELOPER DECISIONS — Developer approves design | Developer considers closure from operational perspective

a project steering group or project manager should be officially in place, but that depends on who is available and the political, strategic, legal and commercial priority of the project.

Consequently, initiating a project can be a hit or miss affair and rules will only partially succeed in regulating the chaos common when a project begins. What follows is a recommended approach. Those managing this process should remember that, at this time more than any other, the organisation may be uncomfortable with the proposed degree of governance, and therefore the need to sell the principles underpinning the whole approach to project management is likely to be greatest.

The project life cycle

Most people appreciate that a project should have a clear start and end, but it also requires structure around what happens between these points. Figure 8.1 shows the life cycle used throughout this book to describe the key deliverables and approval points.

There is an important point to make before considering this life cycle in more detail. Figure 8.1 shows the progression of an idea (described in the project outline) to the realisation of the forecast benefits (described in the benefits realisation report). However, only the initiation, delivery and completion stages fall within the life of the project. It is during these stages that the portfolio management team (or, in their absence, the company's senior management team) have delegated project ownership to the project steering group. They are responsible for steering the project to a successful conclusion so that the benefits will be realised when the main deliverable is used in earnest. During identification and benefits realisation, the project should be firmly in the hands of the wider business. In practice, initiation sees the project handed over from the portfolio management team to the project steering group, so it is normal for a period of transition to exist while the management environment emerges.

Once the project outline has been approved, the idea of a project is now on the roster and a budget has been set aside for its initiation. Ideally, a strict order should be imposed on the activities taking place during initiation; however, most organisations have their own approach to handling budgets, committing resources and decision-making, so it is more useful to consider the outcomes expected from initiation.

A common claim during the initiation stage is that there are too many unknowns to enable the business case and a project governance report to be created. This is a strange argument since the purpose of the initiation stage is to resolve the unknowns. The planning process must resolve as many unknowns as is possible so that the project steering group is clear about the risks. So although it is a difficult stage, it is the only opportunity to develop effectively the project's management environment.

The success of this stage can be judged against the following criteria:

- Is there a well-balanced project steering group?
- Has a project manager been identified and recruited?
- Does the business case propose an acceptable margin between costs and benefits?
- Have the customer's requirements been clearly and fully articulated?
- Does the solution design document address the customer's requirements?
- Does the project governance report, including the project plan, show how it will meet the targets set out in the business case?
- Have all products from this stage been approved by the appropriate authorities?

The business case

The business case underpins any project because it describes success in terms of measurable benefits. To forecast the intended benefits, much thought is needed and the results must find a place in the business case. The sponsor is best placed to develop the business case because it is the sponsor who will be charged with delivering the successful outcome and will probably have pushed for the project to be funded so far. Once completed, the business case should be submitted to the portfolio management team to be approved. If they do so, they should also provide the budget requested.

In practice, it is not unusual for the project manager (if one has been identified) to help to develop the business case, not only because it is an ideal way to become familiar with the project itself, but also because creating the document should be planned, monitored and controlled. However, this document must not be owned nor signed off by the project manager; if this happens, what clearer demonstration could there be of the business's lack of interest or dereliction of responsibility?

The success of a business case should be judged against the following criteria:

- Does it show the difference over time of the costs of the project compared with its intended benefits?
- Are all identified risks accompanied by a mitigation?

- Where alternative solutions exist, does it propose a preferred option?
- Can it be easily compared to other business cases when setting priorities?
- Does it consider not just the project costs alone, but also those that may be incurred beyond its closure?
- Does it enable a clear approval decision to be made?

Table 8.1 lists what should be included in a business case.

Table 8.1 **The business case**

Opportunity or problem	A description of the opportunity or problem that has led to the need for what this project is intended to deliver.
Strategic fit	Shows what contribution the project will make to the organisation's strategic direction.
Interdependencies	An analysis that illustrates the way in which this project may affect, or be affected by, others.
Success criteria	A set of measures by which to describe a successful project outcome.
Options considered	An overview, with supporting analysis, which describes the alternatives to the chosen solution. This should include the "do-nothing" option.
Selected option	A complete analysis of the selected option, including the following:
– Risks	What are the risks of the venture?
– Benefits	What are the merits of the venture?
– Costs	What will be the whole-life costs of the venture?
– Cost/benefit analysis	How well, and when, will the benefits outweigh the costs?
– Deliverables and timescales	What are the key deliverables and their due dates?
– Planning assumptions	What assumptions have been made in developing the business case?
– Benefits realisation plan	How will the benefits be measured and delivered?
– Management by objectives	What incentives will be offered (if any) to encourage a successful outcome?

How the business case is developed is largely up to the individuals, but what it should look like is more readily described.

Opportunity or problem
Opportunities may include the chance for commercial gain, such as a new market, or the chance to develop and sell a new product or service. However, business cases often describe a problem that must be overcome to avoid the organisation being exposed to risk. This section, therefore, provides an introduction to the risks and benefits sections under Selected option (page 138), which provide greater detail.

Strategic fit
This section shows how the project will contribute to the strategic aims of the organisation. This is an opportunity to describe whether the project contribution to each of the balanced scorecard quadrants is direct, indirect, partial or absent and adds a dimension to the business case that is not purely commercial.

Interdependencies
The project may be part of a wider portfolio or programme of work, so it will be helpful to show the principal dependencies with those other initiatives. This not only helps those who will have to manage those dependencies; there are also cases where knowledge of a project's inter-dependencies will help to justify it, for instance where it provides little measurable benefit other than in allowing dependent, benefit-generating projects to take place.

Success criteria
This section should describe fully and clearly what success looks like so that the decision to close the project is relatively easy to take. Examples of success criteria could be:

- Does the new computer system process twice as many trades per day as the previous one?
- Does the new office provide each of the 350 people with at least 36 square feet of desk space?
- Have all new staff been recruited by the end of June?
- Have the new facilities been secured within their quoted budget?
- Have the new office operating procedures been made available to the Tokyo office as a priority?

The last example shows that, where possible, success criteria should be prioritised. It is highly likely that sooner or later, decisions will be needed on some of them. The money may be running short, or perhaps timescales have slipped, or maybe the quality of the intended deliverable looks doubtful. The question to be asked before any such situation arises is: "Where would the project steering group be prepared to compromise their expectations of time, cost and quality?" This is why the project steering group should describe its priorities in the business case.

In aiming for a consensus, it is helpful for the project manager to ask each member to decide whether each criterion is:

- essential;
- desirable;
- nice to have;
- low priority.

These can be drawn together for the project steering group to agree the final list. This will guide the project manager in developing the project governance report.

Options considered

Most problems or opportunities have a range of solutions, more than one of which may be compelling. The business case must successfully outline the solutions most likely to satisfy the need so that only one is selected for full expression. Here are some examples of alternatives for consideration:

- The business case to justify a new building for a company might consider the merits and risks of staying put, moving to a new, preconstructed building or commissioning a purpose-built office.
- An operational inefficiency may be overcome by introducing a new computer solution. As well as living with the inefficiency, the business case could consider whether prepackaged software or a system developed in house would provide the best answer.

In both examples, the do-nothing option must feature. It is an essential part of any business case; not only does it provide a point of reference for other considered options, but it also often presents a compelling argument in favour of the project. Below are some examples of projects where the do-nothing option justified the eventual project:

- ◢ **Automation project.** Two computer systems were not connected but nevertheless were able to communicate because a single person copied data from a report from one system to the other once a month. The business sought to justify the investment needed to automate this process. It was only when it considered the costs of the staff member that it realised the investment needed to connect the two systems would take many years to justify and by then the two systems would already have been replaced. The do-nothing option prevailed.
- ◢ **Regulatory and legal changes.** Companies such as banks are heavily regulated to avoid the risk that money is mishandled. When a bank is informed of a regulatory change that carries a legal penalty for failure to comply, it has little choice but to accommodate it in its systems and operating procedures. The only option may be when to adopt the change.
- ◢ **Year 2000 date change.** During the late 1990s, it became necessary to amend the way in which many computer systems recorded calendar dates. Since many systems held only the last two digits of the year, there was real concern that some computers would fail to differentiate between the year 2000 and the year 1900. The change initiative was not justified by the benefits it would bring. Instead, projects went ahead because they would mitigate the risk of not amending the date. Millions were spent worldwide to avoid planes crashing, sewage plants flooding and hospital equipment failing.

Selected option

The selected option is the one that provides the most compelling argument in its favour. The use of the word compelling is intentional. Although the heart of the business case is formed from a balance of costs and benefits, during the early days of a project much of the debate will be emotional. It is important to avoid becoming either too driven by the stark numbers, or too persuaded by the power of an eloquent but unsubstantiated argument. The words and numbers used to describe the selected option must compel the organisation to put in a calculated figure, to face certain risks and to foresee the likelihood of a return on the investment. The costs, risks and benefits subsections must be expressed robustly.

Selected option: risks

A risk is a possible future event that may have adverse consequences. The business case should identify the risks to a project as well as its benefits from the outset. Although the project outline may have contained a high-level risk assessment, the sponsor will have been focused on selling the idea, so this may be the first opportunity to consider the risks properly. An early example of the risk register might look like Table 8.2.

Table 8.2 **Example of a risk register**

Risk	Likelihood	Impact	Mitigations	
Pre-written, packaged software solution will not hold key sales data needed by marketing team, resulting in their inability to work effectively	High	Medium	1	Continue to use existing sales and marketing system alongside new solution.
			2	Request a specific change from software supplier.
If the live date is missed, legal sanctions may be taken against our business, resulting in reputational and other losses	Low	High	1	Make this project mandatory to ensure it has a priority call on essential resources.
			2	Commence project early to allow for any slippage.

The risk register identifies things that may have an untoward effect on the project and the mitigations that may be possible.

Since the business case is, by definition, not a plan, it is not expected that the costs (in money or time) of mitigation will have been fully assessed. When the project manager starts to create the project plan, these risks (and any others identified) will be subjected to a fuller assessment to determine more precisely their effect on the time, cost and quality expectations of the project. However, a rudimentary assessment will be necessary if the cost of mitigation is likely to increase substantially the timescale or significantly affect the costs/net benefits of the project.

The risk assessment also allows the project's effect on others in the portfolio to be seen. The second example in Table 8.2 shows how a choice made at this stage may affect the provision of resources to, or the duration of, other projects.

Selected option: benefits
This section should describe clearly each benefit in turn, including how they are to be measured and quantified in financial terms.

In preparation for the cost/benefit analysis, it is necessary to show the benefits over time (see Table 8.3).

Table 8.3 **Benefits over time ($)**

	Year 0	Year 1	Year 2	Year 3	Year 4
Increased revenues		**5,000**	**60,000**	**60,000**	**70,000**
Increased customer satisfaction		5,000	10,000	10,000	10,000
Competitor removal			20,000	20,000	20,000
Customers from new market			30,000	30,000	40,000
Cost savings		**8,000**	**10,000**	**11,000**	**11,000**
Headcount savings		5,000	5,000	5,000	5,000
Removal of redundant IT kit		3,000	5,000	6,000	6,000
Total		**13,000**	**70,000**	**71,000**	**81,000**
Cumulative total		**13,000**	**83,000**	**154,000**	**235,000**

Selected option: costs

Every cost associated with the project should be identified so that it can be quantified. Costs should not be only those expected up to the point of project closure; they should also include the operational, maintenance and support of the deliverable the project is producing. There is a good reason for this. The benefits of a project are unlikely to be realised until some time after it has been closed, yet running costs will be incurred while waiting for those benefits. Consequently, they must be shown over the same time period for a realistic comparison of costs and benefits to be made.

Budgets may be needed in:

- company personnel;
- external contract staff;
- consultants;
- hardware;
- software;
- licences;

- property;
- expenses (accommodation, travel, and so on);
- maintenance contracts;
- environment and operations.

To aid the cost/benefit analysis, the costs shown over time should be presented in the same form as the benefits (see Table 8.4).

Table 8.4 **Costs over time ($)**

	Year 0	Year 1	Year 2	Year 3	Year 4
Resources	1,300	12,250	16,820	12,600	19,850
Consumables				1,000	
Hardware			28,000		
Software			17,000		
Environmental				11,000	
Accommodation	500	1,200	1,200	1,200	1,200
Expenses	700	2,400	1,600	1,600	3,200
Total	**2,500**	**15,850**	**64,620**	**27,400**	**24,250**
Cumulative total	**2,500**	**18,350**	**82,970**	**110,370**	**134,620**

Selected option: cost/benefit analysis
This will show whether the project is forecast to deliver a successful outcome and when. It provides a single view of the costs and benefits (see Table 8.5).

Table 8.5 **Costs and benefits ($)**

	Year 0	Year 1	Year 2	Year 3	Year 4
Benefits	0	13,000	70,000	71,000	81,000
Costs	2,500	15,850	64,620	27,400	24,250
Total	**–2,500**	**–2,850**	**5,380**	**43,600**	**56,750**
Cumulative	**–2,500**	**–5,350**	**30**	**43,630**	**100,380**

Payback will be achieved in year 2 but it may also be desirable to show the discounted cash flow (see Table 8.6).

Table 8.6 **Discounted cash flow ($)**

	Year 0	Year 1	Year 2	Year 3	Year 4
Benefits	0.00	13,000.00	70,000.00	71,000.00	81,000.00
Costs	2,500.00	15,850.00	64,620.00	27,400.00	24,250.00
Net	−2,500.00	−2,850.00	5,380.00	43,600.00	56,750.00
Cumulative	−2,500.00	−5,350.00	30.00	43,630.00	100,380.00
Discount factor	1.00	0.94	0.89	0.84	0.79
Discounted net	−2,500.00	−2,688.68	4,788.18	36,607.40	44,951.32
Net present value	−2,500.00	−5,188.68	−400.50	36,206.90	81,158.22

Note: Figures have been rounded.

If the project is part of a wider programme, it may be appropriate to include a financial dependency network to show the relationship between the different parts of the programme, and identify this specific project, like this example from Chapter 5 (Figure 8.2).

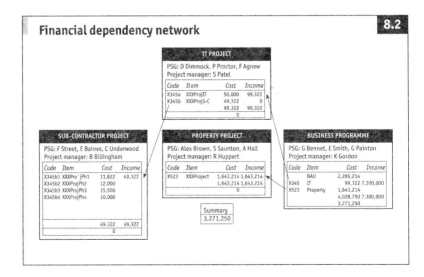

Financial dependency network 8.2

Selected option: deliverables and timescales
The business case has yet to describe what the project will deliver; so far, it is no more than a commercially focused response to a problem or an opportunity. This section presents a chance to describe what the project will produce during its initiation, delivery and closure stages, and when. This will give readers an early understanding of the project's outcome from a non-commercial perspective, identifying target dates by which key milestones should be met.

This is not a plan. A separate set of materials will be produced to describe how, if at all, these dates are to be met. Until the project plan is produced, the high-level deliverables and timescales listed here are only aspirations. However, unrefined as they may be, they are probably an improvement on what was included in the project outline and describe another important dimension of the management environment. Table 8.7 shows what this section may look like.

Table 8.7 **Deliverables and timescales**

Product	Target completion date	Status
Project outline	dd/mm/yy	Complete
Business case	dd/mm/yy	Under way
Project governance report	dd/mm/yy	
User requirements document	dd/mm/yy	
Solution design document	dd/mm/yy	
Developed solution	dd/mm/yy	
Tested solution	dd/mm/yy	
Approved solution	dd/mm/yy	
Project closure report	dd/mm/yy	
Lessons learned	dd/mm/yy	
Benefits realisation report	dd/mm/yy	

Selected option: planning assumptions
None of the numbers or dates in any of the examples in this chapter has been explained. There is no audit trail to describe how they were derived or calculated. Although it is dangerous to make assumptions, by its nature, planning is educated guesswork. Those considering the business case will

wish to know how the numbers and dates quoted were arrived at, so a list of planning assumptions must be included that fully describes the calculations in the business case.

Example planning assumptions include the following:

Benefits
- "Redundant kit" has been valued on the basis of a saving on the monthly lease rate.
- "Competitor removal" has been valued on the basis that the company will gain 30 new clients per month when its closest competitor is removed.

Costs
- People participating in the project will work a standard eight-hour day.
- A flat cost rate has been applied to all internal resources.
- A flat cost rate plus a margin of 30% has been applied to all external resources.
- 20 days' holiday per person have been included.
- No activity is expected during the 14-day Christmas and New Year period.

Selected option: benefits realisation plan
This section describes how the intended benefits will be measured, tracked and delivered. This is discussed in detail in Chapter 12.

Selected option: management by objectives
The last section of the business case recognises that most people need some form of incentive to achieve demanding targets. The business case itself is a series of targets including dates, budgets and "profits", and those engaged in delivering the project may be encouraged if their remuneration is linked to its success.

It is not unusual for the project steering group, and the sponsor in particular, to have their personal reward packages linked to the project delivering payback on the planned date. However, the eventual profitability of the outcome is only partly in the project manager's control, so it is unusual to reward the project manager if the project achieves payback. Rather, project managers should be rewarded on their ability to manage change. They should be offered incentives to apply an effective change control process, maintain the plan against which changes will be measured and apply management by exception so that the right people take the right decisions at the right time.

The business case – a summary

The business case is the single most important document in the project, so it follows that it should be robust, clear and decisive in its recommendation. Yet despite the energy invested in creating it, the organisation may not be much nearer knowing how the targets identified in the business case are to be met. This is the purpose of the project governance report (which includes the all-important project plan). It, too, must be completed by the end of the initiation stage if the essential questions are to be answered before the project moves into the delivery stage.

The project governance report

As soon as the initiation stage has begun, questions will be asked about the project's future. The business case seeks to answer the question: Why is this project necessary? Four more questions must now be answered:

- Who will be involved in the management of the project?
- What will the project deliver?
- When will it deliver it?
- How much will it cost?

The answers are contained in the project governance report. As these challenging questions are posed, the project governance report gradually accommodates ever more detail about the emerging project. At the end of this stage, these questions must have been answered to the full satisfaction of the senior management team so that the portfolio management team can delegate responsibility to the project steering group.

Some organisations attempt to mandate the point at which development of the project governance report should begin. Although there will be many gaps in it at the beginning of the initiation stage, this is not necessarily a bad thing. The gaps demonstrate what remains unknown and thus what needs to be resolved before the project can move confidently into the delivery stage. So, in practice, the project governance report is best begun as soon as the project manager is in place. Even if the business case has yet to be completed, the project governance report is crucial and serves to remind everyone what questions remain to be answered.

Table 8.8 overleaf lists what should be included in the project governance report.

Table 8.8 **Project governance report**

Organisation	
Organisation chart	What are the reporting lines?
Roles and responsibilities	Who are the chosen incumbents and what are their responsibilities?
Communications plan	How will the project's stakeholders be engaged?

Project plan	
Quality plan	What must the project deliver?
– Deliverables	
– Responsibilities	
– Standards	
Planning assumptions	What caveats have been attached to the plan?
Time schedule	When is the project intended to deliver its milestones?
Resource plan	What resources are to be used and when?
Risks	What are the possible challenges that the project may face, and what mitigations are proposed?
Project controls	How will the project be kept on track?
– Control cycle	What interventions have been planned?
– Escalation management	How will problems (real or forecast) be escalated?
– Change control	How will changes be considered?
– Configuration control	How will control be maintained over the project's products?
– Quality control	How will products be tested?
– Risk and issue management	How will risks and issues be managed?

The success of the project governance report can be judged against these criteria:

- ☑ Does it identify and describe the roles and responsibilities of those who will form the project's management team?
- ☑ Does it show how time, cost and quality targets identified in the business case may be met?
- ☑ Are the time, cost and quality components of the plan consistent with each other?
- ☑ Does it describe how the project will be kept on track?
- ☑ Does it enable a clear approval decision to be made?

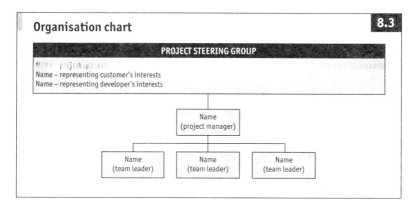

Organisation chart

8.3

PROJECT STEERING GROUP

Name – project sponsor
Name – representing customer's interests
Name – representing developer's interests

Name
(project manager)

Name
(team leader)

Name
(team leader)

Name
(team leader)

Consequently, it should include the following components.

Organisation

Organisation chart
This should identify the roles in the project and the reporting lines between them. As people are identified for each role, their names should be placed clearly in the appropriate boxes. It can be all too easy to deny knowledge of involvement, so this demonstration of their participation is a further means of informing the people chosen, and others, of their role. Something similar to Figure 8.3 is required, replacing the question marks with the names of the participants.

Roles and responsibilities
A title can be misunderstood or misinterpreted, so for each role in the organisation chart, the respective responsibilities must be described fully so that all incumbents are clear about what their own role, and those of the others, entails.

Communications plan
The communications plan will describe:

- what information must be communicated throughout the project and beyond;
- who needs to receive this information;
- what the communication format should be and who should develop or present it;
- when it is needed.

Communication plan table — 8.4

Audience \ Information needs	Continued project viability	Suitability of management environment	Initial time, cost, quality, expectations	Current time, cost, quality targets	Notification report	Project overview	Implementation plan
PMT	A	B		E	H		
PSG	A	B	C	F	H		
PM		B	D	G	H		
Delivery teams			D	G		I	K
Customers						J	L
Developers						J	L

PMT = Portfolio management team
PSG = Project steering group
PM = Project manager

It usually focuses on those communications necessary to ensure that the project's stakeholders remain sufficiently engaged. Principally, this means maintaining suitable lines of communication with the project's management and delivery teams. However, earlier analysis may also have identified important stakeholders outside the immediate project environment, so the plan should accommodate their communication needs too.

A communication plan can be broken into two parts:

- a table, identifying the information needs and audiences;
- a list of communication types, with dates or frequencies, by which those audiences may obtain the information they need.

The table may look like the one in Figure 8.4. The letters (see Table 8.9) provide a key to the form of the communication and when it should occur.

Project governance report – project plan

This is a living document that describes how the targets set in the business case can be met. The project plan contained in the project governance report is a snapshot taken when the initiation stage is about to be completed. It is used by the project steering group to confirm that they are confident of the plan's forecasts of timescale, budget and quality and of

Table 8.9 **Key to communication table**

A	Business case will be updated and presented by the sponsor at each and every stage during the project
B	Project governance report will be developed and submitted during the initiation stage by the project manager to describe the project's management environment
C	The project plan component of the project governance report will be used to accommodate the project steering group's expectations of timescale, cost and quality
D	The project plan component of the project governance report will be used by the project manager to show delivery teams how expectations of time, cost and quality can be met
E	The project forecast report will be used by the project manager to communicate progress and issue a revised forecast every two months
F	The project forecast report will be used by the project manager to communicate progress and issue a revised forecast every month
G	The project forecast report will be used by the project manager to communicate progress and issue a revised forecast every week
H	A notification report will be produced immediately by the project manager if at any time the project is forecast to be completed outside the pre-agreed escalation conditions for time and budget
I	A project overview will be created as a slide show to be presented to the delivery team by the project manager at the end of the initiation stage. This presentation will be sent via e-mail to anyone joining the project after it has begun
J	A project overview will be created as a slide show to be presented to customer and developer stakeholders by the project steering group at the end of the initiation stage
K	A detailed implementation plan will be produced by the project manager early in the delivery stage to obtain the delivery team's commitment to the approach being taken
L	The implementation plan will be presented by the project manager as a slide show to customer and developer stakeholders to ensure they understand the implications for their business-as-usual activity during implementation

taking control from the portfolio management team. This snapshot will be retained as a yardstick for measuring progress. It should never be altered because that would undermine the project manager's ability to manage change. Instead, a copy of the project plan is used to record progress and changes and to show what effect they have had on time, cost and quality expectations.

The project plan must spell out how these time, cost and quality expectations are to be met. It may also suggest at any point in the project's life cycle that they cannot be met. In either case, the project plan provides the evidence. It supports debate between the project steering group and the project manager and helps to prevent the project being driven by emotion alone.

The project plan is based on four components:

◪ quality management and deliverables;
◪ costs (resources and budgets);
◪ timescales;
◪ controls.

Quality plan
This describes how the end product will be developed and delivered to an acceptable standard, on time and to budget.

Quality plan: deliverables
This section must describe the project's deliverables. This means not merely the specified end product, such as a building, a computer system or a set of working practices, but also all other deliverables that must be produced throughout the life of the project and that lead to that specified

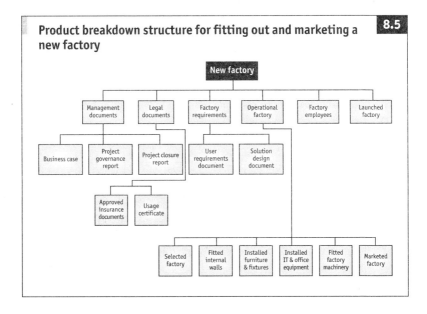

8.5

Product breakdown structure for fitting out and marketing a new factory

Table 8.10 **Product deliverables**

Title	Purpose	Composition	Quality criteria
Project outline	To describe the idea of the project such that a decision may be made to fund the initiation stage	Sponsor Title Objective Benefits Scope Key products Timescale Investment Investment needed for next stage Planning assumptions Risks	Does the document provide sufficient information from which to make a funding decision? Have the benefits been quantified in commercial terms? Are the expressions of timescale and cost consistent with each other? Are the estimates quoted each supported by planning assumptions? Has a specific figure been included for the funding needed for the next stage?

Business case	To confirm the commercial viability of the project so that a go/no-go decision may be made to fund its continuation	Opportunity or problem
		Strategic fit
		Interdependencies
		Success criteria
		Options considered
		Selected option
		   – Risks
		   – Benefits
		   – Costs
		   – Cost/benefit analysis
		   – Deliverables and timescales
		   – Planning assumptions
		   – Benefits realisation plan
		   – Management by objectives
			Does the document provide sufficient information from which to make a go/no-go decision?
			Has the margin between the costs and benefits been explicitly identified?
			Have all calculations been subjected to discounted cash flow analysis?
			Are all success criteria measurable?
			Has it been made clear why options have been discounted?
			Have all risks been evaluated for likelihood and effect?
			Are the estimates quoted each supported by planning assumptions?
			Is there clear evidence to support the chosen option?

Title	Purpose	Composition	Quality criteria
Project governance report	To describe the management environment of the project such that it may be managed to a planned conclusion	Organisation – Organisation chart – Roles and responsibilities – Communications plan Project plan – Quality plan – Deliverables – Responsibilities – Standards – Planning assumptions – Time schedule – Resource plan – Risks Project controls – Control cycle – Escalation management – Change control – Configuration control – Quality control – Risk and issue management	Does the document clearly show whether and how the targets for time, cost and quality set in the business case can be met? Are all risks supported by a mitigation plan? Have all risk mitigations been assessed for their effect on the plan? Have all key deliverables been described by means of a product description? Are all incumbents identified in the organisation section aware of their responsibilities? Are the plans for time, cost and quality consistent with each other? Are the project controls adequate for the type, size and criticality of project?

end product. This is one way of describing the scope of the project and the product breakdown structure from Chapter 6 (reproduced here as Figure 8.5 on page 150) helps to illustrate it.

Each deliverable must be described so that those investing in the project can see what they will get for their investment. This is best described through product descriptions. However, since there may be many of them, they can be put in an appendix, or better still, included in the main document but tabulated to make them more palatable (see Table 8.10 above).

This section can also benefit from showing the order in which the deliverables must be produced. Although this will not include a timescale,

Product flow diagram

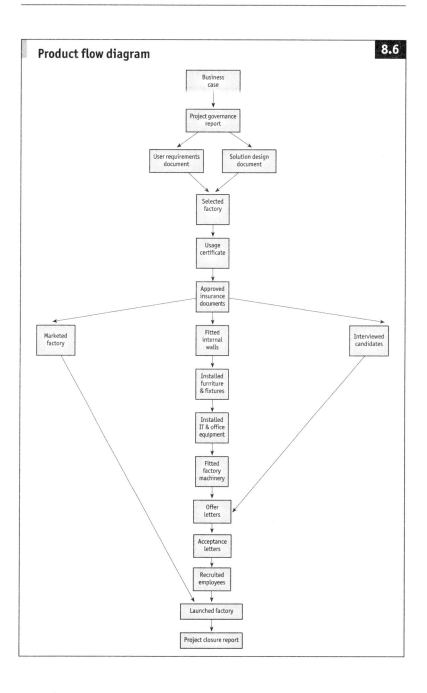

it will show the internal and external dependencies in the project. This is best shown as the product flow diagram developed in Chapter 6 and reproduced here as Figure 8.6 (page 153).

Quality plan: responsibilities
This section describes who will be responsible for which aspects of quality management within the project. It is not a regurgitation of the roles and responsibilities section but specifically identifies the things that named individuals must do to ensure that quality is:

- specified;
- planned;
- built;
- tested;
- accepted.

Consequently, this section may contain statements such as the following:

- The project steering group will agree a set of success criteria from which all expressions of quality will be derived.
- The sponsor will approve time, cost and benefit expectations throughout the project.
- The customer representative will approve the user requirements document on behalf of all end users of the key deliverable.
- The development team representative will approve the solution design document on behalf of the development team(s).
- The project manager will make sure that all key deliverables have been defined in a product description.
- The project steering group will approve all product descriptions before development work starts.
- The project manager will co-ordinate activity according to the plan, taking account of all quality standards to be applied.
- The project manager will make sure that all key deliverables are tested against their quality criteria and according to the method identified in the product description.
- The project steering group will approve all key deliverables once evidence of a satisfactory quality review has been established.
- The customer and developer representatives will decide how many levels of testing are desirable.

Table 8.11 **Sample estimating sheet**

Product	Tasks	Resources	Cost	Assumptions
Product 1	Develop	PR	0.8	PR took this long on previous project
	Review	ST/MW	0.5/0.5	Constrained to half-day as slot for teleconference is already booked
	Amend	PR	0.25	PR took this long on previous project
	Approve	PSG	0.1	Assuming PSG will approve via e-mail
Product 2	Develop	AK	0.5	Based on 0.1 per item x 4 items, plus contingency of 0.1
	Review	PR/MW	0.1/0.1	Estimate based on MW experience
	Amend	AK	0.25	Based on need to rework half original
	Approve	PSG	0.1	Assuming PSG will approve via e-mail
Product 3	Develop	PR	0.8	PR took this long on previous project
	Review	ST/MW	0.5/0.5	Constrained to half-day as slot for teleconference is already booked
	Amend	PR	0.25	Assuming quarter of product to be reworked, plus contingency
	Approve	PSG	0.1	Assuming PSG will approve via e-mail
Product 4	Develop	AK	0.8	AK estimate based on experience
		Train fare	$100	Costs to visit trade show
	Review	ST/MW	0.25/0.25	ST estimate based on experience
	Amend	AK	0.25	Assuming quarter of product to be reworked, plus contingency
	Approve	PSG	0.1	Assuming PSG will approve via e-mail

Note: Costs are in person-days when not monetary.

- The project manager will accommodate the desired level of testing in the project plan.
- The developer representative will approve the completion of all specialist testing.
- The customer representative will approve the completion of user acceptance testing.
- The project steering group will approve the completion of the project and the release of its deliverable into the operational environment.

Quality plan: standards
In any project, there may be prescribed standards that must be met. These may include documentary or procedural standards for:

- specifying the outcome;
- designing the outcome;
- building the outcome;
- testing the outcome;
- operating the outcome;
- managing the project.

This section must describe the standards that must be met for this project.

Planning assumptions
Any planning assumptions made should be listed here. The estimating sheet compiled in Chapter 7 and reproduced here as Table 8.11 (page 155) may also be included.

Time schedule
This should not be regarded exclusively as a project plan because it does not show how cost or quality expectations will be met. A Gantt chart like the one in Chapter 7 and reproduced here as Figure 8.7 may be used in this section.

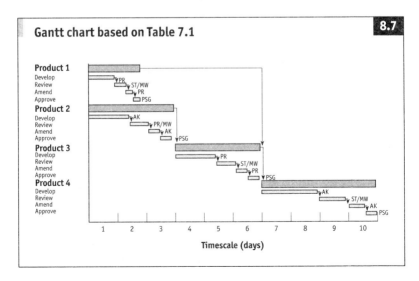

Gantt chart based on Table 7.1 — 8.7

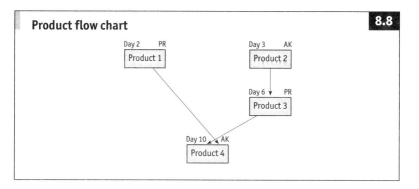

Product flow chart   8.8

An alternative form of graphic can be used to show the project's timing. For instance, the product flow diagram can be adapted to show some of the same information as the Gantt chart (see Figure 8.8).

Table 8.12 **Resource plan with financial information**

Human	Day 1	Day 2	Day 3	Day 4	Day 5	Day 6	Day 7	Day 8	Day 9	Day 10	Total
PR	0.80	0.35		0.80		0.25					2.20
$300/d	$240	$105		$240		$75					$660
ST		0.50			0.50				0.25		1.25
$200/d		$100			$100				$50		$250
MW		0.60			0.50				0.25		1.35
$200/d		$120			$100				$50		$270
AK	0.50	0.50	0.25				0.80			0.25	2.30
$200/d	$100	$100	$50				$160			$50	$460
PSG		0.10	0.10			0.10				0.10	0.40
$400/d		$40	$40			$40				$40	$160
Total human	**1.30**	**2.05**	**0.35**	**0.80**	**1.00**	**0.35**	**0.80**		**0.50**	**0.35**	**7.50**
	$340	**$465**	**$90**	**$240**	**$200**	**$115**	**$160**		**$100**	**$90**	**$1,800**
Non-human travel							$100				$100
Total	$340	$465	$90	$240	$200	$115	**$260**		$100	$90	$1,900

Resource plan

This shows how and when the project is likely to incur its costs. Here reproduced as Table 8.12 (page 157) is an example from Chapter 7.

Risks

This section should further develop the risks identified in the project outline and the business case. The risk register presented in Chapter 5 and reproduced here as Table 8.13 should be included.

Table 8.13 **The risk register**

Risk	Likelihood	Impact	Factor	Mitigations	Cost
Pre-written, packaged software solution will not hold key sales data needed by marketing team, resulting in their inability to work effectively	10	3	30	1 Continue to use existing sales and marketing system alongside new solution. ACTION: JP to advise sales team to prepare for parallel running. 2 Request a specific change from software supplier. ACTION: PT to obtain detailed quotation from supplier.	2 days per month to synchronise systems = $800 15 days' additional fees = $6,000

Risk	Likelihood	Impact	Factor	Mitigations	Cost
If the live date is missed, legal sanctions may be taken against our business, resulting in damage to reputation and other losses	2	11	22	**1** Identify this project as mandatory to make sure that it has priority over essential resources. ACTION: Sponsor to raise at next portfolio management team session. **2** Commence project early to allow for any slippage. ACTION: Sponsor to raise at next portfolio management team session.	Portfolio management team to consider effect on other projects Portfolio management team to consider effect on other projects
Based on supplier's past performance, delivery of equipment required for implementation will be delayed, resulting in delivery delay to client	6	9	54	**1** Identify an alternative supplier. ACTION: SS to ask Procurement for recommendation. **2** Instigate a penalty/ reward clause in the contract ACTION: JP to ask legal department for guidance.	$10,000 premium $5,000 reward provision

Risk	Likelihood	Impact	Factor	Mitigations	Cost
Key people from the legal department will be unavailable during the summer because of their engagement in other projects, resulting in an inability to make critical purchase decisions	6	9	54	**1** Secure the services of an external legal representative. ACTION: Ask legal department for a recommendation. **2** Obtain portfolio management team's authority to use legal team in precedence over other projects during the summer. ACTION: Sponsor to raise at next portfolio management team session.	$1,500 premium
Total risk-based contingency budget					Maximum $23,300

Project controls

Clear controls are needed to describe how the project will be kept on track so that it stands a greater likelihood of meeting its stakeholders' expectations. The project controls section describes the following measures.

Project controls: meetings and reporting
This section describes the way in which various control mechanisms will be used to make sure that progress and forecast information is clearly communicated and that corrective action can be taken when necessary.

Although the communications plan will have identified that some meetings and reports will be necessary, this section must describe how they will keep the project on track.

It is usual for the section to include a table (see Table 8.14).

Project controls: escalation management
This section describes what constitutes a significant issue and what

Table 8.14 **Meetings and reporting**

Control	Participants	Timing	Input	Output
Project initiation meeting	PMT, PSG, PM	At end of initiation stage	Agenda, business case, project governance report, user requirements document, solution design document, next stage plan	Record of actions and decisions, including approval to continue
Team meeting	PM, team leaders	Every week	Agenda, timesheets or records of progress, draft project forecast report	Record of actions and decisions, project forecast report
Scheduled project steering group meeting	PSG, PM	Just before end of each stage	Agenda, business case, updated project plan, next stage plan	Record of actions and decisions, including approval to continue
Unscheduled project steering group meeting	PSG, PM	Exceptional circumstances	Agenda, business case, notification report, revised project plan, revised stage plan	Record of actions and decisions, including approval to continue
Project closure meeting	PSG, PM	At end of closure stage	Agenda, business case, project closure report	Record of actions and decisions, including approval to close project
Lessons learned review	Varies	After closure stage	Agenda, project closure report	Lessons learned report, action plan
Benefits realisation review	PMT, PSG Sponsor	As described in business case	Agenda, draft benefits realisation report	Record of actions and decisions, benefits realisation report

actions should be taken if one arises. Escalation conditions for time, cost and benefits margin should be described (see example overleaf).

Escalation conditions

The project steering group will be subject to the following escalation conditions:

- Time   +/– 4 weeks
- Cost   +/– 50,000
- Margin +/– 100,000

If a breach of these escalation conditions is forecast, the project steering group must immediately alert the portfolio management team and present a notification report on which corrective decisions will be based.

The project manager will be subject to the following escalation conditions:

- Time   +/– 2 weeks
- Cost   +/– 20,000

If a breach of these escalation conditions is forecast, the project manager must immediately alert the project steering group and present a notification report on which corrective decisions will be based.

The team leaders will be subject to the following escalation conditions:

- Time   +/– 1 week
- Cost   +/– 5,000

If a breach of these escalation conditions is forecast, the team leader must immediately alert the project manager and present an action plan on which corrective decisions will be based.

The notification report should describe:

- the circumstances that have caused the project to be forecast being outside the agreed escalation conditions;
- options to address the variance;
- the effect of each option on the project plan/business case;
- the preferred option.

Project controls: change control

This section describes how changes will be dealt with if and when they arise (see example opposite).

Change control

Baseline

The basis on which any requests for changes to requirements or functionality will be assessed are the following documents:

- Business case v1.0
- Project governance report v1.0
- User requirements document v1.0
- Solution design document v1.0

Contingency

A contingency fund has been identified as follows:

Risk mitigation	23,300[a]
Change management	1,000[b]
Approved changes	52,000[c]
Total	**76,300**

a Identified from the risk register.
b Based on 3 person-days needed to assess the effect of any changes during the life of the project.
c Based on an assessment of the changes applied to previous, similar projects.

Process

Should anyone consider a change to the baseline (described above) is needed, the matter will be subject to this change management process. Any item raised in this way will be referred to as a change request. Problems that have arisen will be treated in the same way. New and existing change requests will be reviewed at the weekly meeting between the project manager and the team leaders.

These four steps will be taken, using the organisation's standard pro-forma for identification, assessment, effect and conclusion:

- Change request identification. A change request may be identified by anyone inside or outside the project.
- Change request analysis. The change request will be described fully by the person who has raised it. If further supporting information is needed, this may be provided by a developer, a customer and/or the project manager.
- Change request impact assessment. The change request will be measured against the baseline to decide whether or not it represents a deviation. The contingency change management fund will pay for the necessary assessment.

◪ Conclusion and decision. The conclusion must clearly and unequivocally state whether:
- the change request is a deviation from the baseline;
- its inclusion would take the project outside the escalation conditions.

If the change request is considered worthy of inclusion and can be accommodated within the agreed escalation conditions and approved changes to contingency funds, the project manager can approve the change.

If the change request is considered to be worthy of inclusion but causes the project to be forecast to be completed outside the agreed escalation conditions, the project steering group can approve the change, drawing on the approved changes contingency fund.

If the change request is considered to be worthy of inclusion and falls outside the project steering group's escalation conditions, it must be referred to the portfolio management team.

Responsibilities
This change management process will be facilitated by the project manager. All other responsibilities are identified above.

Project controls: configuration control
This section describes how the project will maintain control of the products it creates. These questions are a guide to what should be included:

◪ Which products are to be subject to control?
◪ Who owns them?
◪ Where will the products be held?
◪ How will back-ups be taken?
◪ How will security be ensured?
◪ How will the products be distributed and redistributed?
◪ How will versions be controlled?
◪ Which version will constitute the baseline?
◪ How will checks be made to make sure that all products are where they should be?

Project controls: quality control
This section describes the tests that will be conducted to increase the

likelihood of delivering an outcome that meets expectations. It can be broken into two:

- **Product quality tests.** This section will describe any special tests to be conducted on particular products. For instance, the solution design document may need a formal review by the solution design committee to make sure it conforms to the organisation's strategic objectives. The form of special tests should also be described more fully. For example, the formal quality review process may be outlined so that senior managers know its depth and value before committing the money necessary to fund it.
- **Project quality tests.** This section describes tests that will be conducted at stages on large projects or ones that involve many products. For instance, a new computer system may undergo system testing, operational acceptance testing and user acceptance testing. The approach to such tests should be described and the project steering group given the opportunity to decide whether they are prepared to allow the time and money needed to accommodate these quality controls.

Project controls: risk and issue management
This section describes how risks and issues will be managed. It must adequately describe:

- how risks and issues will be identified and prioritised;
- the criteria for assigning ownership;
- how mitigating actions will be planned;
- how progress will be monitored and controlled;
- the process by which contingency funds may be drawn.

An example is as follows.

Risk and issue management

Risk and issue identification
Risks will be identified first during the creation of the project outline. An initial risk identification meeting will be held during the initiation stage. The results will be included in both the emerging business case and project governance report as a risk register.

Issues may be identified at any time and by anyone. They will be documented and processed in the same way as a change request.

Risk owners
Risks will be ranked according to their risk factor (see page 85). Those with a factor of 110 will be assigned automatically to the portfolio management team; those with a factor between 57 and 90 will be assigned to the project steering group; those with a factor between 21 and 56 will be assigned to the project manager; and those with a factor of 20 or below will be assigned to the project team.

Risk mitigation
Mitigations will be identified for every risk. Mitigations will be assessed for their potential cost in terms of money and/or time. The summary of all mitigation costs will be included in the contingency budget (see change control, page 163).

Risk management
The risk register will be reappraised at every project controls management meeting. The reappraisal will:

- identify new risks/issues;
- reassess existing risks/issues.

Use of contingency funds
The contingency budget may be drawn upon to mitigate risks, provided those risks have had a contingency sum set aside for mitigation.

The user requirements document

This is used to describe the customer needs the project's outcome must satisfy. Its content will depend on the nature of the project. If the project has to deliver a computer system, it may contain a list of functional and non-functional requirements. If the project is to deliver a new office building, the document should describe graphically the user's vision.

Whatever form it takes, it must provide an adequate means for the project's customers to set out what they want so that their expectations can be met.

The solution design document

This is used to describe how the needs of the users are to be met. It too will depend on the nature of the project. This document might describe the design of a computer system or it could be an architect's blueprint.

Whatever form it takes, it must provide an adequate means for the developers to describe the solution so that it is based on a sound design.

The importance of the initiation stage

The initiation stage has the potential to set the foundations for the successful delivery and closure of the project. Despite the governance described above, it may feel chaotic because the project is in the early stages of formation and no amount of due process will ever replace the importance of allowing people to express their views. Nevertheless, it is essential that the success criteria are established by the end of this stage if the project is to have any chance of being successfully steered through its remaining stages.

9 Project delivery

Once a project has been planned and initiated, its managers must make sure it remains on track. The common-sense control cycle illustrated in Figure 9.1 is no different from that applied to business as usual.

As the plan reveals what needs to be done and by whom, the work must be delegated. As the work is carried out, the management team must continue to know how well the team is performing and whether the project is forecast to deliver according to the time, cost, quality and benefit expectations. Usually, having monitored these elements, some reports are produced to record the findings. They are circulated not merely for information, but to ensure that, where necessary, corrective action is taken to bring the project back on track. Only on completion of the control step can the plan be updated with the actions taken so that the cycle can be repeated.

Anyone who has to manage an aspect of the project should know this cycle and follow it to keep control of the work for which they are responsible.

One feature which ensures the cycle works effectively is the way it depends on effective escalation management. Projects quickly descend into chaos without rules governing who is authorised to make which decision, so there must be a way of determining who has control of the project at any time. The concept and practice of escalation management was described in Chapter 5.

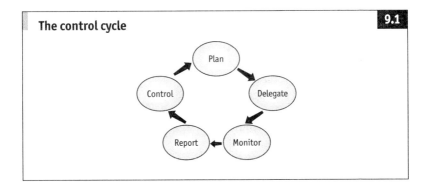

The control cycle 9.1

Plan

The plan provides the road map that describes how the project will achieve its targets. It identifies the deliverables that must be produced and shows to whom the work will be delegated.

Delegate

The portfolio management team delegate responsibility to the project steering group for delivering a commercially or strategically beneficial outcome. The project steering group delegate responsibility to the project manager for delivering the products on time, on budget and to specification. In turn, the project manager will usually have to delegate most of the responsibility for developing those products to the teams working on the project.

When delegating any form of work, care must be taken not merely to describe what is required, but also the constraints within which the work must be carried out. The relationship between the delegator and the delegatee depends on knowing both what must be delivered and the degree of authority within which the delegatee may operate. Therefore, whenever work is delegated, the agreement (formal or informal) must take account of both aspects.

Both parties must agree on the following:

- Product description – to describe what is expected from the delegate.
- Planned start/finish date – to ensure that the work does not commence until a specified date and when it must be finished.
- Planned effort/cost – to clarify what is involved in developing the product and how much budget is available.
- Dependencies – to ensure that the delegatee is aware of who and what else is dependent on the product(s) to be delivered, and what will be required to produce them (a product flow diagram is helpful here).
- Prerequisite products – to allow the delegatee access to previously developed products which may be needed to develop a required new product (for instance, to develop a course definition document, the developer will need the "gathered requirements").

This list focuses on the outcome expected from the delegatee. However, as the delegator remains accountable for the success or failure of the work being undertaken, care must be taken to agree a further set of terms that describe how the delegated work will be controlled:

- Timesheet code – to allow the delegatee to charge hours or costs to the appropriate project account so the delegator can monitor spending.
- Skills/experience required – to make sure the delegatee sufficiently understands the competencies required by the individual(s) who are to do the work (for instance, it may have been specified that the work could be suitable for a trainee).
- Roles – to explicitly describe the responsibilities of each party so that there is no confusion about who is accountable for the work. The delegator remains accountable despite having given some limited authority to the delegatee.
- Reporting arrangements – to make clear when and how the delegator and delegatee will monitor and report progress.
- Escalation conditions – to make sure that the delegatee knows the terms for escalation as soon as any risk to the timescale or budget is identified, thus enabling the delegator to intervene well in advance of the targets being breached.
- Techniques, processes, procedures – to describe any approaches or standards to which the delegatee should conform.

Some projects require a structured approach to delegation, particularly where external suppliers are to do some of the work. In such cases, the arrangement between the delegator (the client) and the delegatee (the supplier) should be set out in the contractual terms of reference and cover the points identified above. Even when not using external suppliers, many organisations use terms of reference to describe the relationship and commitments between client and supplier departments. In large companies especially, these enable project managers to monitor and control the packets of work for which they remain accountable.

Monitor and report

Monitoring is the observation and supervision those in the management team must do to know the condition of their projects. It is not easy to monitor a project or portfolio without a report. Each level in the management hierarchy will need information in a form and at a frequency that will allow the exercising of control without encroaching on the responsibilities of other levels. The worst that can happen is that all levels of management become involved in every corrective decision.

It is also critical that such reports show the extent to which the project is likely to meet its completion expectations, giving any necessary re-forecast of the expectations originally set out in the project plan.

The reports must be designed to satisfy the need of each tier of management for the timely and accurate information necessary for decision making or corrective action.

Portfolio management team

The portfolio management team oversees the wider portfolio of projects. As the portfolio progresses through the year, individual projects will be completed, new projects will be proposed and others will slip or vary in some way. The portfolio management team is ultimately responsible for the state of its portfolio, so the team must meet regularly to evaluate the portfolio's health and answer the question: Is the portfolio on track to deliver its commercial and strategic imperatives?

It is normal for a portfolio management team to meet every month, but also to have a process in place for dealing with exceptional matters at short notice. The regular meeting should have a standard agenda that takes into account the following:

- **Prospects** – where project outlines will have been submitted, suggesting a potential but as yet unproven opportunity. The portfolio management team must decide whether there is sufficient budget to fund the initiation stage in which the business case and project governance report would be developed.
- **Initiated projects** – where newly completed business cases and project governance reports are considered to determine whether the project should continue into the delivery phase, and that the identified project steering group can adopt ownership.
- **Notifications** – where red flags (signalling that the project is likely to breach a key parameter) have been raised.
- **Completions** – where projects have closed but have not yet delivered any benefits.
- **Realisations** – where benefits realisation reports have been submitted to determine the extent to which completed projects have delivered the intended benefits.

Reports from a project register should be used at these meetings so that the state of the portfolio is known at any time. Such a report might look the one in Table 9.1 overleaf, although there is no recognised standard.

The essential data are as follows:

Table 9.1 **Project register**

	Project	First project	Second project
Background	ID	1	2
	Last assessment date	Jan 12th 06	
	Assessor	Pete Robbins	Maggie Jones
	Project start date	Dec 10th 05	Sep 10th 05
PSG	Sponsor	Brad Somerville	Mark Knowles
	Customer representative(s)	Kevin Quinn	Helen Smith
	Developer representative(s)	Mark Johnson	Bupinda Patel
PM	Project manager	Will Stevens	Harry King
Time	Baseline end date	May 31st 06	Jun 10th 06
	Forecast end date	May 31st 06	Sep 30th 06
	Variance (weeks)	*0*	*–16*
	Escalation conditions (weeks)	*2*	*2*
	Within escalation conditions?	*Yes*	*No*
Cost	Baseline budget	$2,026,971	$101,923
	Forecast budget	$2,026,971	$115,000
	Variance	*$0*	*–$13,077*
	Escalation conditions %	*10*	*10*
	Within escalation conditions?	*Yes*	*No*
Benefits	Baseline benefits	$2,703,836	$200,101
	Forecast benefits	$2,703,836	$200,101
	Variance	*$0*	*$0*
	Escalation conditions %	*10*	*10*
	Within escalation conditions?	*Yes*	*Yes*
Business case	Baseline profit	$676,865	$98,178
	Forecast profit	$676,865	$85,101
	Variance	*$0*	*–$13,077*
	Escalation conditions %	*10*	*10*
	Within escalation conditions?	*Yes*	*No*

Background

- ID – the project's identifying code.
- Last assessment date – when the project was last subject to a health check or audit.
- Assessor – who undertook the health check.
- Project start date – when the project was started formally.

Stakeholders

- Sponsor – the person charged with delivering a commercially successful outcome.
- Customer representative(s) – the people charged with authorising the definition and acceptance of the project's outcome from a user's perspective.
- Developer representative(s) – the people charged with authorising the design and development of a robust and reliable solution that will meet the user's needs.
- Project manager – the person charged with planning, monitoring and controlling the delivery of milestones to time, cost and quality expectations.

Time

- Baseline end date – when the project will end as stated in the project governance report.
- Forecast end date – when the project will end as identified in the current project plan, taking account of any actual or forecast variances.
- Variance (weeks) – the difference between the baseline end date and the forecast end date.
- Escalation conditions (weeks) – the amount against which variance is compared to determine whether it should be referred to the portfolio management team.
- Within escalation conditions? – a yes/no response.

Budget

- Baseline budget – the project's intended budget as stated in the project governance report.
- Forecast budget – the project's budget as identified in the current project plan, taking account of any actual or forecast variances.
- Variance – the difference between the baseline budget and the forecast budget.
- Escalation conditions % – the amount against which variance is compared to determine whether it should be referred to the portfolio management team.
- Within escalation conditions? – a yes/no response.

Benefits
- Baseline benefits – the project's intended benefits as stated in the business case.
- Forecast benefits – the project's benefits as currently envisaged, taking account of any actual or forecast variances.
- Variance – the difference between the baseline benefits and the forecast benefits.
- Escalation conditions % – the amount against which variance is compared to determine whether it should be referred to the portfolio management team.
- Within escalation conditions? – a yes/no response.

Business case
- Baseline profit – the project's intended profit (the difference between project/operational costs and benefits over a defined period) as agreed in the business case.
- Forecast profit – the profit as identified in the current business case, taking account of any actual or forecast variances of costs and/or benefits.
- Variance – the difference between the baseline profit and the forecast profit.
- Escalation conditions % – the amount against which variance is compared to determine whether it should be referred to the portfolio management team.
- Within escalation conditions? – a yes/no response.

Table 9.1 on page 172 shows that project 1 seems in good condition with no variances, but project 2 is forecasting variances for both time and cost that will breach the escalation conditions. Although the benefits remain unchanged, the forecast variance for the forecast budget indicates that the intended profit may not be achievable. These multiple forecast variances provide the portfolio management team with the alerts they need to intervene.

The detail in the project register can be summarised further for those organisations undertaking several projects at the same time, giving the portfolio management team an overview of the portfolio on a "corporate dashboard" (see Figure 9.2). It is essential, however, that any report clearly indicates where and what corrective action must be taken. Thus the corporate dashboard also indicates where escalation conditions have been breached so that further detail can be obtained from the project register.

A corporate dashboard

Project costs	Baseline budget	$2,128,894	No. of projects	2
	Forecast budget	$2,141,971	Breaching TIME escalation conditions	1
	Variance	–£13,077	Breaching COST escalation conditions	1
Project benefits	Baseline benefits	$2,903,937	Breaching BENEFIT escalation conditions	0
	Forecast benefits	$2,903,937	Breaching PROFIT escalation conditions	1
	Variance	$0		
Business case	Baseline profit	$775,043		
	Forecast profit	$761,966		
	Variance	–$13,077		

This view has the added advantage of showing how the portfolio is contributing to the organisation's strategic imperatives. The bar chart in Figure 9.3 overleaf illustrates how the projects measure up to the balanced scorecard of targets. The vertical axis identifies the percentage contribution being made by the sum of all projects to each of the four parts of the balanced scorecard. Therefore, the four bars should add up to 100. Ideally, they will be balanced, demonstrating that the projects are contributing evenly across the four measures. In the example, a greater proportion of projects are focused on the financial quartile. Although this is not a particular problem, success may be at the expense of investment in developing customer satisfaction, processes and intellectual growth. This portfolio contribution is usually considered quarterly.

Project steering group
Each project steering group directs an individual project. To do so, it needs a control cycle that regularly tells its participants the status of the project. The project steering group members must also be able to assure themselves that if something exceptional happens to breach the forecast targets, the project manager will alert them immediately.

To maintain a level of control that both supports and gives the project manager his own degree of authority, the project steering group can intervene through:

- project initiation and closure;
- holding meetings at the different stages of the project;
- holding unscheduled meetings;
- holding scheduled meetings;
- project forecast reports.

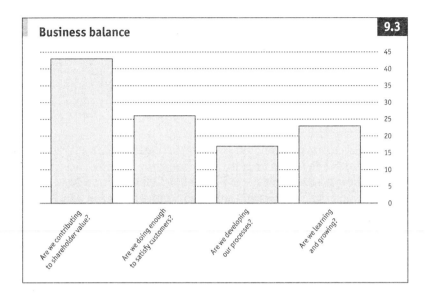

Project initiation and closure
See Chapters 8 and 11.

Stage meetings
The project steering group is required to deliver a successful outcome measured by the extent to which the project's realised benefits outweigh the actual costs. It follows that the balance between forecast costs and benefits will vary throughout the life of the project as estimates and actual spend vary. Therefore, the project steering group should schedule a meeting at the beginning of every planned stage of the project to confirm that it remains viable. At the same point, the group can consider the performance of the project during the previous stage and review and approve the plan for the next stage.

A typical agenda for such a meeting would be as follows:

- Review of previous stage, where the project manager shows how the previous stage performed compared with the plan so that the project steering group can formally approve its closure.
- Review of project plan, where the project manager presents an updated project plan to show the effect of changes and variances during the previous stage and thus whether the project steering group's expectations will still be met. If the escalation conditions

appear to have been breached, this is an opportunity to alert the portfolio management team.

- Review of business case, where the project steering group considers the updated business case to determine the extent to which the project can deliver a profitable outcome. If the escalation conditions appear to have been breached, this is an opportunity to alert the portfolio management team.
- Review of next stage plan, where the project manager presents the plan for the next stage so that the project steering group can provide formal approval for the project manager to assume continued control of the project within defined constraints.
- Approval of controls, where the project steering group confirms the escalation conditions that will apply to the next stage. This provides an opportunity to limit or increase the project manager's authority.
- Approval to proceed, where the project steering group approves the plans so that the project manager can resume control.

Unscheduled project steering group meetings
These should be necessary only if a breach of the escalation conditions is forecast. Escalation conditions can be put on timescale, costs, quality and benefits so the project steering group can be sure that it will be alerted to extreme matters arising between scheduled meetings. The agenda for the meeting is similar to that of a stage meeting, but the review of the previous stage is replaced by a presentation from the project manager outlining:

- what has happened to require notifying the project steering group;
- the effect on the plan;
- the options available to correct or accommodate the matter;
- the recommended solution and its effect on the plan.

Scheduled project steering group meetings
Some managers are uncomfortable with the concept of management by exception. For them, no news does not always mean good news. Consequently, regular project steering group meetings are held, often every month, although this will depend on the duration of the project and the project steering group's need for contact with their project manager. Given that the meeting is not event-based, the agenda is commonly based around the review and approval of the latest project forecast report from the project manager.

Project manager

The project manager is required to plan, monitor and control time, cost and quality. It is probable that during the life of the project there will be pressure from stakeholders to amend one or more aspects of the project as their expectations or needs change. There will also be the unremitting burden of risk – potential problems that may or may not have been identified. The project manager must also motivate the people in the project team to deliver on time, on budget and to the required standard of quality.

These monitoring and reporting mechanisms are the bare essentials for a project manager.

Project team progress meetings

Often the project manager is responsible for a team of people who must be subjected to a regular and repeatable process of delegation, monitoring, reporting and control. Assuming that the project steering group meets every month, it may still want progress reports every two weeks. Figure 9.4 shows how progress data can be gathered, processed, reported and acted on.

This is the agenda for the weekly progress meetings:

- Delivery highlights during previous period – to identify the products started or completed.
- Delivery highlights during next period – to identify the products planned to be started or completed during the next period.
- Timescales – to scrutinise progress and identify variances against the time plan, clarifying the reasons for those variances so that corrective actions can be considered.
- Budgets – to scrutinise progress and identify variances against the cost plan, clarifying the reasons for those variances so that corrective actions can be considered.
- Quality – to scrutinise progress and identify variances against the quality plan (especially where products have been delivered that fall short of the quality criteria) so that corrective actions can be considered.
- Risks and issues:
  - Dependencies – to examine the known dependencies with other projects or outside parties, consider the risk of their being honoured and, where necessary, consider a mitigation plan.
  - Risk mitigation progress – to monitor the progress of agreed

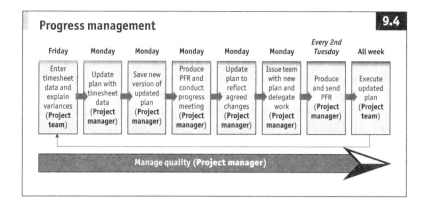

Progress management — 9.4

Friday	Monday	Monday	Monday	Monday	Monday	Every 2nd Tuesday	All week
Enter timesheet data and explain variances (**Project team**)	Update plan with timesheet data (**Project manager**)	Save new version of updated plan (**Project manager**)	Produce PFR and conduct progress meeting (**Project manager**)	Update plan to reflect agreed changes (**Project manager**)	Issue team with new plan and delegate work (**Project manager**)	Produce and send PFR (**Project manager**)	Execute updated plan (**Project team**)

Manage quality (**Project manager**)

mitigating actions so that further corrective actions can be considered.

- Risks for closure – to determine which risks, if any, are of such little significance that they may be considered closed. (It is sensible to let such risks remain on the risk register in case the likelihood of their occurring or their effect changes.)
- New risks – to identify, qualify and evaluate any new or previously unrecognised risks.
▪ Actions and decisions – to review and assign the actions and decisions taken during the meeting.

For the meeting to be effective, reliable and trustworthy management information is essential. This commonly comes in a project forecast report.

Project forecast reports
These are an important way for the project manager to communicate with management stakeholders, the project steering group and the portfolio management team. They are snapshots of the project, taken at regular and frequent intervals throughout its lifetime so that all the project's managers (the project manager included) are aware of both progress and the forecast of completion.

For most members of the project steering group, a summary of key project management information should be sufficient, with the option of being able to scrutinise detail as necessary. A summary project forecast report like the one in Figure 9.5 is usually sufficient for them.

The project manager should have enough detailed information to monitor the progress of individuals in the project team. It is not enough just to show the information in the summary project forecast report; the project manager needs the report on which it is based so that he can identify specific instances of variance where it occurs and the reasons for it. The project plan and the business case should provide that detail and therefore the core data in them must be up-to-date and accurate.

Since the project manager must control timescales, costs, quality and risks, the project forecast report should reflect that content at a level of detail commensurate with the plan. Furthermore, the project steering group may wish the project manager to maintain the business case on their behalf in between project stages. Consequently, in addition to the summary shown in Figure 9.5, it would be usual for a project manager to consider a more detailed report every week or two during the project's lifetime.

These are some of the terms used in Figures 9.6–9.13 (pages 183–92).

Baseline. This is the original set of data agreed by a recognised authority which should be used as a stable foundation against which to track variances. There may be a baseline end date, a baseline budget and a baseline benefit, which were all agreed when the business case and project governance report were approved at the end of the initiation stage. The baseline should not be changed, so the effect of changes can be measured reliably. There are, however, rare circumstances when it is necessary and sensible to amend the baseline; these will be considered later.

Actual to date (ATD). This is a range of measures that should increase as the project progresses. For instance, if $300 of a baseline $500 budget has been spent, the actual to date is $300.

Estimate to complete (ETC). This is a crucial set of information in any project report because it is the latest and most recent estimate. This figure represents the amount to come on top of the actual to date. For instance, if the actual to date is $300 and the baseline was $500, it does not follow that the estimate to complete is $200. The costs may have increased since the baseline was approved and the project forecast report must record this. If the estimate to complete is $400, the new total is $700.

Forecast at completion (FAC). This is the sum of actual to date and estimate to complete – $700 in the example above.

A summary project forecast report

Project Name: Company Annual Seminar
Project Steering Group:
   Sponsor: Howard Smith
   Customer rep.: Annie Ownes
   Developer rep.: Rafiq Shamsal
Project Manager: Danny Frost
Report Date: Monday, February 12, 2007

Highlights

Progress to date has been per plan. The Project Outline, Business Case and Project Governance Report have been completed.

The User Requirements Document has commenced with completion expected to plan

Some budget has been committed to secure the venue and some speakers, and to obtain vital resources for the programme.

Lowlights

The dates for the Draft Programme and Speaker Invitations have been delayed owing to a diary conflict.

However, this will not cause a knock-on delay elsewhere. There will be a delay in obtaining the venue logo as this is being redesigned.

Timescale Summary

There are   22   identified deliverables or milestones.

There are   19   **GREEN** milestones.

There are   3   **AMBER** milestones. The PM should remain in charge, but the PSG should know of these variances.

There are   0   **RED** milestones which should be managed by the PSG.

The intended end date is   20/4/07

The forecast end date is   20/4/07

The variance is   0   days and is **GREEN**

Benefit Summary

The intended benefits were $100,000

The forecast benefits are $100,000

The variance is   0% $0   and is **GREEN**

Budget Summary

The intended budget was $72,250

The forecast budget is $73,000

The variance is   −1%   −$750   and is **AMBER**

Business Case Summary

The intended gross margin was $27,750

The forecast gross margin is $27,000

The variance is   −3%   −$750   and is **AMBER**

Quality Summary

There are   0   **GREEN** quality measures.

There are   0   **AMBER** quality measures which should be managed by the PM.

There are   5   **RED** quality measures which should be managed by the PSG.

Risk Summary

There are   4   identified risks.

There are   2   **GREEN** risks which should be managed by the team.

There are   2   **AMBER** risks which should be managed by the PM.

There are   0   **RED** risks which should be managed by the PSG.

Variance. This is the difference between the baseline and the forecast at completion. In the example above, it is -$200 (the baseline $500 less the forecast at completion $700). When compared with the agreed escalation criteria, this figure enables the red, amber and green alert markers to be created.

Box colours. Grey boxes must be completed whenever a new project forecast report is being produced.

Project forecast report: time forecast
The time forecast (Figure 9.6) lists every product or milestone from the plan and shows the progress made in achieving targets and the extent to which the forecast end date is likely to be met.

Start dates are sometimes excluded, but they have some value; if the development of a product is seen to be starting later, there is a reasonable chance that it will be completed behind schedule too.

Using the same columns to represent forecast and actual dates is simply explained: if the date is before the date of the report, it is an actual date. If it is after the date of the report, it is a forecast date. Once an actual date has been entered, there should no reason to change it.

Project forecast report: cost forecast
There are a number of ways of reporting the costs of the project. Figures 9.7 and 9.8 show two different ways of expressing the same data. The cost forecast (Figure 9.7 on page 184) lists the resource types, including all the people and non-human costs.

Figure 9.8 on page 185 lists the costs by product. This is important if earned value analysis is to be carried out (see page 188). This example identifies a matter that may interest the project steering group: despite the project having started only a few days ago, money has been committed to some products that have been reported elsewhere as not started (reserved venue, agreed speakers and draft programme).

An alternative used by many organisations is to separate the capital and revenue costs and show them as two summarised rows. However, this may lead to difficulties when attempting to discover the reason for a variance.

Project forecast report: project quality forecast
The project quality forecast (Figure 9.9, page 186) identifies the intended success criteria and shows how close the project is to meeting those

9.6

Project forecast report: time forecast

Project name: Company annual seminar
Project manager: Danny Frost

ESCALATION		From	To
RED=	Off track, requires project steering group's intervention	6	100
AMBER=	Off track, but within project manager's control	1	5
GREEN=	On track to deliver on intended delivery date	0	0

ID	Milestone	Team member responsible	Baseline Start	Baseline End	Forecast/actual Start	Forecast/actual End	Variance/ R/A/G (TIME)	Reason
1	Completed and internally approved project outline and business case	PR	03/02/07	09/02/07	03/02/07	09/02/07	0	
2	Completed project governance report	JK	10/02/07	10/02/07	10/02/07	10/02/07	0	
3	Completed user requirements document	JK	11/02/07	14/02/07	11/02/07	14/02/07	0	
4	Draft agenda and topics	JK, PR	15/02/07	15/02/07	15/02/07	15/02/07	0	
5	Identified venue	SP	15/02/07	15/02/07	15/02/07	15/02/07	0	
6	Reserved venue	LA	11/02/07	19/02/07	11/02/07	19/02/07	0	
7	Marketing plan	LA	15/02/07	19/02/07	15/02/07	19/02/07	0	
8	Confirmed date	DK	19/02/07	19/02/07	19/02/07	19/02/07	0	
9	Agreed speakers	LA	10/02/07	19/02/07	10/02/07	19/02/07	0	
10	Draft programme	PR	10/02/07	01/03/07	10/02/07	03/03/07	2	Diary conflict
11	Approved speaker invitations	JK	01/03/07	05/03/07	01/03/07	08/03/07	3	Diary conflict
12	Despatched speaker invitations	LA	19/02/07	21/02/07	19/02/07	21/02/07	0	
13	Completed speaker confirmations	DK	21/02/07	10/03/07	21/02/07	10/03/07	0	
14	Received venue logos	SP	15/02/07	15/03/07	15/02/07	19/03/07	4	Logos being redesigned
15	Booked and paid venue	PR	15/02/07	20/03/07	15/02/07	20/03/07	0	
16	Completed delegate packs	LA	15/02/07	25/03/07	15/02/07	25/03/07	0	
17	Approved marketing materials	LA	15/02/07	25/03/07	15/02/07	25/03/07	0	
18	Printed and despatched marketing materials and invitations	DK	25/03/07	04/04/07	25/03/07	04/04/07	0	
19	Received speaker speeches	PR	10/03/07	04/04/07	10/03/07	04/04/07	0	
20	Produced and despatched running plans	SP	04/04/07	15/04/07	04/04/07	15/04/07	0	
21	Final approval meeting	LA	16/04/07	16/04/07	16/04/07	16/04/07	0	
22	Event	ALL	20/04/07	20/04/07	20/04/07	20/04/07	0	

9.7

Project forecast report: cost forecast by type

Project name: Company annual seminar
Project manager: Danny Frost
Summary variance: -$750.00

Off track, requires project steering group's intervention
Off track, but within project manager's control
On track to deliver to intended budget

ESCALATION		
RED=	-3,000	-1,000,000
AMBER=	-1	-3,000
GREEN=	0	0

ID	Resource	Baseline			Actual to date (COST)			Estimate to complete			Forecast	Variance/ R/A/G	Reason
		Items	Unit	TOTAL	Items	Unit	TOTAL	Items	Unit	TOTAL			
1	Marketing team (10 person days @ $300 per day)	10.00	$300	$3,000	10.00	$300	$3,000	0.00	$0	$0	$3,000	$0	
2	Technology team (5 person days @ $350 per day)	5.00	$350	$1,750	4.00	$350	$1,400	2.00	$350	$700	$2,100	-$350	One extra day needed to source kit
3	Marketing materials	1.00	$5,000	$5,000	1.00	$5,000	$5,000	1.00	$0	$0	$5,000	$0	
4	Copywriting fees	1.00	$3,000	$3,000	1.00	$3,000	$3,000	1.00	$0	$0	$3,000	$0	
5	Editing in house	1.00	$3,000	$3,000	1.00	$3,000	$3,000	1.00	$0	$0	$3,000	$0	
6	Fulfilment	1.00	$1,500	$1,500	1.00	$1,500	$1,500	1.00	$0	$0	$1,500	$0	
7	Transportation	1.00	$500	$500	1.00	$800	$800	1.00	$0	$0	$800	-$300	Estimates failed to include supplier price increase
8	Stationery	1.00	$1,200	$1,200	1.00	$1,300	$1,300	1.00	$0	$0	$1,300	-$100	Estimates wrongly based on last year's figures
9	Signage	1.00	$300	$300	1.00	$300	$300	1.00	$0	$0	$300	$0	
10	Airfares	5.00	$600	$3,000	0.00	$600	$0	5.00	$600	$3,000	$3,000	$0	
11	Venue	1.00	$20,000	$20,000	0.00	$20,000	$0	1.00	$20,000	$20,000	$20,000	$0	
12	Hotel accommodation	60.00	$400	$24,000	60.00	$400	$0	60.00	$400	$24,000	$24,000	$0	
13	Audio visual	1.00	$3,000	$3,000	0.00	$3,000	$0	1.00	$3,000	$3,000	$3,000	$0	
14	Food and drink	60.00	$50	$3,000	0.00	$50	$0	60.00	$50	$3,000	$3,000	$0	
	TOTAL			$72,250			$19,300			$53,700	$73,000	-$750	

Project forecast report: cost forecast by product

Project name:	Company annual seminar
Project manager:	Danny Frost
Summary variance	-$750.00

Off track, requires project steering group's intervention
Off track, but within project manager's control
On track to deliver on intended delivery date

	ESCALATION	From	To
	RED=	-3,000	-1,000,000
	AMBER=	-1	-3,000
	GREEN=	0	0

ID	Milestone	Team member responsible	Baseline	ATD	ETC	TIME FAC	Variance/ R/A/G	Reason
1	Completed and internally approved project outline and business case	PR	$1,200	$1,200	$0	$1,200	$0	
2	Completed project governance report	JK	$300	$300	$0	$300	$0	
3	Completed user requirements document	JK	$700	$700	$0	$700	$0	
4	Draft agenda and topics	JK, PR	$700	$0	$700	$700	$0	
5	Identified venue	SP	$760	$0	$760	$760	$0	
6	Reserved venue	LA	$10,000	$10,000	$350	$10,350	-$350	One extra day needed to source kit
7	Marketing plan	LA	$1,200	$0	$1,200	$1,200	$0	
8	Confirmed date	DK	$300	$0	$300	$300	$0	
9	Agreed speakers	LA	$3,790	$3,790	$0	$3,790	$0	
10	Draft programme	PR	$3,500	$3,310	$190	$3,500	$0	
11	Approved speaker invitations	JK	$700	$0	$700	$700	$0	
12	Despatched speaker invitations	LA	$900	$0	$900	$900	$0	
13	Completed speaker confirmations	DK	$7,000	$0	$7,000	$7,000	$0	
14	Received venue logos	SP	$400	$0	$400	$400	$0	
15	Booked and paid venue	PR	$17,800	$0	$17,800	$17,800	$0	
16	Completed delegate packs	LA	$12,300	$0	$12,300	$12,300	$0	
17	Approved marketing materials	LA	$700	$0	$700	$700	$0	
18	Printed and despatched marketing materials and invitations	DK	$8,900	$0	$9,300	$9,300	-$400	Increase in prices from suppliers
19	Received speaker speeches	PR	$100	$0	$100	$100	$0	
20	Produced and despatched running plans	SP	$300	$0	$300	$300	$0	
21	Final approval meeting	LA	$700	$0	$700	$700	$0	
22	Event	ALL	$0	$0	$0	$0	$0	
	TOTAL		$72,250	$19,300	$53,700	$73,000	-$750	

9.9

Project forecast report: project quality forecast

| Project name: | Company annual seminar |
| Project manager: | Danny Frost |

ESCALATION

On track to deliver as intended	GREEN= 100%	100,000%
Off track, but within project manager's control	AMBER= 75%	99%
Off track, may require project steering group's intervention.	RED= 0%	74%

METRICS

ID	Quality measure	Baseline	Actual to date	Success/ R/A/G	Reason for variance
1	Speaker acceptances	7	2	29%	Ahead of schedule – none expected at this stage
2	Employee registrations	300	0	0%	On plan – invitations not yet sent
3	Number of external press attending	3	0	0%	Event not yet completed
4	No shows	30	0	0%	Event not yet completed
5	Evaluation forms completed	200	0	0%	Event not yet completed

expectations. It will be particularly important to the project steering group because they want to know that the project is likely to meet not only its time and budget targets but also its quality targets. They set these targets, so they should take a keen interest in seeing the progress towards meeting them. However, ultimately the project manager will be measured on his ability to balance, control and meet the project steering group's expectations for time, cost and quality. Thus the project quality forecast provides a means of knowing how near to or far from meeting its target the project is, and, importantly, what should be done to manage any variances.

Project forecast report: product quality log
The product quality log (Figure 9.10, page 189) lists the key deliverables or milestones and shows the status of each with regard to their fitness for their purpose. It provides a more detailed means of monitoring and reporting progress by recording the progress achieved in meeting each product's success criteria. Thus if the time forecast shows that a product is forecast to be delivered late, the product quality log may show that the delay is due to a failure related to quality.

The product quality log is a simple report that follows the life cycle of each product, showing to what extent each of the product's steps have been successfully achieved. These steps are:

- draft complete;
- review complete;
- changes completed;
- approved fit for purpose (FFP).

Specific columns identify the date on which each step has been completed so that progress can be better managed.

Project forecast report: benefits forecast
Most projects have to be completed before their benefits can be delivered. Therefore, there may be limited value in reporting progress in achieving benefits during the life of the project. However, there are occasions when it can be helpful to assess progress in achieving benefits during the life of the project (Figure 9.11, page 190), such as the following:

- The forecast benefits change. The baseline forecasts were underestimated or overestimated. For example, the intended customers from a new market are no longer anticipated.

- Some benefits have been delivered during the project. For example, redundant computer equipment has been removed during the project rather than after completion, resulting in lower maintenance charges.
- There is a desire to compare benefits and costs dynamically during the project. The project steering group is responsible for delivering benefits that outweigh costs by an agreed margin. If it is to take well-informed decisions throughout the project life cycle, it will help to have management information about the project's accruing and forecast benefits, as well as the costs.

Project forecast report: risk register
The risk register (Figure 9.12, page 191) will help the project manager when reviewing the project. The "Factor" column alerts the project steering group to risks or issues requiring their intervention.

Timesheet
The forecast at completion and variance can be calculated automatically, but the actual to date and the estimate to complete must be obtained to allow that to happen. Every time a project forecast report is produced, these figures must be included if it is to have any value. The source of such information will be the people to whom the work has been delegated, so a timesheet is the best way to gather the data. In Figure 9.13 on page 192, the person completing the form is required to enter data in the grey boxes; all other boxes contain information derived from the project plan.

Earned value analysis
Using reports to determine whether or not a set of expectations will be met is a necessary aspect of effective management. It is also helpful to gain some confidence that a project is currently where it was expected to be. Earned value analysis objectively measures a project's accomplishments in respect of its performance against the time, cost and quality targets.

Earned value analysis depends on a detailed and up-to-date plan being available and it relies on being able to calculate the extent to which any product is complete. Therefore, it is a prerequisite that the plan against which progress is being tracked is product-based.

Figure 9.14 on page 193 tells the project management team very little about the current state of the project. The planned cost is a measure of what should have been spent at each point throughout the project's life

Project manager: Danny Frost

A — Approved
ASTA — Approved subject to amendments
RAR1 — Revise and reschedule – product unready
RAR2 — Revise and reschedule – product needs significant change
RAR3 — Revise and reschedule – insufficient reviewers
RAR4 — Revise and reschedule – unqualified reviewers
RAR5 — Revise and reschedule – unprepared reviewers

								METRICS						
ID	Milestone	Quality reviewers	Approval authority	Draft complete	Invitation sent	Baseline review	Review complete	Outcome	Number of changes	Changes complete	Approved FFP	Baseline approval	Variance RAG	Observations
1	Completed and internally approved project outline and business case	PR, TC, US	PSG	05/02/07	03/02/07	07/02/07	07/02/07	ASTA	12	08/02/07	09/02/07	09/02/07	0	
2	Completed project governance report	PR, TC, MM	PSG	10/02/07	05/02/07	10/02/07	10/02/07	ASTA	8	10/02/07	10/02/07	10/02/07	0	
3	Completed user requirements document	MM, SP, TC	PSG	13/02/07								14/02/07		
4	Draft agenda and topics	MM, SP, TC	PSG	15/02/07								15/02/07		
6	Reserved venue	PR, TC, MM	PSG	18/02/07								19/02/07		
7	Marketing plan	MM, SP, TC	PSG	18/02/07								19/02/07		
9	Agreed speakers	MM, SP, TC	PSG	18/02/07								19/02/07		
10	Draft programme	PR, TC, US	PSG	02/03/07								01/03/07		
11	Approved speaker invitations	MM, SP, TC	PSG	07/03/07								05/03/07		
15	Booked and paid venue	MM, SP, TC	PSG	19/03/07								20/03/07		
16	Completed delegate packs	MM, SP, TC	PSG	24/03/07								25/03/07		
17	Approved marketing materials	PR, TC, US	PSG	24/03/07								25/03/07		
18	Printed and despatched marketing materials and invitations	MM, SP, TC	PSG	03/04/07								04/04/07		
19	Received speaker speeches	PR, TC, US	PSG	03/04/07								04/04/07		
20	Produced and despatched running plans	PR, TC, MM	PSG	14/04/07								15/04/07		

9.11

Project forecast report: benefits forecast

Project name:	Company annual seminar		
Sponsor:	Howard Smith		
Summary variance	$0		0%

Escalation		From	To
Off track, may require project steering group's intervention.	RED=	−50%	−100,000%
Off track, but within project manager's control	AMBER=	−1%	−49%
On track, project manager remains in control	GREEN=	0%	0%

		Baseline	Actual to date	Estimate to complete	Forecast	Variance $	%
1	Increased employee satisfaction resulting in reduced staff wastage	$100,000	$0	$100,000	$100,000	$0	0%
2							
3							
4							
5							
6							
7							
	TOTALS	$100,000	$0	$100,000	$100,000	$0	0%

9.12

[Project forecast report: risk register

| Project name: | Company annual seminar |
| Sponsor: | Howard Smith |

	0 None			Green	
	2 Very Low	3 Activity may suffer		1	20	Share – allow a partner to share the burden of risk
	4 Low	5 Product may suffer			Amber	Endure – accept that the risk may become an issue
Green – anyone can be assigned ownership	6 Medium	7 Stage may suffer		21	56	Avoid – prevent the risk from transpiring
Amber – project manager assigned ownership	8 High	9 Project may suffer			Red	Lessen – reduce the likelihood and/or impact
Red – project steering group assigned ownership	10 Certainty	11 Business may suffer		57	110	

ID	Risk	Likelihood	Impact	Factor	Mitigation
1	Employees do not sign up in sufficient numbers resulting in loss of benefit	4	9	36	Sponsor to send personal invitation
2	Food poisoning incident from last year is repeated resulting in bad will and potential legal sanctions	2	9	18	New caterers have been identified
3	Venue is lost to a competitor resulting in last minute attempt to secure an alternative	4	9	36	Venue is secured with payment much earlier than usual
4	Speakers say something controversial resulting in company position being compromised	6	3	18	Speeches to be pre-vetted

Timesheet

9.13

Project name:	Company annual seminar
Team member name:	Jackie King
Date:	12/01/07

ID	Milestone	TIME						COST				
		Original		Forecast/actual				Original effort	Actual to date	Estimate to complete	Forecast	Reason
		Start	End	Start	End	Reason						
1	Completed project governance report	10/02/07	10/02/07	10/02/07	10/02/07			1.0	1.0	0.0	1.0	
2	Completed user requirements document	11/02/07	14/02/07	11/02/07	14/02/07			1.0	0.0	1.0	1.0	
3												
4												
5												
6												
7												
8												
9												
10												
	TOTAL							2.0	1.0	1.0	2.0	

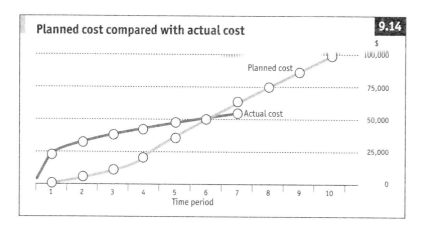

Planned cost compared with actual cost

9.14

cycle. For example, the project should have spent $50,000 at period 6, $75,000 at period 8 and its whole budget by the end of period 10.

In Figure 9.14 it appears that the actual cost has exceeded the planned cost until period 6, but after that the cumulative actual cost appears to be less than expected. This is not necessarily a time to celebrate, however. This view takes no account of what has actually been delivered at each point, so if the project were suddenly to finish at period 8, although it may be under budget, it may also have produced less than was intended.

Assuming that the project manager has drawn up a product-based plan at the start of the project, it should have been possible to determine the value of each product and its total cost of production. Shown over time, this is called the planned value. At the end of every period, the project manager calculates the value of every product created so far, allowing a proportionate amount for partly completed products. This is the earned value. As progress is tracked, instead of simply comparing the planned cost with the actual cost, the earned value of the products delivered can be compared with the planned value expected (Figure 9.15 overleaf).

Figure 9.15 shows that progress was better than planned to begin with but fell behind at period 8. However, when the earned value is compared with the actual cost figures used earlier (Figure 9.16 overleaf) it is higher than the actual cost, which implies that the products that have been delivered have contributed a greater value than the spend to date. Therefore, the project is in a markedly better state than originally illustrated.

Given the emphasis on the cost of production and the variances that the project manager may wish to identify, the terms "planned value" and "earned value" are often replaced by two better descriptions:

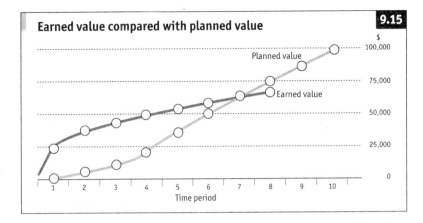

Earned value compared with planned value 9.15

- budgeted cost of work scheduled (BCWS) – the budgeted cost of work planned in the period being measured;
- budgeted cost of work performed (BCWP) – the planned cost of work completed in the period being measured.

However, for the technique to work, a third measure is needed:

- actual cost of work performed (ACWP) – the cost of work completed to date.

Now it is possible to calculate:

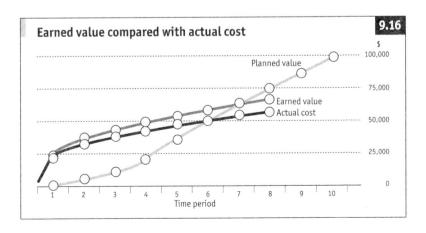

Earned value compared with actual cost 9.16

- cost variation – the budgeted cost of work scheduled minus the actual cost of work planned (how much should have been spent to date based on what has been achieved, minus the amount actually spent);
- schedule variation – the budgeted cost of work performed minus the budgeted cost of work scheduled (how much should have been spent to date based on what has been achieved, minus the amount that was planned to have been spent);
- schedule delay – when the budgeted cost of work scheduled is the same as the budgeted cost of work performed, less the date when the data was captured, measured in days.

Therefore, the example can be extended. Figure 9.17 shows a project that is:

- underspent – the actual cost of work performed is less than the budgeted cost of work performed, so the cost variance is positive;
- behind schedule – the budgeted cost of work scheduled is greater than the budgeted cost of work performed so the schedule variance is negative.

Therefore, having given a value to each product, earned value analysis provides a view of project data that can significantly enhance the management team's understanding of the state of the project.

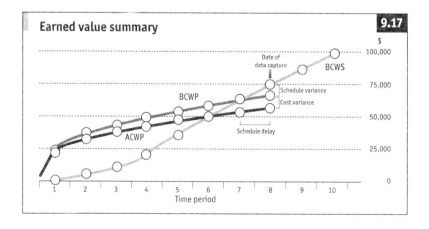

Earned value summary 9.17

Quality reviews

Earned value analysis depends on being able to measure the completeness of a product. Without it, performance is only measurable in terms of money spent over time. But regardless of whether earned value analysis is being used as a monitoring and control technique, the successful execution of the plan depends on managing quality as well as time and cost. It follows, therefore, that the project's products' fitness for their purpose should also be actively managed.

While the product quality log tracks the project's progress in meeting milestone targets, it only records the results of a more substantial product review process to which all key deliverables should be subjected. Only in this way can those approving their completion have confidence that they are measurably fit for their purpose.

As a product is being developed, the product description should be used as a definition of what a successful outcome should look like. In particular, the quality criteria set out the specifier's quality expectations so that the developer can be sure to build them into the product. So, if the quality criteria section asks, "Will the report be limited to no more than 30 pages?", the author can be sure to meet that expectation.

Given that the product description can be complex and that there is usually room for misinterpretation, a quality review is often advisable. This compares the draft product and the product description to determine how far the product can be considered complete.

There are different forms of quality review, each suitable for a particular type of product:

- Testing – where a physical test is necessary, for example a pressure test of a tyre to determine the point at which it would explode.
- Inspection – where a product or service is scrutinised to determine its fitness, for example a visit to premises to evaluate whether they meet health and safety standards.
- Demonstration – where the potential errors are identified by a display, for example a prototype car is demonstrated on a track.
- Formal quality review – where a group of carefully identified reviewers are invited to challenge a product's ability to meet predefined success criteria. This enables errors to be identified and corrected, for example a marketing plan is scrutinised by experts.
- Informal quality review – a less structured version of a formal quality review, where the product is circulated by mail or e-mail so that errors can be identified and corrected.

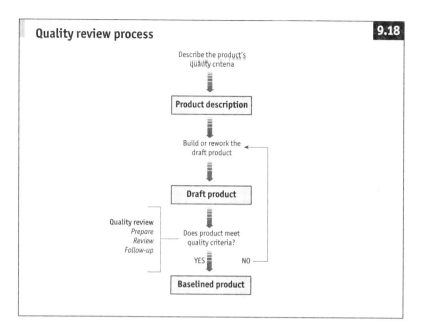

Quality review process 9.18

Describe the product's
quality criteria

Product description

Build or rework the
draft product

Draft product

Quality review
Prepare
Review
Follow-up

Does product meet
quality criteria?

YES   NO

Baselined product

In many projects, the formal quality review is an effective means of monitoring and reporting the fitness for their purpose of many of its products. The process was first outlined by Michael Fagan in 1976, and he developed it further ten years later. Although originally intended for the software industry, it lends itself perfectly to any form of documentation that has been defined by means of a product description (see Figure 9.18).

Quality review: preparation. This begins during initiation when the product descriptions against which the products will be compared for their fitness for purpose are developed and approved by the project steering group as part of the project plan. The quality plan (a component of the project plan) will contain all product descriptions, together with a list of quality responsibilities identifying who will be responsible for reviewing and approving each product.

Reviewers should be selected with care. They should fulfil these roles:

- chair – to ensure that a clear conclusion is drawn from the review;
- scribe – to record the actions and decisions arising from the review;

- author – to offer insight into the product and its construction;
- reviewers – to identify errors.

The project manager or team leader should also be prepared to attend since the outcome will affect the plan in some way.

To make sure the review is balanced, reviewers should be drawn from a variety of commercial, customer and developer backgrounds. An invitation should be sent to all reviewers informing them of their role. It should include:

- an error list for recording the errors the reviewer identifies;
- a copy of the product description to provide the baseline definition against which the draft product should be compared;
- the draft product to be reviewed.

The scribe should also receive an action form for recording actions and decisions arising from the review. All reviewers should prepare for the meeting by comparing the draft product to the product description, noting errors on their error lists.

A room should be booked and sufficient time allowed to review the product.

Quality review: review. The meeting should start with an introduction of the participants and an explanation of the purpose of the review. Assuming the product is a document, there are several ways to proceed:

- Significant errors are identified as a priority. Thus if the product is critically flawed, a decision to propose rework can be taken before the review has progressed too far.
- Reviewers present and describe their error lists in turn. This lets each reviewer express their particular concerns about the product. The disadvantage is that by the time the last reviewer is reached the errors listed may have been identified and presented by someone else, leaving them feeling as though they have made no contribution.
- Each page of the document is considered in turn. Each reviewer has an equal opportunity to contribute. Furthermore, if the review has to be cut short or overruns, everyone will have reviewed the product to the same place.
- Each quality criterion in the product description is considered

in turn, which means that the quality criteria against which to measure the fitness of the product must be sufficiently reliable and that the product descriptions must be of a high standard.

When conducting a review:

- participants should be expected to have prepared thoroughly;
- everyone should aim to work within agreed time limits;
- the authority of the chair should be respected;
- all participants should be tactful and diplomatic;
- the chair should be prepared to reschedule the review if there are too few participants or if they are underqualified;
- the product should be reviewed, not the author;
- the product should always be compared with the product description, not with any personal opinions about what constitutes a "fit" product;
- during the review, errors should be identified, not solutions;
- irrelevant debate should be avoided;
- each reviewer should annotate the product with trivial matters, such as spelling errors.

As the review progresses, the scribe should record the actions and decisions agreed on the action form, being sure to assign each action to an agreed participant. In practice, most of the actions usually fall to the author, who will be expected to produce the necessary amendments. When the review has been completed, the scribe should read back the items on the action form to make sure that they reflect the debate and that those required to take action understand their obligations. They should gather the reviewers' copies of the products annotated with spelling and grammatical errors, together with the errors lists.

The chair is responsible for making sure that the review concludes decisively. The options are:

- approved – the product can be accepted;
- approved subject to amendments – the product can be approved once the actions on the action form are undertaken;
- revise and reschedule (product not ready) – the product is not sufficiently complete or of a suitable standard for review;
- revise and reschedule (product needs significant change) – the product is critically flawed and requires radical redevelopment;

- revise and reschedule (insufficient reviewers) – not enough reviewers attended;
- revise and reschedule (unqualified reviewers) – the reviewers attending were insufficiently qualified;
- revise and reschedule (unprepared reviewers) – the reviewers attending were insufficiently prepared.

Quality review: follow-up. If the review showed that the product was complete subject to corrections, the scribe should give everyone a copy of the action form. The scribe should also give the author the annotated copies of the product.

The author should consider the changes necessary, determine whether they can be accommodated within the time and budget remaining available for this product and inform the project manager of the effect. In turn, the project manager should update the product quality log and after considering the time and cost implications decide whether the author should go ahead and make the changes.

Assuming that the changes can be accommodated according to the plan, the author amends the product using the action form and the annotated copies as a guide. A revised version is then circulated so that reviewers can confirm that the errors they identified have been corrected and that all other actions have been satisfied. Once they have provided proof of their acceptance, the chair can approve the product. This confirms that it meets the planned quality expectations and is fit for its purpose.

Informal quality review. This a common form of product appraisal which, if managed well, has many of the benefits of the formal quality review but is cheaper to implement. Instead of gathering reviewers together, the product is sent to them via mail or e-mail. The author asks them to identify errors, which he then seeks to rectify in a further version.

While this might appear faster and cheaper than a formal review, it is often less rigorous and may not identify errors in sufficient quantity or quality.

To make sure that the informal quality review is as effective as possible, the author should:

- identify a balanced selection of reviewers to represent commercial, customer and developer viewpoints;
- set a time by which reviewers should return their identified errors;

- ☑ provide a budget within which reviewers should work and a cost code to which their time and any costs should be attributed;
- ☐ provide a product description against which the reviewers will compare the product, or at the very least, a list of quality criteria to limit the scope of the review (this will stop errors being created by opinions rather than fact).

Both the formal and informal quality reviews seek to lift the fitness of a product to a point at which it is acceptable for use. Creating a product that is fit for its purpose takes time and money, so managers need to be prepared to invest in quality.

Control

Monitoring and reporting will not be effective without control. Once the various reports have been considered, the control cycle moves towards its final position where any corrective actions and decisions are taken to pull the project back onto its intended track. This must be subject to tight governance because the project might easily find itself in a worse position if the wrong decision is made or taken by someone without the appropriate authority.

The variances identified in the reports may well have been unforeseen and risk management may have failed to anticipate some of the things that have affected the project. Timescales may have slipped, costs may have overrun and quality expectations may not have been met. These are "issues" – matters the project must manage. But there are also potential changes that are neither risks nor issues. As the project exists in a changing environment, there is bound to be continued pressure on its timescale, costs, quality, scope, risks and benefits. Thus there are "change requests" – potential alterations to the project's parameters that must be considered in order to determine whether they are suitable.

The process by which both issues and change requests are handled is identical so that the right people are given the best information on which to make the decision they believe to be right. This process makes sure that, if the project's parameters have to change, it is a conscious, intended management control. It is reasonable for a project's timescale to be extended, its budget doubled, or its output to look very different from that originally planned, so long as these changes are agreed under a predetermined management process and overall the project remains financially justifiable. The control process is illustrated in Figure 9.19 overleaf.

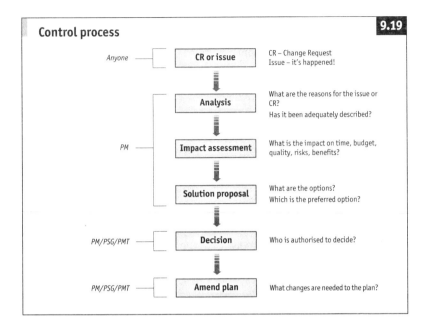

Control process 9.19

CR or issue — Anyone
CR – Change Request
Issue – it's happened!

Analysis — PM
What are the reasons for the issue or CR?
Has it been adequately described?

Impact assessment — PM
What is the impact on time, budget, quality, risks, benefits?

Solution proposal
What are the options?
Which is the preferred option?

Decision — PM/PSG/PMT
Who is authorised to decide?

Amend plan — PM/PSG/PMT
What changes are needed to the plan?

Change request or issue
Change must be managed, so anyone may raise a change request or an issue on a freely available form (these are often summarised in a change log to give an overview of every change request made and issue raised in order to keep track of progress). This is preferable to allowing changes without control.

Analysis
Everything known about the issue or change request should be included on the form, which may be circulated widely. The reason for the issue may well be contained in any of the project forecast report's "Reasons" columns. The reasons may be complex, so the project manager should oversee the analysis to make sure the background is clearly explained.

Impact assessment
The effect an actual or potential change may have on the project can be significant and expensive and therefore needs to be evaluated. The project manager must make sure that critical baseline documents are available so that the effect of the change can be assessed accurately. These are the principal baseline documents:

- business case – to assess the effect on benefits;
- user requirements document – to assess the effect on scope;
- solution design document – to assess the effect on the solution's robustness;
- project plan – to assess the effect on timescale, costs and quality;
- risk register – to assess the effect on the riskiness of the project.

If several change requests and issues arise, it may be necessary to have a team of people to assess their effects. This will have a cost implication for the project and is why the control of such changes is linked to the contingency budget. Even if a team is not required, impact assessment can be expensive, especially where the project is complex. The budget needed is not easy to estimate, but if managers record what they have invested, future projects can use the figures as a guideline.

Impact assessment answers these questions:

- What are the time and money implications of this issue or change request?
- How will this issue or change request affect the robustness of the design?
- How will this issue or change request affect the operability of the solution?

To find an appropriately balanced solution, the impact assessment process must involve someone with a commercial focus, a developer to consider the effects on the design and a customer or user to judge how the solution will be affected. The project manager should manage the process and may well promote a particular perspective; however, in the interests of balance, the project manager should take account of other views. Nevertheless, it is not surprising that the effects on time, cost and benefits usually take precedence, because a focus on the commercial point of view is often uppermost in many stakeholders' minds.

Solution proposal
There may well be a number of options and the project manager must make sure they are outlined clearly so that a recommendation can be made. No matter how many solutions there are, all will have an impact on time, cost or quality, and possibly also the benefits of the project, because they are inextricably linked. For instance, if more time is needed, this is likely to affect cost. If the budget must be contained, the product's

quality may be impaired. If more functionality or content is required, both the time and cost targets may be compromised. Any solution will usually require a compromise regarding the original expectations. Here is a list of compromises needed to achieve a desired outcome:

- To accommodate a solution while keeping to a fixed deadline:
  - more resources may be necessary;
  - faster resources may be needed;
  - quality and/or quality checks may have to be reduced;
  - the scope of what is delivered may have to be reduced;
  - overtime/weekend work may have to be increased;
  - holidays may have to be cancelled.
- To accommodate a solution while working within a fixed budget:
  - cheaper resources may be required;
  - fewer resources may be employed;
  - quality and/or quality checks may have to be reduced;
  - the scope of what is delivered may have to be reduced;
  - delivery dates may have to be delayed;
  - overtime/weekend work may have to be reduced;
  - holidays may have to be cancelled.
- To accommodate a solution while meeting the original quality and content expectations:
  - more resources may be necessary;
  - "better" resources may be needed;
  - quality processes, including tests, may have to be improved;
  - customer expectations may have to be better managed;
  - delivery dates may have to be delayed;
  - discounts may have to be offered;
  - some components may have to be deferred until later.

The need to control quality can be mitigated by strengthening the organisation's ability to specify, plan, build and test products by:

- identifying senior and authorised customers to participate in the project steering group;
- accommodating requirements through user forums;
- clarifying and baselining requirements at the start of the project;
- allowing changes to requirements only through formal change control;
- keeping customers involved throughout;

- involving business analysts throughout as advocates for customers;
- prototyping solutions;
- setting clear "quality gates" such as the number of faults tolerated at each stage of testing;
- training those who will take part in testing;
- managing end-date expectations to avoid compressing the testing;
- providing incentives for quality, not just timeliness and keeping to budget.

In all cases, further but stark options include:

- delivering late, despite intentions not to do so;
- delivering over budget, despite intentions not to do so;
- delivering lower quality or reduced scope, despite intentions not to do so;
- if the business case is compromised, cancelling the project.

Decision

If a baseline for time, cost, quality, risks and benefits has been agreed during the initiation stage, the assessment should have produced a clear statement of how the project will be affected by the change request or issue. This is important to determine not only the extent to which those parameters may be affected, but also who should decide whether to accept the proposed solution. It is all too common for critical decisions to be passed down the organisation structure rather than upwards. The project organisation has been specifically designed with degrees of authority given to each level of management that must be respected. Determining who should make a decision to accept or decline a change to the project's parameters is made simpler by using red, amber and green escalation conditions. For instance, if, on assessing the effect of an issue that has taken the project by surprise, it is now forecast to be completed in the project manager's red zone, he must ask the project steering group for a decision. If the forecast completion date falls outside the project steering group's red zone, the decision must pass further upwards to the portfolio management team. If the escalation condition is amber, control remains with the management tier in question, but those above should be alerted.

In all the reports described in this chapter, the red, amber and green escalation conditions are clearly identified so it is instantly possible to determine who is authorised to decide which solution is to be adopted.

Amend plan

Having decided upon a certain course of action, the control cycle has come full circle and either the business case or the project plan, or both, will need updating.

If the solution was approved by the project manager, the updates may include altering the forecast timescales, budgets or quality expectations in keeping with the (now) approved solution.

If the effect of the change request or issue was significant enough to involve the project steering group or portfolio management team, additional changes to the project plan and/or the business case may be required. They will need to approve the new version to make sure it contains the revised parameters created by the impact assessment. These new parameters, possibly involving amended timescales, altered budgets or changed quality expectations, will form the project's revised baseline against which future variances will be measured.

If the degree of change has heightened the anxiety of the most senior authorities in the project, they may decide to make the escalation conditions more sensitive. This will make it more likely that the decision to accept proposed solutions to issues and change requests will be referred upwards either earlier or more often. This gives each level of management dynamic control over the authority of those below.

The importance of effective control

The control process is a sound basis for managing significant change. However, most competent managers delegate, monitor, report and control progress as a matter of course, taking decisions regularly and frequently without recourse to such governance. Even so, overconfidence can be a manager's downfall. Small changes can have a significant and lasting effect on a project. When added together, a number of small, seemingly insignificant variances can quickly add up to a critical slippage that may not only require referring upwards, but also affect the underlying justification of the project.

Effective control mitigates the risk of a project failing one day at a time.

10 Support and assurance

Working on a project can be confusing and demanding for people new to change management. Even those familiar with the language, the processes and the responsibilities will need some help.

A common way of providing help is to use a support/assurance function to:

- assist the project manager and project team;
- assure the project steering group that the project management environment is, and continues to be, fit for its intended purpose;
- assist and assure the portfolio management team in their governance of the portfolio.

The support/assurance function can have a variety of names, such as:

- Project office
- Project support office
- Project management office
- Programme office

There is no typical structure, position or remit for a support/assurance function since it provides a tailored set of products and services to a specific audience whose needs are many and various.

The need for, and benefits of, a support/assurance function

A support/assurance function is not always essential. Much will depend on the size, criticality and risks of the changes being delivered and the needs and experience of the people working on the project and within the wider organisation.

Project managers may benefit from having some administrative responsibilities removed, freeing them to manage more effectively. The project steering group may benefit from the independent assurance that their project is in safe hands. The portfolio management team may be unable to function effectively without the regular management information they need to make critical decisions.

The variety of people that the support/assurance function is there to

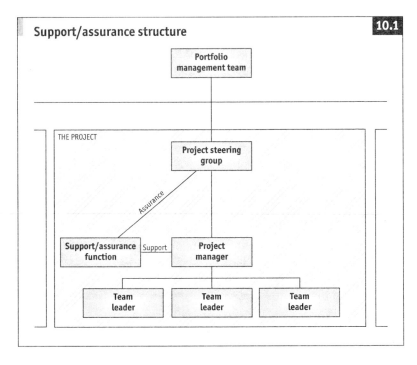

10.1 Support/assurance structure

serve suggests that its positioning is critical. The structure illustrated in Figure 10.1 will support a project manager and assure the project steering group.

However, to serve a portfolio management team, the support/assurance function should be outside any individual project, as in Figure 10.2.

A combination of both may be needed if the project manager, project steering group and portfolio management team all need support and assurance, as in Figure 10.3 on page 210.

Therefore, the help provided by the support/assurance function and the way it is delivered will depend on who is to be served. Given this, the benefits of an effective and efficient support/assurance function can be:

- ◢ better use of scarce skills;
- ◢ development arena for project management expertise;
- ◢ faster and more accurate impact assessment of changes and risks;
- ◢ application of common standards;
- ◢ stronger application of a common management discipline;

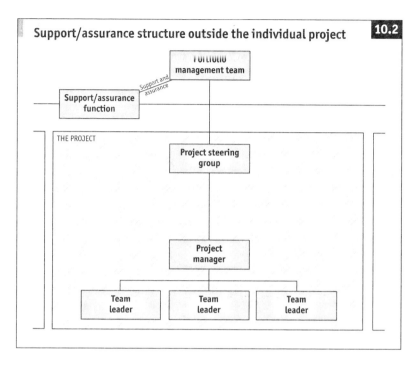

Support/assurance structure outside the individual project `10.2`

- central and single repository for management information;
- flexible service provision according to need;
- greater confidence in alignment of projects to strategic imperatives.

Introducing and operating a support/assurance function entails costs. In addition to running overheads, the satisfaction of one audience usually comes at a cost to another. For instance, providing management information to the portfolio management team suggests that the project managers will be required to gather the necessary project data but they will see no benefit from doing so. Therefore, the support/assurance function must have a clear and approved remit.

Support and assurance definition report

This document describes what a support/assurance function offers and how it will do so. Its success will be judged by answering these questions:

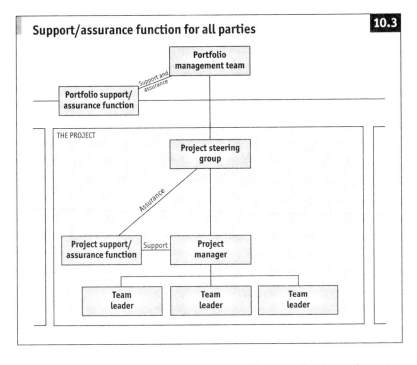

Support/assurance function for all parties   10.3

- Does it identify a steering group of sufficient authority to direct it to a successful outcome?
- Does it identify a support/assurance function manager of sufficient experience to plan, monitor and control it effectively?
- Does the solution address the identified issues and opportunities?
- Have all potential constraints been addressed?
- Is its position in the organisation clear?
- Are customers of the support/assurance function specifically identified?
- Have the products and services it is there to provide been prioritised to make sure the benefits are realised swiftly?

A support and assurance definition report should cover the areas listed in Table 10.1.

Table 10.1 **Support and assurance definition report**

Background	An outline of how the proposal for a support/assurance function has come about so that the environment within which it is to be introduced may be fully understood.
Issues and opportunities	A detailed explanation of the reasons a support/assurance function is considered to be an appropriate solution.
Constraints	What matters will constrain the way in which the support/assurance function operates?
Governance	How will the support/assurance function be structured?
Products and services	What will the support/assurance function provide, to whom and in what order of priority?

Background

As many people will have an opinion about what needs the support/assurance function must satisfy, this section must describe the principal drivers. These will be more fully expressed in a business case, but until then, this section must provide a background of sufficient depth to make sure it is clear why the support/assurance function is being considered.

Issues and opportunities

This section must fully express the challenges and opportunities faced by each customer of the support/assurance function. The section can be divided by customer type (project manager, project steering group, portfolio management team, and so on). Failure to clearly identify the issues and opportunities may result in an expensive support/assurance function that adds little value.

Constraints

Many factors will affect the remit of the support/assurance function. This section should consider the following areas, not all of which will be relevant in every case:

- **Who is to be served?** This statement must be consistent with the needs expressed in the issues and opportunities section.
- **Customer expectation.** How will each of those to be served judge the success of the support/assurance function? Are their expectations

contradictory? Have their expectations been prioritised?

- **Shared resource.** Is the support/assurance function to be responsible for providing project resources across a portfolio? For instance, are people with project planning experience to be made available according to project demand?
- **Organisational scope.** Where will the line be drawn between its responsibilities and those of the finance team, the resource demand/supply team, the management information team, the head of project management, and so on?
- **Skills and experience availability.** To what extent are the specialist competencies already available within the organisation? Will they need to be sourced from outside?
- **Internal structure.** What internal organisation structure will be suitable? How senior must it be? What will be the internal reporting structure?
- **Delivery structure.** Will specialist services be delivered by support/assurance function team experts or will all its team members deliver all services?
- **Professional development.** Will participants be drawn from the project management resource pool, or will they seek to join it? What would be the next career step for the support/assurance function manager?
- **Administrative support.** Is the support/assurance function expected to deliver administrative services either wholly or in addition to other offerings?
- **Advisory.** To what extent will it be expected to provide "expert" support and assurance? Would the team members be known for their proficiency as project management professionals?
- **Culture.** Is there a history of attempts made at implementing a support/assurance function? Is the concept new to the organisation? How ready is the organisation to accept the investment it will need to make?
- **Phasing/growth/maturity.** Will it be a permanent or temporary function? If it is not expected to outlive the project(s) it supports, how will it be disbanded?
- **Location.** Will it need to be physically based in a particular location? Can it operate "virtually"? Could the team be split, and if so, how?
- **Technology.** How can technology be used to help deliver its products and services? How much is already automated and centralised? To what extent would technology be needed to allow

the products and services to be effectively utilised?
- **Systemised approach.** Will it be expected to develop and/or administer the organisation's approach to project management?
- **Impartiality.** Where will the line be drawn between the responsibility to support and potentially having to audit the project? Will the people working in the support/assurance function be mature enough to manage such challenges? What form of assurance could it offer: project management health checks, internal project audits, externally resourced project audits?
- **Value for money.** Will the team charge for its services? If so, how? How will the quality of service be assured?

Failure to overcome such constraints could lead to the increased likelihood of serious risks. For example, the support/assurance function may:

- be seen as an ivory tower, resulting in a loss of respect and reputation;
- fail to deliver real value and create instead a financial burden for the organisation;
- not deliver soon enough, resulting in a loss of faith in its ability to support the organisation;
- not offer its members a development path towards a clear and desirable objective, resulting in their demotivation.

Governance

The definition report must show how the support/assurance function will be structured and governed. It might be relatively simple to create a team or department within the line structure to deliver the necessary products and services, but this suggests a permanency that may not be appropriate. If the team are to support and assure those temporary management environments called projects, it is sensible to develop the support/assurance function along similar lines; it would not become a fixed body and would need to demonstrate its continued relevance throughout its lifetime, just like a project.

In this way, the support/assurance function would be:

- justified by a business case;
- owned and directed by a team of sponsors;
- managed by a project manager;

- controlled by a plan;
- required to deliver value in stages, throughout its life, adding more value at each stage;
- able to close when its purpose has been achieved.

Since the purpose and value of a support/assurance function are often questioned, treating it like a project demonstrates to its customers that it faces the same challenges as a project, will benefit from the application of principles and techniques described in this book, and is shown to be credible by the way it responds to them.

Therefore, if it is to be justified by a business case, its intended benefits must be clearly outlined and quantified by a set of sponsors. Whether or not they are called a project steering group is up to them; it may be more appropriate to call them a support/assurance function steering group, comprising the following:

- **Sponsor.** A person representing the body that will commercially sponsor the support/assurance function, who might be an existing project sponsor, a department line manager or possibly a member of the portfolio management team.
- **Developer representative(s).** A person (or people) who can offer an authoritative view on how the support/assurance function is to be constructed, governed and made active. They may have operated one previously or come from a third-party project management specialist.
- **Customer representative(s).** This person (or persons) would be very important, providing the success criteria by which the support/assurance function would be judged. Depending on the audiences to be served, the customer representative could be a project manager, a project steering group member, a member of the portfolio management team, or a combination of all three.

The project manager, or more appropriately the support/assurance function manager, will be responsible for development and implementation according to an approved plan drawn up to satisfy the expectations set out in the business case. It must show how the support/assurance function can be enabled to deliver value to its customers as soon as possible, and how that the value can be maintained or increased over time.

Products and services

Below are some common products and services demanded from a support/assurance function

To support and/or assure the portfolio management team

- contribute to the development and continued management of the portfolio plan;
- develop and maintain the organisation's systemised approach to project management;
- monitor progress of all projects against the portfolio plan, prepare portfolio forecast reports and alert the portfolio management team to variances;
- assure the integrity of products being delivered by the portfolio particularly regarding:
  - scope, to confirm that duplication or omissions are minimised;
  - value, to provide assurance that projects are delivering to cost with a clear focus on benefits management;
  - competencies, to ensure that the organisation's skills are being applied effectively and efficiently;
  - timescale, to determine that projects remain focused on time targets and that dependencies are being honoured;
  - strategic fit, to assure the portfolio management team that projects have been prioritised to meet the organisation's strategic imperatives;
  - compliance, to demonstrate that standards and procedures are being respected;
- conduct health checks and propose solutions;
- assess and advise on the implications of changes to the portfolio plan;
- provide support in using tools or techniques for managing the portfolio or projects;
- identify and satisfy training needs;
- develop and maintain a register of the organisation's project resources and skills;
- facilitate portfolio co-ordination and communication sessions;
- track and measure the realisation of benefits from projects.

To support and/or assure the project steering group

- help to link projects to the organisation's strategic imperatives;
- advise on initiation procedures;

- advise on identifying and managing benefits in the business case;
- help the sponsor to maintain the business case;
- help to prepare project steering group meetings;
- propose and/or conduct project health checks;
- advise on closure procedures;
- support the sponsor during the benefits realisation stage.

To support the project manager
Planning:
- help the project manager to prepare the project plan;
- facilitate and/or administer planning sessions;
- assist in developing estimates;
- help the project manager prepare changes to plans where escalation conditions have been breached;
- propose recovery actions where escalation conditions have been breached.

Control:
- make sure that time recording and forecast reporting procedures are being applied;
- produce the project forecast report for the project manager, alerting him to key variances;
- administer change control procedures;
- assess the effect of change requests and issues;
- facilitate the regular identification of risks;
- maintain and update the business case, particularly regarding costs;
- make sure that all quality controls are applied through maintaining the product quality log;
- attend quality reviews when appropriate to make sure they are adequate;
- assist in closing the project.

Administration:
- co-ordinate all quality control activities;
- check or complete timesheet information on behalf of all project resources;
- minute all project meetings;
- administer the project's configuration management;
- identify training requirements and assist in their resolution;
- gather improvements to the systemised approach to project management.

Consultancy:
- coach project personnel in project management;
- provide project planning support and assistance to all project personnel;
- provide guidance on assorted specialist matters;
- develop and/or support automated tools or techniques;
- provide support to improve the accuracy of estimates.

When the products and services desired are identified, needs should be prioritised so that a pilot phase can provide the most important ones to start with, adding others over time.

Defining, validating and implementing a support/assurance function

The product flow diagram in Figure 10.4 overleaf shows how to implement the support/assurance function as a project.

This approach allows for effective project management principles to be applied to developing and implementing the support/assurance function while its operation is subject to continued phased benefit reviews to determine whether or not it is delivering value.

Key products in the approach are as follows:

- **Business case.** To justify why the support/assurance function is necessary and to set targets against which it must be seen to perform.
- **Support/assurance function definition report.** As described above.
- **Communications document.** To describe the audiences, methods of communication and messages needed to promote the support/assurance function so that all essential stakeholders are engaged.
- **Recruited support/assurance function personnel.** To develop and deliver the range of products and services. This may begin with support from specialist third parties but can eventually be delivered internally.
- **Developed tranche one products and services.** The support/assurance function must offer a range of products and services that will be popular with and benefit its customer(s). The first tranche must satisfy an immediate demand and make sure the investment in the support/assurance function can be justified.
- **Operational environment.** This may be a physical space for the

Product flow diagram

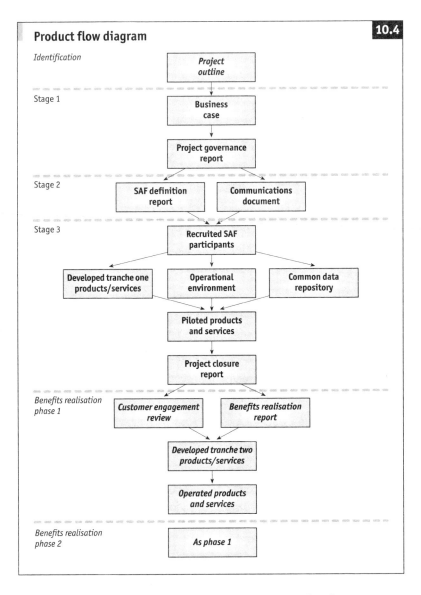

Identification — Project outline

Stage 1 — Business case → Project governance report

Stage 2 — SAF definition report, Communications document

Stage 3 — Recruited SAF participants → Developed tranche one products/services, Operational environment, Common data repository → Piloted products and services → Project closure report

Benefits realisation phase 1 — Customer engagement review, Benefits realisation report → Developed tranche two products/services → Operated products and services

Benefits realisation phase 2 — As phase 1

10.4

support/assurance function to occupy or a virtual web or intranet environment through which it can operate.

▪ **Common data repository.** Since it is almost inevitable that the support/assurance function will be asked for project management information, the core data must be gathered and held somewhere. This usually begins as a spreadsheet from which some of the reports described in Chapter 9 are produced. However, most organisations quickly outgrow the storage capacity and capabilities of a spreadsheet and need to develop ever-more sophisticated data management tools. This list gives an idea of the data fields needed to produce sensible management information:

- Project name
- Project manager
- Project sponsor
- Customer representative(s)
- Developer representative(s)
- Dependent projects
- Milestones/deliverables name
- Time escalation conditions – red, from and to
- Time escalation conditions – amber, from and to
- Time escalation conditions – green, from and to
- Milestone/deliverable quality reviewers
- Approval authority
- Baseline start date
- Baseline end date
- Forecast/actual start date
- Forecast/actual end date
- Start date variance (calculated)
- End date variance (calculated)
- Time within escalation conditions? (calculated)
- Reason for time variance
- Draft completion date
- Quality review "invitation sent" date
- Quality review "baseline review" date
- Quality review "review complete" date
- Quality review outcome
- Quality review number of changes
- Quality review "changes complete" date
- Quality review "approved fit for purpose" date
- Resource name
- Resource escalation conditions – red, from and to
- Resource escalation conditions – amber, from and to
- Resource escalation conditions – green, from and to
- Resource baseline items

- Resource baseline unit value
- Resource baseline total (calculated)
- Resource actual to date items
- Resource actual to date unit value
- Resource actual to date total (calculated)
- Resource estimate to complete items
- Resource estimate to complete unit value
- Resource estimate to complete total (calculated)
- Resource forecast (calculated)
- Resource variance (calculated)
- Resource within escalation conditions? (calculated)
- Reason for resource variance
- Quality measure
- Quality escalation conditions – red, from and to
- Quality escalation conditions – amber, from and to
- Quality escalation conditions – green, from and to
- Quality measure baseline
- Quality measure actual to date
- Quality measure success % (calculated)
- Quality within escalation conditions? (calculated)
- Reason for quality measure variance
- Benefit name
- Benefit escalation conditions – red, from and to
- Benefit escalation conditions – amber, from and to
- Benefit escalation conditions – green, from and to
- Benefit baseline
- Benefit actual to date
- Benefit estimate to complete
- Benefit forecast (calculated)
- Benefit variance ($ and %) (calculated)
- Benefit within escalation conditions? (calculated)
- Reason for benefit variance
- Risk description
- Risk escalation conditions – red, from and to
- Risk escalation conditions – amber, from and to
- Risk escalation conditions – green, from and to
- Risk likelihood
- Risk impact
- Risk factor (calculated)
- Risk mitigation

- Risk contingency amount
■ **Piloted products and services.** This is the first time that the tranche one products and services will have been provided to a real customer of the support/assurance function.
■ **Project closure report.** This will close the project and initiate the benefits realisation phase(s).
■ **Customer engagement review.** This will determine how far the customers of the support/assurance function are satisfied with the quality and form of its products and services. It must not only determine their happiness with what has been delivered, but should also ascertain their future needs so that the support/ assurance function can respond.
■ **Reassessed business case.** This will ensure that there remains sufficient enthusiasm, a market and enough funding for the support/assurance function to continue.
■ **Developed tranche two products and services.** The second tranche must satisfy the maturing needs of the support/assurance function's customers. Usually, their number and sophistication increase, but the support/assurance function must be prepared to reduce its offerings if the market so demands, or to close if necessary.
■ **Operated products and services.** As each benefits realisation phase progresses, more refined products and services may be provided.

A flexible function

A support/assurance function should always be sensitive to the needs of those it serves. Since its value will be judged by its customers, it should not be seen as permanent but rather as a flexible part of an ever-changing environment. Therefore, the support/assurance function should be developed as the product of a managed project so that its value is assessed at every stage.

11 Project closure and beyond

A project can be closed too quickly as people seek to extricate themselves and identify their next role. They believe remaining involved would be worthless because if the work planned has been completed, what can be gained from any further project stages?

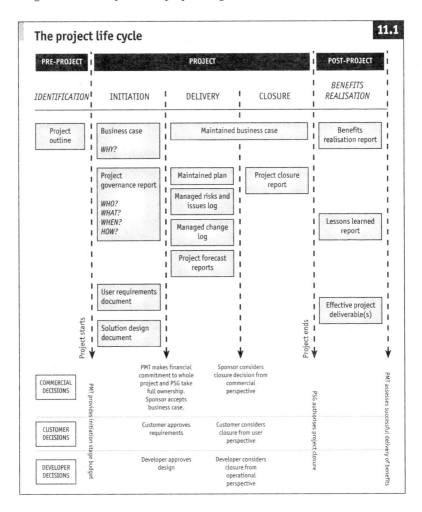

The project life cycle   11.1

When a project is completed in a well-considered way it provides the chance to learn valuable lessons, to make sure the project delivered everything in the way it was intended and, most importantly, to measure the benefits it promised to deliver.

To do this, it is helpful to separate completion into two stages:

- Project closure – where the project is closed down with the same management rigour as when it was initiated.
- Benefits realisation – where the emerging benefits promised in the business case are monitored, measured and, where possible, controlled to a point where they finally outweigh the whole-life investment.

A project is complete when the closure stage is deemed successful. Benefits realisation is a post-project stage owned and administered by those who commissioned the project, as illustrated by the project life cycle (Figure 11.1).

Project closure

This formal stage enables the management environment to be dismantled only when the project has met the project steering group's success criteria. They keep control of the project until they – and only they – agree it can be disbanded.

Closure asks whether the project has resulted in a product of sufficient quality, within acceptable timescales and budgets, and that should deliver the intended benefits. Therefore, the project steering group must find out from the project manager to what extent the expected time, cost and quality targets have been met.

The project closure report

The project manager answers by drawing up a project closure report (see Table 11.1 overleaf) which provides quantitative measures for the project steering group to use in making their decision to close the project.

The report's success will be judged on the answers to these questions:

- Does it provide sufficient information for the project steering group to close the project with confidence?
- Is the information accurate and up-to-date?
- Is all information internally consistent?

Table 11.1 **Project closure report**

Baseline documentation	The documents against which successful completion is being measured.
Background	An outline of the project's history so that any anomalies are fully understood.
Project summary	A detailed review of planned versus actual measurements to determine whether the variances would prevent a decision to close the project.
Matters outstanding	Any matters that remain unsettled.
Post-project governance	What management environment is needed for the post-project period leading towards the final measurement of realised benefits?
Other closure criteria	What additional closure criteria must be satisfied, if any, for the project steering group to make their decision?
Recommendations	What options are there for closing the project?
Proposed action	What outcome does the project manager propose? How will post-project governance be implemented?

- Does it clearly outline a course of action for the benefits realisation stage?
- Does it fully describe the roles and responsibilities of those who will take part in the benefits realisation stage?
- Does it provide enough information about the governance of the benefits realisation stage for the portfolio management team to approve the post-project management environment?

Baseline documentation
Generally, the documentation will be the business case (success criteria section), project governance report (containing the project plan), the user requirements document and the solution design document. Version numbers should be listed to make sure that success is being measured against the most recently approved versions of the documentation.

Background
The composition of the project steering group should be described to make it clear that those seeking to close the project are those who have directed it so far. The course of the project's progress should be outlined,

identifying changes relevant to understanding its state and variances at the point of closure.

Project summary
This section should list the following:

- Project success criteria. These are outlined in the business case. The report must show how far these success criteria have been met (see Table 11.2 overleaf, for example).
- Budget (see Table 11.3 on page 227, for example). The project steering group will want to know the reasons for any variances and the details should be noted here. In Table 11.3, even a positive variance of $500 is shown as amber, representing money requested but not used and which must be handed back to the portfolio management team.

  The project steering group should also know about monies committed but for which the liability has not yet been recorded (usually because the invoice has not been received). This identifies costs to be attributed to the project after closure and for which the cost codes must remain open.
- Timescales (see Table 11.4 on page 228, for example). The project steering group must know the reasons for any variances and details should be noted here.

Matters outstanding
This section should list the following:

- Additional products –any products included beyond those originally anticipated.
- Excluded products – any products which, although planned, were not delivered (for instance, "documented operating manual").
- Additional benefits – any benefits added to the business case or augmented since its original approval.
- Excluded benefits – any benefits removed from the business case or reduced since its original approval.
- Change requests and issues – the change log will show the status of change requests and issues at the point of closure. Some changes may have been deferred until a later phase or release or may have been declined altogether.

Table 11.2 **Project success criteria**

Baseline project success criteria	Actual project success	Variance	Reason
Does the new computer system process twice as many trades per day as the previous one?	Original system processed 950 trades per day. New system has been shown to process 1,900 trades per day successfully.	0 **GREEN**	
Does the new office provide each of the 350 staff with at least 36 sq ft of desk space?	Office provides 400 people with at least 36 sq ft of desk space.	+50 people **AMBER**	Capacity was allowed for staff who may join office in the future.
Have all new staff been recruited by the end of June?	All new staff were recruited by August, but at no risk to the project.	−2 months **AMBER**	Three of the nine intended staff were unable to join by June. However, they were not critical to the success of the project.
Have the new facilities been secured within budget?	See budgetary review below.	See budgetary review below.	See budgetary review below.
Have the new office operating procedures been made available to the Tokyo office as a priority?	Tokyo office received new operating procedures before other colleagues.	0 **GREEN**	

Post-project governance

The benefits realisation stage does not fall within the project's governance. If closing the project means that every aspect of the management environment will be dismantled, there is an increased likelihood of not knowing fully whether the benefits will be achieved.

This section of the project closure report must cover the following:

- ☑ The outcome expected of the benefits realisation stage – the report required, its content and the success criteria which, when met, will determine that it is complete.

Table 11.3 **Budget**

1	2	3	4	5	6	7
Resource item	Original baseline	Last authorised baseline	Invoiced at completion	Forecast total	Variance with original baseline	Variance with last authorised baseline
Human resources	$32,000	$42,000	$42,000	$42,000	–$10,000 RED	$0 GREEN
Non-human resources	$29,500	$29,500	$25,500	$29,000	$500 AMBER	$500 AMBER
Capital costs	$4,000	$4,000	$4,000	$4,000	$0 GREEN	$0 GREEN
Total	$65,500	$75,500	$71,500	$75,000	–$9,500 RED	$500 AMBER

Notes:
Column 1: resource type, summarised from project plan
Column 2: as approved in project governance report
Column 3: as approved in notification (where relevant), dated dd/mm/yy
Column 4: as identified on finance ledger, dated dd/mm/yy
Column 5: taking account of committed and planned spend, not yet invoiced
Column 6: variance if the amended baseline had not been approved by the project steering group on dd/mm/yy
Column 7: variance, based on approved changes to the project plan following notification (where relevant), dated dd/mm/yy

- The time it will take.
- Who will monitor the stage, identifying those responsible for measuring the benefits and any operational costs that accrue during it.
- The data and/or metrics to be used to measure them; these need to be identified for each project benefit together with the specific means by which its realisation will be measured.
- When and how benefits will be monitored, measured, compared with those planned and (if necessary) steered towards a successful outcome. Pre-scheduled events should be listed to update the business case with actual costs and benefits.

Other closure criteria
There should be few other closure criteria. Examples are:

- Has a suitable post-project governance been proposed?

Table 11.4 **Timescales**

1	2	3	4	5	6
Product/ milestone	Original baseline	Last authorised baseline	Actual end date	Variance with original baseline	Variance with last authorised baseline
Initiation	10/04/05	01/05/05	01/05/05	–20 days RED	0 days GREEN
Delivery Stage 1	30/07/05	28/08/05	28/08/05	–29 days RED	0 days GREEN
Delivery Stage 2	28/09/05	30/10/05	30/10/05	–32 days RED	0 days GREEN
Closure	30/10/05	30/11/05	30/11/05	–31 days RED	0 days GREEN

Notes:
Column 1: key deliverables or stages summarised from the project plan
Column 2: as approved in the project governance report
Column 3: as approved in notification (where relevant), dated dd/mm/yy
Column 4: as contained in the most recent project plan, dated dd/mm/yy
Column 5: variance if the amended baseline had not been approved by the project steering group on dd/mm/yy
Column 6: variance, based on approved changes to the project plan following notification (where relevant), dated dd/mm/yy

- Are all participants in the post-project governance comfortable and familiar with their roles and responsibilities?
- Have all project cost codes been prepared for closure?

Recommendations
This section should describe the circumstances under which the project should be closed. This may mean that a straightforward decision is required to close the project as planned. Alternatively, it may be necessary to recommend a postponement of some of the project to a supplementary stage, for example where a part of the project cannot be delivered within the planned time or budget. In more extreme circumstances, it may be recommended that the key deliverables are not to be used in the operational environment, for instance where the product does not meet quality expectations. In any case, the recommendation should not come as a surprise to the project steering group, which should have been kept informed of progress throughout the project.

Without such governance being placed around project closure, benefits realisation can all too easily become unmanaged and unfocused, resulting in a failure to monitor realised benefits adequately and, ultimately, not knowing whether the project was a success.

Proposed action
This describes the steps that must be taken to reach the closure decision and to put in place the governance of the post-project benefits realisation stage described in the post-project governance section.

It is important to state when the benefits reviews will take place so that those involved can note them in their diaries. Additionally, the responsibility for delivering and approving the final benefit realisation report must be made clear so there is no doubt about ownership.

Project closure process

The project closure process (see Figure 11.2 overleaf) is relatively straightforward, although since closure means different things to different people, it must satisfy their varied needs.

For the project steering group closure means:

- The investment made in the project has come to an end.
- A period is beginning during which the emerging benefits must be seen to outweigh the actual project costs and increasing operational costs.
- The customer representative(s) must make sure that the business-as-usual environment is able to operate the project's product.
- The developer representative(s) must make sure that support is available to customers.

For the project manager closure means:

- Work identified on the project plan is complete, so the plan must be brought up-to-date and filed.
- Post-project actions must be handed over to the post-project governance team, whatever that may be.
- Project cost codes must be prepared for closure, making sure that only committed and authorised spend is charged to them.
- Project team members must be told of the closure and their line managers instructed to seek new engagements for them.
- The project manager must give feedback to each team member for use during their regular performance appraisals.

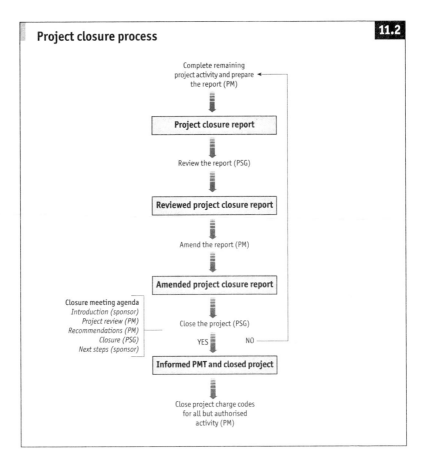

Project closure process — 11.2

☑ Sufficient budget must remain available to fund a "lessons learned" meeting, which should be scheduled for a time that suits as many project participants as possible.

Lessons learned report
This is the result of a lessons learned review, which gathers and communicates as much information as possible to generate greater future management efficiencies.

The report is often less valuable than the review itself; it is hard to think of many projects where the first step has been to review the lessons learned from the past. In many organisations, individual learning contributes to the improvement of company procedures and standards more than the rectification of systemic faults and anomalies when a project has been completed. However, the report may provide useful information to a new project's first risk identification workshop.

The success of a review of how the project was governed can be judged by whether:

- representatives of all levels of management were involved in the review;
- it was held near enough to the end of the project so that participants in the review remembered things clearly and accurately;
- both positive and negative aspects of project management were given sufficient consideration;
- improvement actions were clearly identified;
- the individuals responsible for carrying out those actions have been identified;
- each action has a timetable for completion.

The report's proposed structure (see Table 11.5) helps to determine how the review is conducted.

Table 11.5 **Lessons learned report**

Project background	A brief outline of the project itself for readers who are not participants in either the project or the review.
Objectives	What is the purpose of the review, and what are the measures of success?
Scope	How widely is the management of the project being reviewed? What exclusions are there, if any?
Observations	What observations did the participants identify?
Lessons learned	What lessons can be learned from those observations?
Action plan	What is the plan to implement the lessons?

Project background
This can be copied from the project closure report.

Objectives
These depend upon how open the organisation is about learning and growing. A common set of objectives is:

231

- ◪ to allow all participants to feel that they have had the opportunity to contribute to the growth of the organisation's project management capabilities;
- ◪ to identify specific project management improvements that can be implemented in future.

A lessons learned review can be conducted not merely at the end of a project, but also at the end of a project stage. Clearly it can help improve project management if there is a willingness to learn and improve throughout the project rather than just at the end.

Scope
The purpose of the lessons learned review is to consider how well the project was managed. To avoid confusion, it may be necessary explicitly to exclude non-management matters, such as a technical review of the computer system or bridge or building that the project delivered. Inclusions can be described by listing the area of project management to be considered, such as:

- ◪ organisation, roles and responsibilities;
- ◪ communications and stakeholder management;
- ◪ plans, planning and delegation;
- ◪ monitoring, reporting and management information;
- ◪ project control, including change control;
- ◪ quality management;
- ◪ risk management;
- ◪ benefits management.

Observations
A lessons learned review should promote good practice and help eliminate poor habits. The observations should be straightforward statements without qualification. For example, a positive observation from a debate about monitoring and reporting might be: "The project forecast report was used for the first time and helped to identify variances." A negative observation might be: "Too many preventable issues arose because the monthly risk identification session was too infrequent."

Lessons learned
This section describes the lessons to be learned from the positive and negative observations and is the reason for the report. For example, a

lesson to be learned from the positive observation above could be: "All projects should be encouraged to use project forecast reports (and, at the very least, make sure that variances are clearly identified)." A lesson to be learned from the negative observation above could be: "Risk identification sessions should be more frequent for all similarly sized/scoped projects."

Action plan
This shows how the lessons are to be embedded in the organisation's project management culture (see Table 11.6, for example).

Table 11.6 **Action plan**

Number	Lesson	Action(s)	Success criteria	Who?	Due date
1	All projects should be encouraged to use project forecast reports (and, at the very least, make sure that variances are clearly identified)	Introduce project forecast report to Project Ace, Project King and Project Queen.	Projects Ace, King and Queen adopt the project forecast report and use it fully without supervision.	DK	dd/mm/yy
2	Risk identification sessions should be more frequent for all similarly sized/ scoped projects	Increase frequency of risk identification sessions for Project Jack.	Project Jack conducts two-weekly risk identification sessions.	PT	dd/mm/yy

Lessons learned review
This usually takes place a week or two after the project has been closed. Those invited to take part should come from all levels of the project's management, including team members, team leaders, the project manager, the project steering group, customers, suppliers, the project steering group and, if the project was of sufficient size, criticality or risk, members of the portfolio management team.

Given the importance of allowing everyone to contribute fully and equally, the review is usually best managed by an external or impartial, seasoned and assured facilitator, possibly found in, or through, the support/assurance function.

The agenda should be as follows:

- introduction;
- ground rules;
- observations;
- break;
- lessons learned;
- action plan.

Introduction
The introduction should be made by a member of the project steering group, ideally the sponsor. This lends authority to the review and provides an opportunity to promote the value of the output to all participants. The introduction must also allow the sponsor to state the objectives of the session. Given that some participants may not have been involved throughout the whole life cycle, some limited project background will be necessary. This will also help set the scope of the review.

Ground rules
An occasion where unhappy memories may have to be revisited can be upsetting for individuals and disruptive. Emotions can cloud the desired outcome, so the facilitator should set out the rules of engagement at the outset. The list below is not exhaustive, but is a starting point for developing a set of rules participants should abide by:

- **Park issues.** If a matter is debated for longer than five minutes without resolution, it is "parked" on a flip chart and revisited outside the session.
- **Work within the agenda.** The agenda approved by the sponsor should be respected. If there is not sufficient opportunity to discuss something, it may be parked.
- **Respect the facilitator.** The facilitator is there to allow the session to progress effectively and efficiently.
- **Prepare in advance.** Participants should be encouraged to think in advance about the observations and lessons they wish to raise.
- **Criticise the governance, not individuals.** If criticisms are to be made, they should be levelled at the project's governance rather than the people who developed or operated it.
- **Speak one at a time.** This will enable observations and solutions to be identified more quickly.

- **Make your point clearly.** Think about what you wish to raise and use language participants will understand.
- **Make your point once.** Time is limited, so avoid labouring a point.
- **Make your point politely.** Do not allow emotions to create unnecessary tension.

Observations

Everyone attending will be keen to offer their views, positive or negative, so some structure is necessary. The two approaches below depend on breaking the group into smaller teams:

- **Tailored group topics.** Each group has a specific set of topics they must review, including those identified in scope (see Lessons learned report above). A set of starter questions may be provided to help each group explore the issues relating to their topic. For instance, one group may be assigned risk management and their starter questions might include: Were risk management events conducted sufficiently frequently? How effective was the project in mitigating risks?
- **Common group topics.** Each group is presented with a list of all topics falling within the scope of the review. The same starter questions may be provided to assist groups. This approach has merit if everybody wants to cover every topic.

The result is a flipchart sheet listing the positive and negative observations arising from each group's discussion, with three or four highlighted as the most significant (see Figure 11.3 overleaf).

During the session, the facilitator should move around the groups to make sure they are progressing to schedule and that the output is as required. At the end of the session, each group should be given a few minutes to present their highlighted observations.

Break

The observations session can be draining, not least because people often focus on the negative aspects of the project. The break allows participants to recover and prepare for the next session, which is intentionally upbeat and focused on improvements.

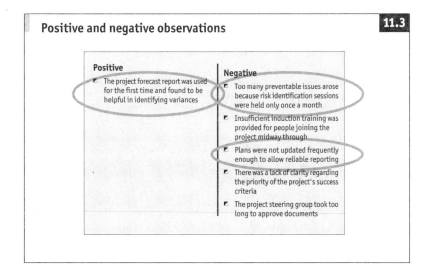

Positive and negative observations

11.3

Positive
- The project forecast report was used for the first time and found to be helpful in identifying variances

Negative
- Too many preventable issues arose because risk identification sessions were held only once a month
- Insufficient induction training was provided for people joining the project midway through
- Plans were not updated frequently enough to allow reliable reporting
- There was a lack of clarity regarding the priority of the project's success criteria
- The project steering group took too long to approve documents

Lessons learned

Participants return to their groups to consider the highlighted observations. Their objective must be clearly stated: to identify improvements that can be introduced to the project management approach. For each highlighted observation, they should identify at least one practical way of overcoming the issues and promoting those matters considered positive.

Each group's results can be noted on a sheet of flipchart paper (see Figure 11.4).

During the session, the facilitator should move around each group with an eye to the schedule and the required output. At the end of the session, each group should be given a few minutes to present the lessons it has identified.

Action plans

It is essential to create an action plan for the event to have any value. It is not sufficient to have identified lessons within the review; the changes necessary to the project management governance must be made if the improvements are to make any difference.

The action plan must state what the action entails, how its completion will be measured, who has responsibility for completing it and by when. The responsibility for making sure the actions are carried out should be assigned only to participants in the room.

Once the action plan is agreed, the sponsor who backed the review

Positive and negative observations and lessons learned   **11.4**

Positive	Negative
◪ The project forecast report was used for the first time and found to be helpful in identifying variances	◪ Too many preventable issues arose because risk identification sessions were held only once a month
◪ *LESSON LEARNED: All projects should be encouraged to use project forecast reports and, at the very least, to ensure that variances are clearly identified.*	◪ *LESSON LEARNED: Risk identification sessions should be more frequent for all similarly sized/scoped projects*
	◪ Plans were not updated frequently enough to allow reliable reporting
	◪ *LESSON LEARNED: Project plans must be updated at a frequency no less than every two weeks*

must publicly take responsibility for seeing it to a successful conclusion. The project manager should not take on this burden; he may well be assigned to another project and his responsibilities will lie elsewhere. The sponsor, however, has continuing accountabilities after the project has ended, including the continuous improvement of the organisation's systemised approach to project management. Contributions to this will come from the actions taken as a result of the lessons learned review.

This is not the sponsor's only remaining responsibility. Having proposed that a package of benefits may be delivered by the project on or after its completion, the organisation may rightly expect each sponsor to remain responsible for, and committed to, the realisation of those benefits.

Benefits realisation

This stage follows the closure of the project; it is when the intended benefits are expected to grow. The governance put in place for the project is no longer present and besides, it would be unnecessary and inappropriate for the activities ahead. The objective of the benefits realisation stage is to make sure that the benefits outweigh the investment according to the targets outlined in the business case.

For the stage to be successful, these questions must be asked:

◪ Who has responsibilities during the stage?
◪ How will the mounting costs and benefits be monitored, measured and controlled?

237

- When can the stage come to an end?
- How will the organisation reward success or failure?
- Can the benefits be shown to have contributed to planned business objectives?

Roles and responsibilities

Since it commissioned the project, the portfolio management team has ultimate responsibility for both a successful conclusion to the stage and the realisation of benefits that sufficiently outweigh the investment. It is also responsible for commissioning projects that contribute to the strategic growth and development of the organisation. Consequently, although the sponsor promoted the project and persuaded others to follow, it was the portfolio management team who considered it sufficiently worthwhile to merit investing the organisation's money.

The sponsor may have a line role to which he must return, but he has the additional responsibility of monitoring, measuring and controlling the mounting costs and benefits during this stage, so many organisations provide help, often from the support/assurance function. Specifically, the sponsor can draw upon the skills of a project specialist who can devote time to the monitoring and measurement of costs and benefits. Where a project/programme support function does not exist, an expert may be identified to take on the monitoring and measuring role. In either case, this frees the sponsor to exercise authority where variances in expected costs or benefits are identified. The sponsor alone is expected to bring the realisation of benefits back on plan.

Once a project has been completed, it is not uncommon for its sponsor to work in an entirely different part of the organisation. If that makes it impractical for the sponsor to discharge his continuing responsibilities for benefits realisation, the portfolio management team should identify someone to do so. Without such an authority in place, the benefits and costs may not grow at their intended rate and the project might yet be deemed a failure.

Monitoring, measurement and control

Tracking benefits and costs during the benefits realisation stage should be reasonably straightforward if:

- the monitoring and measurement mechanisms have been expressed clearly enough in the business case; and
- changes to the intended benefits, costs or monitoring and

measurement mechanisms have been accommodated in the business case during the project.

Each benefit and cost item must be monitored and measured separately. Table 11.7 gives an example of some benefits identified in a business case in Chapter 5.

Table 11.7 **Quantifying benefits ($)**

	Year 0	Year 1	Year 2	Year 3	Year 4
Increased revenues	–	**5,000**	**60,000**	**60,000**	**70,000**
Increased customer satisfaction	–	5,000	10,000	10,000	10,000
Competitor removal	–	–	20,000	20,000	20,000
Customers from new market	–	–	30,000	30,000	40,000
Cost savings	–	**8,000**	**10,000**	**11,000**	**11,000**
Headcount savings	–	5,000	5,000	5,000	5,000
Removal of redundant IT kit	–	3,000	5,000	6,000	6,000
Total	–	**13,000**	**70,000**	**71,000**	**81,000**
Cumulative total	–	**13,000**	**83,000**	**154,000**	**235,000**

The relevant facts extracted from the business case are as follows:

- ◪ Customer satisfaction is measurable before, during and after the project through a survey.
- ◪ A 5% improvement in customer satisfaction between year 0 and year 1 is envisaged as a direct result of this project.
- ◪ In year 2, it will increase by a further 5%.
- ◪ It will remain stable during years 3 and 4
- ◪ The increase in revenue will come from newly satisfied customers spending more on the organisation's products and services.
- ◪ The 5% improvement in customer satisfaction will lead to a $5,000 increase in sales in year 1, a further $5,000 in year 2, and then stabilise at $10,000 for the remainder of the whole life of the venture.

- The lower costs will come from headcount savings because fewer customer service staff will be required.
- The 5% improvement in customer satisfaction will lead to a reduction in headcount, creating savings of $5,000 per year, every year for the remainder of the whole life of the venture.

Therefore, during the benefits realisation stage, the sponsor is responsible for making sure the benefits accrue according to the benefits realisation plan. In the example in Table 11.7, this means that the plan must allow for the following to be measured or recorded in a consistent way:

- customer satisfaction before the project begins and at least every year thereafter;
- customer revenue before the project begins and at least every year thereafter;
- the number of customer service staff before the project begins and at least every year thereafter;
- the operational costs of the implemented solution.

The benefits realisation stage is as much about monitoring and controlling the operational costs of implementing the solution to make sure that they do not exceed the planned amount as it is about monitoring the benefits. The margin, the difference between costs and benefits, is ultimately what matters as stated in the business case.

The costs identified in the business case in question are shown in Table 11.8.

If the project was completed at the end of year 0, the subsequent costs must be monitored and controlled, and the way in which they are to be measured must be recorded in the benefits realisation plan.

Each measurement of costs or benefits must be planned to take place at a certain time, to cost no more than a specified budget and to satisfy a set of success criteria. For this example, these would be as follows:

- Does the plan enable customer satisfaction, customer revenue and headcount levels to be determined in a way that can be measured year after year in the same way?
- Where possible, have survey dates been selected to coincide with other organisation-wide events to minimise the duplication of effort?
- Can it be shown that the variances in customer satisfaction, revenue and headcount may be attributed to this project?

Table 11.8 **Costs over time ($)**

	Year 0	Year 1	Year 2	Year 3	Year 4
Resources	1,300	12,250	16,820	12,600	19,850
Consumables				1,000	
Hardware			28,000		
Software			17,000		
Environmental				11,000	
Accommodation	500	1,200	1,200	1,200	1,200
Expenses	700	2,400	1,600	1,600	3,200
Total	2,500	15,850	64,620	27,400	24,250
Cumulative total	**2,500**	**18,350**	**82,970**	**110,370**	**134,620**

- ◪ Where possible, has the same person been responsible for monitoring throughout the benefits realisation stage?
- ◪ Have all elements contributing to operational costs been separately and accurately measured?

By showing how the time, cost and quality expectations of the benefits realisation stage are to be managed, the benefits realisation plan bears many of the hallmarks of a regular project plan and should be treated no differently. As the plan is used to determine where variances have occurred, the sponsor is responsible for keeping the costs and benefits in line with the plan. Throughout this stage the sponsor's responsibilities are similar to those of the project manager during the project itself.

Achieving strategic change

The monitoring, measurement and control of costs and benefits during the benefits realisation stage described above are sufficient if the benefits have been stated in commercial terms. However, if the project was undertaken to enable the success of a programme or to contribute to the wider strategic needs of the organisation, the portfolio management team will expect that link to be demonstrated.

Particularly where information technology is concerned, it is sometimes more difficult to show the extent to which a contribution has been made to strategic, rather than overtly commercial, success factors. However, there is a way to trace the audit trail from project outcome to strategic

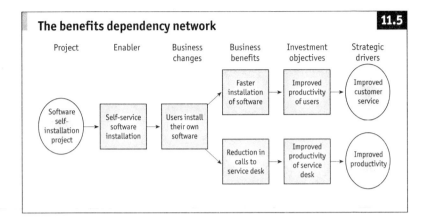

The benefits dependency network   11.5

imperative. Called the "benefits dependency network", it was developed by John Ward and Joe Peppard of Cranfield University in their book, *Strategic Planning for Information Systems* (3rd edition, John Wiley and Sons, 2002).

Figure 11.5 shows how the software self-installation project on the left can be shown to contribute to two of the organisation's strategic imperatives on the right. The link between them is formed by the assertion that the project will deliver an "enabler", a feature that facilitates achieving a change in the way the business works. In this case, users are able to pick software from a list to self-install without recourse to experts. This change, if carried out, will benefit the business through faster installation of software and fewer calls to the service desk. These fit the business's investment objectives, which were to improve user and service-desk productivity, both of which are measurable. If the productivity improvements meet the intended targets, progress will be made in achieving the organisation's strategic drivers. Service will improve as users have more time to spend with customers, and productivity will improve as the service-desk team are able to do more with their time.

Additionally, since Table 11.9 was created when the portfolio was being developed, it can and should be used to determine each project's actual contribution to the organisation's strategy. As each project is completed and enters its benefits realisation phase, each statement should be changed from the original "Will this project contribute to...?" to "Did this project contribute to...?".

Table 11.9 **Project contribution to strategy**

Strategic imperative	Project 1	Project 2	Project 3
The company securing $500,000 worth of recurring revenues during the coming year from clients that have always previously paid one-off payments.	Direct	Indirect	Absent
The company delivering three implementations during the coming year of its standard product in seven weeks rather than nine.	Absent	Absent	Absent
The company implementing its own project management method based upon an industry-recognised standard during the coming year.	Indirect	Absent	Absent
Contributing to the company delivering two projects in the coming year using the new project management method.	Absent	Absent	Absent
The company reducing its turnover of staff of more than ten years' experience by 20% during the coming year.	Absent	Direct	Absent

The benefits realisation report

The sponsor should produce regular benefits realisation reports for the portfolio management team. Depending on how long the benefits realisation stage lasts, they may be needed every three months to a year. The concept and content are similar to that of the project forecast report. The project forecast report provides a regular update on progress towards the intended project target; the benefits realisation report takes a snapshot of the mounting post-project costs and benefits, and clearly shows variances so that the stage can be managed and brought to a successful outcome.

The success of a business realisation report can be judged by whether it:

- shows what progress has been made since the preceding report;
- identifies variances in intended operational costs and benefits;
- explains fully how variances arose;
- describes how variances will be addressed;
- determines who is responsible for any proposed corrective actions.

With these criteria in mind, Table 11.10 overleaf lists what should be included in a business case.

Table 11.10 **Business realisation report**

Summary	A table to summarise the actual and forecast operational spend and benefits realised, identifying variances and escalation conditions.
Variances	An analysis of the key variances.
Corrective actions	A description of what will be done by whom to address the key variances.
Changes to benefits realisation stage governance	A narrative to determine what, if anything, must be done to change the governance of this stage to increase the likelihood of success.
Conclusion	To provide an opportunity for the author to summarise the outcome of the review.
Recommendations	To allow the author to propose how the benefits realisation stage should continue, if at all.

Summary

A table like Table 11.11 can be included.

This example is based on an assessment of costs and benefits during year 2 of the business case, and illustrates the following points:

- Variances are shown "to date" (the difference between the planned to date and actual to date figures) and as forecast "on completion" (the difference between the baseline and forecast figures). This enables the sponsor to assess the likelihood of the intended margin between costs and benefits being achieved.
- Variances, whether positive or negative, are subject to red, amber and green escalation conditions because the portfolio management team should be alerted to any significant variances. For instance, "removal of redundant kit" has realised its full benefit after year 2, but was not planned to occur until after year 4. The portfolio management team may wish to examine this because it may indicate the kit was removed before it was sensible to do so.
- Since the original business case was developed, two new benefits have been identified, "improved employee morale" and "avoidance of identified risks". These are shown with a zero baseline because they were not anticipated. This makes sure the portfolio management team is alerted to their recent inclusion.

Table 11.11 **Actual benefits and costs**

Benefits	Baseline	Planned to date	Actual to date	Estimate to complete	Forecast	Variance	
						to date	on completion
1 Increased customer satisfaction	35,000	15,000	15,000	20,000	35,000	0	0
2 Competitor removal	60,000	20,000	20,000	40,000	60,000	0	0
3 Customers from new market	100,000	30,000	35,000	70,000	105,000	5,000	5,000
4 Headcount savings	20,000	10,000	9,000	11,000	20,000	-1,000	0
5 Removal of redundant kit	20,000	8,000	20,000	0	20,000	12,000	0
6 Improved employee morale	0	0	1,000	4,000	5,000	1,000	5,000
7 Avoidance of identified risks	0	0	1,000	10,000	11,000	1,000	11,000
BENEFITS TOTALS	235,000	83,000	101,000	155,000	256,000	18,000	21,000
Costs							
1 Consultancy	2,500	2,500	2,500	0	2,500	0	0
2 Human resources	61,520	29,070	35,000	32,000	67,000	-5,930	5,480
3 Consumables	1,000	0	0	1,000	1,000	0	0
4 Hardware	28,000	28,000	29,000	0	29,000	-1,000	1,000
5 Software	17,000	17,000	17,000	0	17,000	0	0
6 Environmental	11,000	0	500	11,000	11,500	-500	500
7 Accommodation	4,800	2,400	2,500	2,300	4,800	-100	0
8 Expenses	8,800	3,000	3,000	5,800	8,800	0	0
COSTS TOTALS	134,620	81,970	89,500	52,100	141,600	-7,530	6,980
NET	100,380	1,030	11,500	102,900	114,400	-10,470	14,020

Variances
The benefits realisation report must contain all the information needed to answer any questions it raises. Variances should be described fully, not merely by referring to the numbers in the table.

Corrective actions
Corrective action must be proposed for every variance, and an intention to do nothing should be also documented. A simple table can be used (Table 11.12).

Table 11.12 **Corrective actions**

	Actions	Success criteria	Responsibility	Due date
1				
2				
3				
4				
5				

Changes to governance
The benefits realisation stage may take several years to be completed, so it is not unusual for those involved in it to move to new positions or for changes to the wider organisation to affect the emerging costs and benefits. The sponsor should use this section to record the changes.

Conclusion
The author should summarise the report, clearly stating the extent to which the realisation of benefits is on track.

Recommendations
This section allows the author to propose a course of action to the portfolio management team. This may suggest that the realisation stage is complete and that no further reviews will be necessary, or alternatively that subsequent reviews must be carried out. Whatever the recommendation, it must be made sufficiently clear so that the portfolio management team know how they are expected to respond.

Project success

On the assumption that

- the original business case was robust and reliable;
- it was maintained during the life of the project;
- there was effective management of time, costs, quality, risks and change;
- the "lessons learned" report identified improvement actions that have been accommodated into the systemised approach;
- there has been a determination to maximise the benefits and minimise the operational expenses during the benefits realisation stage;

there is every chance that the final benefits realisation report will show that the realised benefits outweighed the actual project and operational costs by the amount anticipated in the business case. If, happily, this is the case, it can be said that effective project management has led, intentionally, to project success.

12 Embedding effective project management

A systemised approach for using projects to deliver lasting business change may represent a change in itself for many people in an organisation. To succeed, any approach to designing, implementing and embedding a new way of working must take account of the fact that it must be a culture-changing exercise. If project management behaviours are not modified at both the individual and organisational levels, the desired transformation will not take place.

As in many projects, realising the benefits of introducing a new approach will take time. During this time, the leaders of the change must manage carefully the expectations of the many stakeholders who will be affected by the outcome. For some, it may be a difficult experience; their workload may increase, or they may be required to work in a way that is not instinctive. Others will relish the opportunity to embrace practices that they see as enhancing their professional lives. Those who seek to design, implement and embed the new approach will need to deliver an outcome that neither panders to, nor exiles, either of these two extremes. A managed approach is essential, so using a project to embed project management in an organisation is an effective way of accomplishing it. For the rest of this chapter, this project will be referred to as the project management improvement initiative.

Establishing a case for change

It is important to demonstrate the link between projects and business change objectives – one delivers the other – so there must be a clear indication from the outset that an investment in project management will directly contribute to the organisation's ability to meet its agenda for change.

It is sensible to remind managers of their personal and organisational objectives so that they grasp the relevance of the proposed changes. Some examples of business objectives which effective project management can contribute to are:

- ◪ achieving demanding financial targets;
- ◪ overcoming competitive challenges;

- being able to respond swiftly to change;
- being recognised for excellence in product and service delivery;
- offering opportunities for staff development;
- learning without customers having to identify improvement opportunities.

The case for a project management improvement initiative can be made more compelling by comparing the organisation's existing project management capabilities against an index. This puts aspirations into context and shows how challenging it may be to achieve the desired level of expertise. A capability maturity model provides simple measures of an organisation's state of development. There are five levels:

- Initial – where a chaotic, unstructured approach is self-evident. Success depends on a combination of chance and the personal energy of those driving change.
- Repeatable – where there is evidence of prior success being repeated.
- Defined – where a systemised approach to project management is evident and documented.
- Managed – where the approach is integrated with wider business management and measurement of performance is possible.
- Optimised – where feedback from practice and innovation is incorporated into the organisation's documented and cultural approach to project management so that it becomes self-improving and self-sustaining.

Table 12.1 overleaf presents a capability maturity model for project management, covering the topics contained in this book.

The analysis can be illustrated. Table 12.2 on page 254 shows an organisation's position on a simple scale of project management maturity. Despite some limited peaks, this organisation's maturity is no more advanced than the lowest measuring item, and is therefore level 1.

There are several models of maturity for project management. Among the more structured is the Project Management Institute's Organisational Project Management Maturity Model (commonly called OPM3). It seeks to provide a way for organisations to understand project management and to measure their maturity against a comprehensive, broad-based set of best practices. It also helps organisations wishing to increase their project management maturity to plan for improvement.

Table 12.1 **Capability maturity model**

	Level 1: Initial	*Level 2: Repeatable*
Project alignment to business imperatives	No alignment of projects to business strategy. There is no clear expression of a portfolio of projects, or a change agenda.	Mandatory and strategic projects are identifiable. Most attract senior sponsorship.
Benefits management	Projects are initiated without any cost/benefit analysis being undertaken. The benefits delivered are never measured.	The scope of mandatory and strategic projects is defined, enabling cost/benefit analysis to be regularly undertaken.
Systemised approach to project management	There is no articulated, systemised approach to project management. Project work is mostly indistinguishable from business as usual.	Only core processes and deliverables are documented and applied to mandatory and strategic projects. Knowledge of a systemised approach is shared among a limited few. Support tools are used sporadically.
Stakeholder management and project organisations	Projects are managed using the business-as-usual structure. The terms "project manager" and "project sponsor" are occasionally used.	In the organisation there are individuals who are known for their ability to manage or sponsor projects. Other stakeholders are identified but rarely engaged. Project steering groups are formed for mandatory or strategic projects.

Level 3: Defined	Level 4: Managed	Level 5: Optimised
A defined portfolio of projects exists for which each has a clear sponsor. Each project's intended contribution to the organisation's advancement is described.	Decisions about which projects to promote and pursue are based on business and project performance metrics.	The planned or actual contribution made by each project to the organisation's strategic advancement is regularly reappraised and used to improve future change agendas.
An approach to benefits management exists. Scope is defined for all projects. A cost/benefit analysis is completed for all projects.	The benefits management approach is applied to all projects. Benefit-related data are gathered throughout the life cycle and used to facilitate stop/start decisions.	The actual benefits delivered by each project are measured and used to determine choices for forthcoming projects. Sponsor rewards are linked to the delivery of benefits.
All processes and deliverables are documented. Some integration with business-as-usual systems and procedures exists. Project data are being gathered centrally. Immature support/assurance function in place. Support tools used consistently.	Processes and deliverables are being applied in common across all projects. Project and business-as-usual systems and procedures fully integrated. Decisions based on reliable information. A mature support/assurance function employs sophisticated tools and techniques.	Projects, and the systemised approach, regularly examined to identify and implement improvements. Recognised project management standards set by accredited bodies could be met.
The project roles are understood. Project practitioners are a recognised group. A portfolio management team manages the portfolio. Project steering groups exist for most projects. An approach to stakeholder identification exists.	The competencies of project managers and members of the project steering group are known, allowing the selection of a tailored project management team to be more precise. The project management team operates to a commonly understood process. Stakeholders are actively managed.	The organisation's change agenda is delivered by tailored project, portfolio and programme structures which accommodate relevant stakeholders.

	Level 1: Initial	Level 2: Repeatable
Quality management (planning, monitoring, reporting and control)	Project success criteria are misunderstood and undefined. Project delivery focuses only on achieving time and/or budgetary targets. Quality control and assurance activities are rare.	Project success criteria are defined for mandatory and strategic projects. Some common project deliverables have been identified and described. Assurance and control activity is applied to key projects and deliverables.
Resource and cost management (planning, monitoring, reporting and control)	Resources and costs are managed through existing business-as-usual channels. Project resource and cost plans do not exist, or can only be constructed under instruction. Budget targets are frequently missed.	Techniques exist for estimating resources and costs. Standard reports are available for key projects. Resource tracking and cost management are applied to mandatory and strategic projects.
Time management (planning, monitoring, reporting and control)	Project time schedules do not exist, or can only be constructed under instruction. Delivery dates are frequently missed.	Techniques exist for estimating timescales. Standard reports are available for projects. Time management techniques applied to mandatory and strategic projects.
Risk management	There is no approach to risk management. Projects are regularly surprised by unforeseen events. The organisation invests in troubleshooters to fix problems.	Some organisational risk management is applied to select priority projects. An approach to risk management is used for mandatory and strategic projects.

Level 3: Defined	Level 4: Managed	Level 5: Optimised
An approach to quality management is well documented. Most projects are subjected to some form of independent quality assurance. Most deliverables are subjected to quality definition and control.	All projects apply the quality management approach, allowing quality expectations to be specified, planned, built, tested and accepted. Evidence exists of all completed deliverables. The support/assurance function provides support and assurance services. Libraries of common project deliverables exist.	Project and deliverable success/quality criteria are regularly reappraised in light of changes. Projects regularly commission quality assurance activities (eg, health checks). Recognised quality standards set by accredited bodies could be met.
Resource selection and cost estimation approach is applied by most projects. Reporting is standardised. Demand and supply management is understood as a concept and practised to some degree.	Resource control and cost management is integrated with organisation's other systems and procedures. Management information is available in a variety of tailored formats. Demand and supply management works effectively.	Lessons are learned from underestimates and overestimates. Demand forecasts are regularly used to facilitate resource movement across the organisation. Management information is used extensively to facilitate control.
Timescale estimation approach is applied by most projects. Reporting is standardised. Links between time, cost and quality are understood but not fully managed.	Timescale management is integrated with organisation's other systems and procedures. Management information is available in a variety of tailored formats. Time, cost and quality are managed through an integrated plan.	Lessons are learned from underestimates and overestimates. Management information is used extensively to facilitate control. Time, cost and quality expectations are commonly traded to meet strategic or commercial targets.
A risk management approach exists and is applied to most projects. Metrics are used to identify contingency amounts. Risk mitigation is allocated to those with suitable authority.	Project, portfolio and programme risk management is aligned to organisation-wide risk management. An approach to contingency management is commonly applied.	Well-articulated contingency amounts are a common feature of project, portfolio and programme plans, and are traceable to identified risk mitigation activities. Lessons are learned from exposure to risk so that future change initiatives accommodate suitable mitigations.

	Level 1: Initial	Level 2: Repeatable
Change management	Little or no management of project scope takes place, resulting in fluctuating expectations of time, cost, quality and benefits.	Baselines for time, cost, quality and benefits are set for mandatory and strategic projects. Some change control is applied to such projects.
People management	Project management expertise largely unrecognised. High turnover of project-related staff. Project expertise remains undeveloped.	Key staff engaged in multiple projects. Exposure to more complex or risky projects is the only development route.

Although many potential sponsors may be persuaded by the prospect of a comparison with an industry norm, many will wish to judge their

Table 12.2 **Project management maturity**

	Level 1: Initial	Level 2: Repeatable	Level 3: Defined	Level 4: Managed	Level 5: Optimised
Business alignment					
Benefits management					
Systematised approach					
Stakeholder management					
Quality management					
Resource and cost management					
Time management					
Risk management					
Change management					
People management					

Level 3: Defined	Level 4: Managed	Level 5: Optimised
A change control process exists and is applied to most projects. Metrics are used to manage the demand on contingency budgets.	Project change control is aligned to portfolio change management. Approved authorities are in place at all levels of the organisation to agree or decline changes, subject to clearly stated escalation conditions.	The organisation plans its contingency budgets based on the amounts required by previous projects.
Multiple development paths defined to facilitate project management career progression. The support/ assurance function facilitates recruitment of project practitioners.	Individual performance aligned to career development. Demand and supply management of specific skill types is widely practised.	The performance of project practitioners is measured and managed, ensuring that the organisation develops the competencies it needs. Project management career path integrated with industry standards. Tailored recruitment campaigns facilitated by active skills management.

organisation's improvements against its own past performance. This helps them see progress in project management being measured in more relevant, and possibly commercial, terms.

The questionnaire in Table 12.3 overleaf helps to identify and consolidate the perceptions of different groups of people. It allows them to show how far they disagree or agree with each statement. The results of this survey paint a picture of the concerns of different levels of management at a point in time, providing an indication of where the organisation's priorities lie and a further mandate for change. Further surveys can be conducted during the life of the project management improvement initiative to determine how far improvements are being realised.

Depending on who is invited to take part, the analysis may identify some clear but probably contradictory priorities. For instance, potential sponsors may strongly agree that "projects routinely miss time, cost and quality targets". Project managers may strongly agree that "expectations fluctuate so much that we are rarely able to state the scope of our projects with any certainty". The solution lies in a carefully planned and unified approach to making improvements.

Table 12.3 **Questionnaire**

No.	Current state	Disagree		Agree

Project alignment

PA1	Our company strategy does not exist in documented form	☐☐☐☐☐☐☐☐☐ 123456789
PA2	Our company strategy contains contradictions and/or gaps	☐☐☐☐☐☐☐☐☐ 123456789
PA3	Most projects proceed, regardless of their relative contribution to our strategic objectives	☐☐☐☐☐☐☐☐☐ 123456789
PA4	The priority of business or change opportunities depends on the seniority of the sponsor	☐☐☐☐☐☐☐☐☐ 123456789
PA5	We do not have a commonly understood expression of our projects' contribution to our company strategy	☐☐☐☐☐☐☐☐☐ 123456789
PA6	We do not use our company strategy to validate our selection of projects	☐☐☐☐☐☐☐☐☐ 123456789

Benefits management

BM1	All projects proceed, whether or not there is an articulated justification	☐☐☐☐☐☐☐☐☐ 123456789
BM2	Project success is measured only in terms of meeting time, cost and quality expectations	☐☐☐☐☐☐☐☐☐ 123456789
BM3	At the end of a project, we cannot quantify what benefits were delivered	☐☐☐☐☐☐☐☐☐ 123456789
BM4	We have never established whether a project delivered us the desired outcome	☐☐☐☐☐☐☐☐☐ 123456789
BM5	Once a project has begun, we do not revisit its justification	☐☐☐☐☐☐☐☐☐ 123456789
BM6	We have lacked the information and/or authority to stop projects when necessary	☐☐☐☐☐☐☐☐☐ 123456789
BM7	We reward revenue generation	☐☐☐☐☐☐☐☐☐ 123456789
BM8	We do not offer rewards to those involved in delivering successful projects	☐☐☐☐☐☐☐☐☐ 123456789

No.	Current state	Disagree	Agree

Systemised approach

SA1 Project work is largely indistinguishable from business as usual activity, and is delivered by people who work mostly in the business as usual environment

☐☐☐☐☐☐☐☐☐
1 2 3 4 5 6 7 8 9

SA2 We have limited or no access to an impartial assurance service

☐☐☐☐☐☐☐☐☐
1 2 3 4 5 6 7 8 9

SA3 We are failing to either gather or apply lessons that we should have learned from previous projects

☐☐☐☐☐☐☐☐☐
1 2 3 4 5 6 7 8 9

SA4 We invest in project management tools that deliver little value

☐☐☐☐☐☐☐☐☐
1 2 3 4 5 6 7 8 9

Project organisations

PO1 There are multiple, independent sponsors who provide direction to single projects

☐☐☐☐☐☐☐☐☐
1 2 3 4 5 6 7 8 9

PO2 When changes are made to our business's organisation structure, it affects the organisation of our projects

☐☐☐☐☐☐☐☐☐
1 2 3 4 5 6 7 8 9

PO3 The organisation's ability to implement change depends on the complex co-ordination of multiple departments, many of which cannot or will not work with each other

☐☐☐☐☐☐☐☐☐
1 2 3 4 5 6 7 8 9

PO4 Participants often move in and out of management positions within individual projects

☐☐☐☐☐☐☐☐☐
1 2 3 4 5 6 7 8 9

PO5 When those involved in a project are unable to make a decision, they turn to the line management structure

☐☐☐☐☐☐☐☐☐
1 2 3 4 5 6 7 8 9

PO6 Responsibility for delivering project success lies with the project manager

☐☐☐☐☐☐☐☐☐
1 2 3 4 5 6 7 8 9

PO7 We expect the project manager to make every decision necessary to deliver the project successfully

☐☐☐☐☐☐☐☐☐
1 2 3 4 5 6 7 8 9

PO8 The clients of our projects have little or no authority in the way in which the project is managed

☐☐☐☐☐☐☐☐☐
1 2 3 4 5 6 7 8 9

PO9 The suppliers engaged in our projects have little or no authority in the way in which a project is managed

☐☐☐☐☐☐☐☐☐
1 2 3 4 5 6 7 8 9

PO10 People are unclear about their respective responsibilities and boundaries of authority

☐☐☐☐☐☐☐☐☐
1 2 3 4 5 6 7 8 9

No.	Current state	Disagree	Agree

Planning and control

PC1	Project success criteria are rarely stated	□□□□□□□□□
		1 2 3 4 5 6 7 8 9

PC2	Project plans consist mainly of a timeline or bar chart	□□□□□□□□□
		1 2 3 4 5 6 7 8 9

PC3	There is no detailed, clearly articulated list of the specific deliverables that each project will deliver	□□□□□□□□□
		1 2 3 4 5 6 7 8 9

PC4	While our projects have phases and stages, we rarely halt the project in order to consider its continued viability	□□□□□□□□□
		1 2 3 4 5 6 7 8 9

PC5	We have frequent senior management project meetings	□□□□□□□□□
		1 2 3 4 5 6 7 8 9

PC6	We have little confidence in project time and cost estimates	□□□□□□□□□
		1 2 3 4 5 6 7 8 9

PC7	Key resources become unavailable at short notice	□□□□□□□□□
		1 2 3 4 5 6 7 8 9

PC8	Time, cost and quality expectations are frequently at odds	□□□□□□□□□
		1 2 3 4 5 6 7 8 9

PC9	Projects are funded month by month	□□□□□□□□□
		1 2 3 4 5 6 7 8 9

PC10	Project plans are updated irregularly if at all	□□□□□□□□□
		1 2 3 4 5 6 7 8 9

PC11	Although we could probably find out how much a project has cost to date, it would be a major exercise for someone to do so	□□□□□□□□□
		1 2 3 4 5 6 7 8 9

PC12	We are skilled in monitoring spend to date, but rarely do we re-evaluate our earlier estimates	□□□□□□□□□
		1 2 3 4 5 6 7 8 9

PC13	We report all variances of any amount to senior managers	□□□□□□□□□
		1 2 3 4 5 6 7 8 9

PC14	By the time a problem is identified, it is too late for any corrective action to have any effect	□□□□□□□□□
		1 2 3 4 5 6 7 8 9

PC15	At best, we have an informal peer review system in place, but mostly, we don't put any of our project deliverables through a review process	□□□□□□□□□
		1 2 3 4 5 6 7 8 9

No.	Current state	Disagree	Agree

Risk management

RM1	We pride ourselves on our ability to manage issues and problems	□□□□□□□□□ 1 2 3 4 5 6 7 8 9
RM2	We alert our senior managers to most risks or issues that we have identified	□□□□□□□□□ 1 2 3 4 5 6 7 8 9
RM3	Risks or issues are rarely discussed outside the project environment	□□□□□□□□□ 1 2 3 4 5 6 7 8 9

Change management

CM1	Projects routinely miss time, cost and quality targets	□□□□□□□□□ 1 2 3 4 5 6 7 8 9
CM2	Expectations fluctuate so much that we are rarely able to state the scope of our projects with any certainty	□□□□□□□□□ 1 2 3 4 5 6 7 8 9
CM3	The impact of changes is difficult to determine resulting in our being led into an acceptance of them all	□□□□□□□□□ 1 2 3 4 5 6 7 8 9
CM4	A change is implemented if the person who requested it is persuasive enough	□□□□□□□□□ 1 2 3 4 5 6 7 8 9
CM5	The project manager has to decide whether or not a change is accepted	□□□□□□□□□ 1 2 3 4 5 6 7 8 9

People management

PM1	It is important for us to resource our project management teams with people who understand the technical nature of the project	□□□□□□□□□ 1 2 3 4 5 6 7 8 9
PM2	We have a high turnover of project-related personnel	□□□□□□□□□ 1 2 3 4 5 6 7 8 9
PM3	We have one or two key project practitioners who are in constant demand	□□□□□□□□□ 1 2 3 4 5 6 7 8 9
PM4	The career path for any project practitioner is to engage in more, or more complex, projects	□□□□□□□□□ 1 2 3 4 5 6 7 8 9
PM5	We have little idea how to obtain the necessary project competencies we will need in the coming years	□□□□□□□□□ 1 2 3 4 5 6 7 8 9

Table 12.4 overleaf is an extension to Table 12.3. It assumes that the "consolidated responses" have been gathered, giving some guidance about priorities. Adding some corresponding "future states" allows the overview to be expressed more elaborately.

Table 12.4

No.	Current state	Consolidated responses Disagree Agree	Future state
Project alignment			
PA1	Our company strategy does not exist in documented form	□□□□□□□■□ 1 2 3 4 5 6 7 8 9	Our company strategy exists in documented form
PA2	Our company strategy contains contradictions and/or gaps	□□□□□□□■□ 1 2 3 4 5 6 7 8 9	Our company strategy is internally consistent
PA3	Most projects proceed, regardless of their relative contribution to our strategic objectives	□□□□□□□□■ 1 2 3 4 5 6 7 8 9	All new and existing initiatives are regularly prioritised against strategic objectives
PA4	The priority of business or change opportunities depends on the seniority of the sponsor	□□□□□□□□■ 1 2 3 4 5 6 7 8 9	Successful project prioritisation comes as a result of each initiative's alignment to commercial or strategic objectives
PA5	We do not have a commonly understood expression of our projects' contribution to our company strategy	□□□□□□□□■ 1 2 3 4 5 6 7 8 9	Projects are derived from and measured against our company strategy
PA6	We do not use our company strategy to validate our selection of projects	□□□□□□□□■ 1 2 3 4 5 6 7 8 9	We measure the extent to which each project contributes to our strategy
Benefits management			
BM1	All projects proceed, whether or not there is an articulated justification	□□□□□□■□□ 1 2 3 4 5 6 7 8 9	Only projects justified by a business case are sponsored
BM2	Project success is measured only in terms of meeting time, cost and quality expectations	□□□□□□□■□ 1 2 3 4 5 6 7 8 9	Project success is measured in terms of the benefits delivered to our clients and to ourselves

No.	Current state	Consolidated responses Disagree Agree	Future state
BM3	At the end of a project, we cannot quantify what benefits were delivered	□□□□□□□■□ 1 2 3 4 5 6 7 8 9	Retrospectively we can calculate project profitability
BM4	We have never established whether a project delivered us the desired outcome	□□□□□□□■□ 1 2 3 4 5 6 7 8 9	We evaluate completed projects to determine the benefits they delivered to us commercially, and to our strategic vision
BM5	Once a project has begun, we do not revisit its justification	□□□□□□□□■ 1 2 3 4 5 6 7 8 9	The project's justification is revisited and revalidated throughout the project's lifetime
BM6	We have lacked the information and/ or authority to stop projects when necessary	□□□□□□■□□ 1 2 3 4 5 6 7 8 9	We would be prepared and able to stop a project if it looked as though it could fail us
BM7	We reward revenue generation	□□□□□□□■ 1 2 3 4 5 6 7 8 9	We reward profit margin delivery
BM8	We do not offer rewards to those involved in delivering successful projects	□□□□□□□□■ 1 2 3 4 5 6 7 8 9	We reward those involved in the project to deliver a defined, articulated commercial or strategic benefit

Systemised approach

No.	Current state	Consolidated responses	Future state
SA1	Project work is largely indistinguishable from business-as-usual activity, and is delivered by people who work mostly in the business-as-usual environment	□□□□□■□□□ 1 2 3 4 5 6 7 8 9	Projects are conducted according to a clear and commonly understood approach

No.	Current state	Consolidated responses Disagree Agree	Future state
SA2	We have limited or no access to an impartial assurance service	☐☐☐☐☐☐☐■☐ 1 2 3 4 5 6 7 8 9	We have access to a range of independent, impartial sources of assurance to mitigate project risk and confirm the effectiveness of our management
SA3	We are failing to either gather or apply lessons that we should have learned from previous projects	☐☐☐☐☐■☐☐☐ 1 2 3 4 5 6 7 8 9	We have a means by which improvements can be both captured and applied
SA4	We invest in project management tools that deliver little value	☐☐■☐☐☐☐☐☐ 1 2 3 4 5 6 7 8 9	The organisation benefits from a range of integrated tools that support the management of projects

Stakeholder management and project organisations

No.	Current state	Consolidated responses	Future state
PO1	There are multiple, independent sponsors who provide direction to single projects	☐☐☐☐☐■☐☐☐ 1 2 3 4 5 6 7 8 9	The portfolio is managed by a single, unified body which empowers tailored groups to own and direct individual projects
PO2	When changes are made to our business's organisation structure, it affects the organisation of our projects	☐☐☐☐☐☐■☐☐ 1 2 3 4 5 6 7 8 9	Delivery of our operational imperatives is independent of our organisational structure
PO3	The organisation's ability to implement change depends on the complex co-ordination of multiple departments, many of which cannot or will not work with each other	☐☐☐☐☐☐☐☐■ 1 2 3 4 5 6 7 8 9	Projects are managed and delivered by a tailored group of people, independent of the line structure, who accommodate the demands of all parties

No.	Current state	Consolidated responses Disagree ⟶ Agree	Future state
PO4	Participants often move in and out of management positions within individual projects	□□□□□□□■□ 1 2 3 4 5 6 7 8 9	There are distinct, tailored groups of people who deliver individual projects
PO5	When those involved in a project are unable to make a decision, they turn to the line management structure	□□□□■□□□□ 1 2 3 4 5 6 7 8 9	Our project organisations contain the authority within themselves to make the decisions necessary to the project's continued progress
PO6	Responsibility for delivering project success lies with the project manager	□□□□■□□□□ 1 2 3 4 5 6 7 8 9	Authority and responsibility for delivering project success lies with the project steering group
PO7	We expect the project manager to make every decision necessary to deliver the project successfully	□□□□□□■□□ 1 2 3 4 5 6 7 8 9	We make a clear separation between project "ownership" and its "daily management"
PO8	The clients of our projects have little or no authority in the way in which the project is managed	□□□□□□□■□ 1 2 3 4 5 6 7 8 9	The clients of our projects form part of the management team of the project
PO9	The suppliers engaged in our projects have little or no authority in the way in which a project is managed	□□□□□■□□□ 1 2 3 4 5 6 7 8 9	The key suppliers of major components of our projects form part of the management team of the project
PO10	People are unclear about their respective responsibilities and boundaries of authority	□□□□□□■□□ 1 2 3 4 5 6 7 8 9	All individuals to whom project roles have been assigned have been acquainted with their responsibilities and are comfortable with them

No.	Current state	Consolidated responses Disagree Agree	Future state
Planning and control			
PC1	Project success criteria are rarely stated	□□□■□□□□□ 1 2 3 4 5 6 7 8 9	Project success criteria are listed and prioritised by those who will take receipt of the project's deliverables
PC2	Project plans consist mainly of a timeline or bar chart	□□□□□□□■□ 1 2 3 4 5 6 7 8 9	All plans detail time, cost and quality components
PC3	There is no detailed, clearly articulated list of the specific deliverables that each project will deliver	□□■□□□□□□ 1 2 3 4 5 6 7 8 9	Our plans clearly identify deliverables, not just activities
PC4	While our projects have phases and stages, we rarely halt the project in order to consider its continued viability	□□□□□□□■□ 1 2 3 4 5 6 7 8 9	We divide projects into non-overlapping stages
PC5	We have frequent senior management project meetings	□□□□□□□□■ 1 2 3 4 5 6 7 8 9	Senior management project meetings are pre-planned, event-driven sessions at which key decisions are made
PC6	We have little confidence in project time and cost estimates	□□□□□□□□■ 1 2 3 4 5 6 7 8 9	Time and cost estimates are demonstrably based on clearly described deliverables
PC7	Key resources become unavailable at short notice	□□□□□□□□■ 1 2 3 4 5 6 7 8 9	Demand forecasts are regularly used to facilitate resource movement across the organisation
PC8	Time, cost and quality expectations are frequently at odds	□□□□□□□□■ 1 2 3 4 5 6 7 8 9	Time, cost and quality expectations are commonly traded to meet strategic or commercial targets

No.	Current state	Consolidated responses Disagree — Agree	Future state
PC9	Projects are funded month by month	□□□□□□■□□ 1 2 3 4 5 6 7 8 9	Funds are identified and set aside when each project is approved
PC10	Project plans are updated irregularly if at all	□□□□■□□□□ 1 2 3 4 5 6 7 8 9	All projects have an up-to-date plan
PC11	Although we could probably find out how much a project has cost to date, it would be a major exercise for someone to do so	□□□□□□□■□ 1 2 3 4 5 6 7 8 9	We know how much any project has cost us to date
PC12	We are skilled in monitoring spend to date, but rarely do we re-evaluate our earlier estimates	□□□□□□■□□ 1 2 3 4 5 6 7 8 9	We regularly re-estimate and report forecast costs
PC13	We report all variances of any amount to senior managers	□□□□□□□□■ 1 2 3 4 5 6 7 8 9	We manage significant variations through escalation conditions so that senior manager deal only with matters for which others are unauthorised or unqualified
PC14	By the time a problem is identified, it is too late for any corrective action to have any effect	□□□□□□□□■ 1 2 3 4 5 6 7 8 9	Project progress reports and meetings are timed to allow sufficient opportunity to anticipate and fix problems
PC15	At best, we have an informal peer review system in place, but mostly, we don't put any of our project deliverables through a review process	□□□□■□□□□ 1 2 3 4 5 6 7 8 9	We review and approve deliverables according to their defined success criteria

Risk management

No.	Current state	Consolidated responses	Future state
RM1	We pride ourselves on our ability to manage issues and problems	□□□□□□□□■ 1 2 3 4 5 6 7 8 9	We pride ourselves on our ability to prevent issues and problems through effective risk management

No.	Current state	Consolidated responses Disagree Agree	Future state
RM2	We alert our senior managers to most risks or issues that we have identified	☐☐☐☐☐☐☐☐■ 1 2 3 4 5 6 7 8 9	We alert senior managers only to those risks or issues for which their attention is deserved
RM3	Risks or issues are rarely discussed outside the project environment	☐☐☐☐☐☐☐☐■ 1 2 3 4 5 6 7 8 9	There is an escalation route for risks and issues that may affect the wider organisation

Change management

No.	Current state	Consolidated responses Disagree Agree	Future state
CM1	Projects routinely miss time, cost and quality targets	☐☐☐☐☐☐☐☐■ 1 2 3 4 5 6 7 8 9	Expectations and estimates are regularly reappraised and approved to allow appropriate contingencies to be identified to mitigate risks and accommodate change
CM2	Expectations fluctuate so much that we are rarely able to state the scope of our projects with any certainty	☐☐☐☐☐☐☐☐■ 1 2 3 4 5 6 7 8 9	Every project has a set of baselined statements of time, cost, quality and benefits expectations
CM3	The impact of changes is difficult to determine resulting in our being led into an acceptance of them all	☐☐☐☐☐☐■☐☐ 1 2 3 4 5 6 7 8 9	All proposed changes are subject to consideration via an acknowledged process
CM4	A change is implemented if the person who requested it is persuasive enough	☐☐☐☐☐☐☐■☐ 1 2 3 4 5 6 7 8 9	Changes are assessed by a balanced combination of people before a recommendation is made

No.	Current state	Consolidated responses Disagree · · · · · Agree	Future state
CM5	The project manager has to decide whether or not a change is accepted	□□□□□■□□□ 1 2 3 4 5 6 7 8 9	Approval to accommodate a change is granted only by authorised members of the management team

People management

No.	Current state	Consolidated responses	Future state
PM1	It is important for us to resource our project management teams with people who understand the technical nature of the project	□□□□□■□□□ 1 2 3 4 5 6 7 8 9	We have a balance of users, technicians and commercial skills in our project management teams
PM2	We have a high turnover of project-related personnel	□□□□□□□■□ 1 2 3 4 5 6 7 8 9	Our project practitioners develop through continued participation in, and contribution to, our portfolio of projects
PM3	We have one or two key project practitioners who are in constant demand	□□□□□□□■□ 1 2 3 4 5 6 7 8 9	We have access to a community of experienced project practitioners
PM4	The career path for any project practitioner is to engage in more, or more complex, projects	□□□□■□□□□ 1 2 3 4 5 6 7 8 9	There is a clearly defined development path for all project practitioners
PM5	We have little idea how to obtain the necessary project competencies we will need in the coming years	□□□□□□□■□ 1 2 3 4 5 6 7 8 9	We have recruitment campaigns that satisfy our considered project competency demands

Given the direction provided by these statements, the vision need not be complex. It may be enough to express it like this:

- The "future state" cultural change will be achieved by dd/mm/yy through the implementation of self-sustaining measures.

Obtaining a mandate for change

Expressing clearly the opportunities for change is not enough. A sponsor, or sponsors, will be needed to drive, fund and direct the project management improvement initiative. The more senior they are in the organisation, the better. This is not to say, however, that anyone is suitable. Nor is it enough that there is a groundswell of enthusiasm for change. Without sponsorship, the initiative will either fail to start successfully or falter soon after. If the project management improvement initiative is to be managed according to the principles of effective project management, they must be applied in selecting a suitable project steering group to own and direct it.

The sponsor should be a recognised promoter of change, ideally someone who has previously sponsored significant change initiatives for the organisation. He should not be involved exclusively in business as usual, no matter how competent he is in managing business operations. He should be senior enough to command the respect of his peers since the role will involve selling and promoting concepts that may be alien or unpalatable to others. Significantly, he should have access to funds and be prepared to commit them over what may be a long period. Ideally, the sponsor will be the person who identified the need for change and who has driven the project management improvement initiative this far.

The developer representative must be an expert in managing projects and understand intimately the "systemised approach", as he must assure the organisation that it will be a robust and reliable solution to its challenges. Sometimes a project management consultant will be hired for this role. It is possible that a second person may be required in an organisation that already has a significant number or complexity of existing systems and processes into which the project management approach is to be accommodated. This person might come from the finance department because of its central role in so many management processes.

The customer representative must make sure that the delivered solution meets the needs of the organisation. It is sensible to choose two people who represent communities that will be affected differently by the project's outcome – the sponsors and the project managers. Consequently, one candidate could be a highly regarded project manager and the other could come from the pool of project sponsors, possibly allowing the sponsor to adopt this as an additional role. Whatever the solution, if it is to work and last, it must satisfy these two people.

Much will depend on selecting an appropriate project manager, not just to make sure that the project management improvement initiative is well planned, monitored and controlled, but also that it is a beacon for best practice. If the initiative is poorly managed, there will be little chance of the benefits it seeks to promote becoming entrenched elsewhere. If the organisation does not have a candidate with the necessary qualifications, the person could be recruited from a project management consultancy. The commitment to a suitable individual should not be underestimated; a project management improvement initiative for a medium-sized organisation may take two years or more to complete.

With a powerful, guiding coalition in place (if only informally at this stage), and an identified project manager waiting to be instructed, the fledgling project management improvement initiative is ready to use the evidence it has gathered to justify its case for change.

Justifying the investment

Most organisations should look for commercial benefits from a project management improvement initiative. Too often, the change is instigated by junior managers who argue that a consistent approach to project management will inherently deliver rewards, but that argument does not adequately support what might be a considerable investment. Working in a common way will, at best, help to avoid repeating work, but that will not persuade the senior management team to adopt the initiative. Instead, having sold the concept to the wider senior management team, those promoting the project management improvement initiative should build a substantial business case to show the range of benefits it can generate.

Typically, these benefits fall into three categories which together make a more persuasive case for the investment. Table 12.5 lists some examples and how they could be quantified.

Table 12.5 **Benefits of a project management improvement initiative**

Item	Planning assumption	Value
Increased revenue and margin		
Business opportunities will be increased through existing clients' exposure to the organisation's project management excellence.	Clients buy more products and services from our organisation rather than building them in-house.	n additional projects per year of, say, nn days' effort, which returns a revenue of $nn per year.

Item	Planning assumption	Value
Clients recognise the value that the organisation's approach to project management creates.	Existing clients (who are not currently paying for project management) pay for project management.	n projects per year of, say, nn days' elapsed duration where a project manager is allocated full time. Value $nn per year.
Clients recognise that all the organisation's project managers can successfully deliver projects because the approach to project management (supported by training and career development) will ensure better availability of project management practitioners with management skills.	The organisation's sales opportunities are not limited by the availability of project managers.	n additional projects are delivered during the year, the profit from which would be, say, $nn.
The organisation's project management expertise is recognised and so it is used in preference to third-party contractors.	Clients use the organisation's project management.	Revenue for one project manager for one project (full-time for nn days at $nn per day). Value $nn.
Developing a business case for each project will result in improved prioritisation of projects.	All projects will be prioritised according to their value to the business and some projects will be rejected.	One project per year is selected over another on the basis of its greater margin, increasing profit by, say, $nn.
Senior managers will be more able to direct the progress of the organisation towards its strategic goals via the management of a portfolio of business cases.	All business cases are linked to the organisation's strategic aims.	Strategic success increases the organisation's profitability by nn%, say $nn per year.

Reduction in costs

As a result of effective planning and reporting, clients recognise their own responsibilities where slippage occurs.	Clients pay the full value of invoices charged to their project.	The discount given to clients via credits in the past year due to disputes was $nn, and the chargeable time not billed was $nn. A nn% improvement would represent $nn annual saving.

Item	Planning assumption	Value
Definition of products and quality criteria will reduce rework.	More products are delivered to specification, resulting in less rework.	nn% reduction in the cost of rework, and so a saving of, say, $nn per year based on nn person days per month.
Senior managers and project managers will become more efficient at executing projects.	Reduction in the cost of executing project.	A nn% percent reduction in the cost of all projects, say $nn.
Project managers become more focused on project matters and less distracted by line management pressures.	Project managers spend less time resolving line management issues.	n project managers each save nn days per month. This time could be charged elsewhere, giving revenue of $nn.
Mitigation of risk		
With better planning and risk management, the organisation can competitively bid for fixed-price contracts with a reduced risk of financial loss on the contract.	Fixed-price projects are completed with less variance from cost budget.	Assume $nn of fixed-price work during the previous financial year, including a variance of nn%. The project management improvement initiative reduces variance from nn% to nn%, creating an annual saving of $nn.
Better risk management will reduce the cost to the organisation of the management of issues.	Risks are mitigated before becoming issues.	A nn% reduction in the cost of all projects, say $nn.
The effort to identify and manage risks is reduced by learning from previous projects.	An established risks register is available to all project managers.	Saving of nn days per month for nn project managers. This time is charged elsewhere at $nn per day giving revenue of $nn

The list in Table 12.5 is not exhaustive, and although it suggests how the benefits of a project management improvement initiative can be demonstrated, it is highly likely that the figures quoted will be disputed in the same way that forecasts usually are. After discussion, the proposed revenue increases, cost savings and mitigation of risks may well be lower, but ideally they should outweigh the proposed costs of the initiative, which may be substantial. In any case, if the organisation is not open to using a disciplined project management approach, a business case is unlikely to persuade it otherwise. In that case, it may be necessary to wait until events (such as a failure to deliver a project) force the issue.

Delivering the change

Figure 12.1 was used in Chapter 1 to show the components of effective project management.

Every organisation is different, but the order in which these components become understood and entrenched often begins with project sponsors and owners and moves clockwise, ending with the most mature organisations conducting benefit reviews. With this outline sequence in mind, a plan can emerge. The project manager must consider that to reach the desired future state, these components must be selected, put in sequence and delivered. Figure 12.2 suggests how the components can be addressed in phases, forming a progressively firmer foundation for future enhancements of the approach to project management.

Phase 1 stresses the importance of putting the foundations in place. This includes generating enthusiasm and competence among senior managers so that they commission and lead projects which will deliver their strategic imperatives. They will need a method to work by (the system-

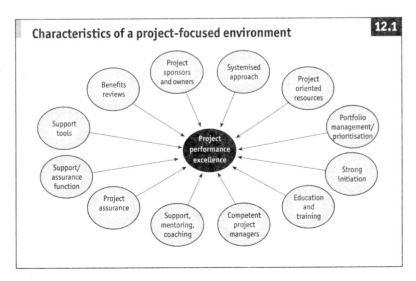

Characteristics of a project-focused environment 12.1

The project's components divided into phases `12.2`

CURRENT STATE ⟶ FUTURE STATE

PHASE 1
- Project sponsors and owners
  Focused, motivated and informed leaders to justify and direct change initiatives
- Systemised approach
  To articulate the method by which projects are to be managed
- Project oriented resources
  To understand and drive change initiatives
- Portfolio management/prioritisation
  To prioritise and align projects to the organisation's strategic imperatives
- Strong initiation
  To provide a means of articulating the project's viability throughout its lifetime
  To identify and form clearly defined project management environments
- Education and training
  To obtain a common understanding and competence among all participants

PHASE 2
- Competent project managers
  To plan, monitor and control projects to a successful conclusion
- Support, mentoring, coaching
  To provide all project participants with the support they require as they engage in project work
- Project assurance
  To identify opportunities to address the health of the organisation's approach to project management

PHASE 3
- Support/assurance function
  To support the organisation's efforts to develop and deliver an effective approach to project management
- Support tools
  To automate some processes and to enhance the provision of management information

PHASE 4
- Benefits reviews
  To determine how successful a completed project has been in meeting its intended success criteria

ised approach) and a core of educated, trained participants. However, the organisation-wide training and education programme that is often commissioned at huge expense at the beginning of a project management improvement initiative is not yet necessary. Education should be provided for sponsors and other senior stakeholders as a priority so that they can persuade others to adopt the approach. Training project managers too early wastes both a precious opportunity and resources. Trainees will return from their courses, enthusiastic and capable, only to be thrust into an environment not yet ready for them. Consequently, the position of training and education in the sequence should be considered, using these criteria:

- **Can potential trainees be prioritised according to their**

seniority? A first round of senior management briefings will be essential if the drive for change is to come from the top of the organisation. The use of the word "briefing" as opposed to "training" is important as it takes account of the sensitivities of executives who may believe that, for them, training is unnecessary. Trainees should be selected from a carefully considered, prioritised range of participants.

▪ **Can potential trainees be prioritised by the importance of the projects in which they are engaged?** Some projects may benefit if their participants are trained in project management, but others may be at such a critical point that the introduction of a new approach to project management may do more harm than good. Trainees should be selected from a prioritised range of projects.

▪ **Can potential trainees be prioritised according to their development needs?** There will be some for whom an introduction to project management will be an invaluable boost to their confidence and competence. For others, the training will be frustrating and exacerbate existing issues. Involving people of all backgrounds and expertise in projects does not mean that they must all be trained in the principles and techniques of project management. It is better to focus on those for whom the management of projects is an essential skill. In the early stages at least, this may rule out the need to train and educate those who are not involved in the project's management. Trainees should be selected according to their development needs.

A training needs analysis is an important product of the first phase since it allows these points to be accommodated in a thoughtful and planned approach to education. Training is also a way of describing the systemised approach to project management so that a new, commonly understood language can be introduced into the organisation. The training needs analysis becomes both a means of describing how the educational needs of the organisation will be satisfied and the basis of a plan for communication. It can be shown in a simple matrix (Figure 12.3).

Groups of participants are shown on the vertical axis and the proposed training events are listed on the horizontal axis. The ticks indicate the events thought appropriate for each audience. The events seek to satisfy markedly different objectives:

Training needs analysis | 12.3

	Sponsors' project management briefing	Practitioner's project management	Condensed project management overview	Operational project management techniques
Portfolio management team	✓			
Project steering groups	✓			
Project managers		✓		
Project team leaders		✓		
Project team members			✓	
Operational managers			✓	
Operational team members				✓

- ◪ Sponsors' project management briefing – to familiarise project sponsors with their obligations so they can communicate clearly with each other and consistently direct the organisation's pool of project managers.
- ◪ Practitioners' project management – to provide practitioners with the skills and knowledge to practise the principles and techniques of project management in the organisation.
- ◪ Condensed project management overview – to provide non-participants with sufficient knowledge to understand the principles of project management and the organisation's approach to its application.
- ◪ Operational project management techniques – to provide non-participants with sufficient skills to practise the techniques of project management in operational areas of the organisation.

These four events allow all potential delegates from project and operational backgrounds to obtain sufficient knowledge and/or skills to participate constructively in a project-focused environment.

Phase 1 must deliver some successful projects. Without some early wins to promote the approach, few will see the benefit of the investment. It follows that in selecting projects to which the approach is to be applied, timing must considered carefully. This will make sure there are milestones throughout the project management improvement initiative that show the value it is delivering.

Phase 2 is characterised by a need to embed the approach and support those engaged in project management. A sensible tactic is to support both the projects and the people who are being subjected to the new approach. This helps to make sure that the organisation develops healthy projects and healthy project participants. Healthy projects are encouraged by using health checks and other assurance measures; healthy participants are encouraged to develop and flourish through support and guidance from the wider project management community.

Phase 3 sees more infrastructure included to support the organisation. Since the introduction of a support/assurance function and some supporting technology will require significant outlay and cause disruption, it is important that the investment so far has delivered measurable rewards.

As project benefits reviews begin, phase 4 not only marks the end of the project management improvement initiative, but also suggests that a significant level of maturity has been reached. Desirable as it may be to conduct benefits reviews in phase 1, it is unlikely that the essential principles underpinning the approach to project management will be understood sufficiently and widely enough to allow that to happen. Only because an investment to develop, build and embed an approach to project management has been made in the three previous phases is it culturally acceptable, and possible, to measure realised benefits.

Enjoying the benefits

Introducing a new approach or method to an organisation is, above all, a change to its management culture. In his book *Leading Change*, John Kotter wrote:

> *In the final analysis, change sticks when it becomes "the way we do things around here", when it seeps into the bloodstream of the corporate body. Until new behaviours are rooted in social norms and shared values, they are subject to degradation as soon as the pressure for change is removed.*

The pressure to optimise competence in project management must be not only continuous and unrelenting but also entire across all parties. It takes an organisation to deliver a project; no single individual or group can do it alone. Those who seek to promote and embed the benefits of effective project management must be committed to what may be a lengthy and challenging process.

However, the benefits of effective project management are there to be enjoyed. They offer clear commercial and competitive advantages. They can help to reduce operating costs, but more compelling still, they answer the question that should keep any risk-aware executive awake at night: "What might be the consequence of my failure to effectively manage my organisation's projects?"

Glossary

Cross-references are in SMALL CAPS.

Action form A pro forma used by a SCRIBE on which are written the decisions taken and the necessary actions identified during a QUALITY REVIEW.

Activity network A technique used to determine a PROJECT'S DURATION and CRITICAL PATH from the activities (or DELIVERABLES) and their dependencies.

Actual cost of work performed (ACWP) In EARNED VALUE ANALYSIS, what has been spent on the PROJECT to date.

Actual to date (ATD) The amount of BUDGET or time which has been spent to date.

Analogy estimating technique A way to estimate the time and cost needed to develop a DELIVERABLE by comparing it with another deliverable which has similar features and characteristics.

Approved subject to amendments (ASTA) A QUALITY REVIEW outcome which allows for the DELIVERABLE to be approved on the condition that all recorded amendments have been completed and agreed by those who identified them.

Assessment date The date upon which a project HEALTH CHECK was last conducted.

Assumption A condition used for forecasting purposes which has not been proven. An assumption may therefore be considered a risk.

Balanced score card (BSC)	A means by which to measure a company's performance taking into account not only financial outcomes but also matters such as customer relationships, business processes and employee skills and engagement that contribute to those outcomes. It was developed by Robert S. Kaplan and David Norton.
Baseline	An approved date or financial value against which all changes (intended or otherwise) may be compared to determine VARIANCE.
Benefits	The positive outcome sought from a PROJECT that outweighs the investment made in it.
Benefits dependency network	A technique for tracing the audit trail from PROJECT OUTCOME to strategic imperative. It was developed and described by John Ward and Joe Peppard of Cranfield University.
Benefits realisation	The project phase or process where planned benefits are brought to fruition.
Benefits realisation plan	The section of a BUSINESS CASE which describes how the organisation intends to measure and deliver the planned benefits.
Benefits realisation report	A document used after project closure to determine to what extent the intended benefits have been realised and what further action may be needed to bring them to fruition.
Benefits review/ benefits realisation review	A session to determine to what extent the intended benefits have been realised and what further action may be needed to bring them to fruition.
Bottom-up estimating	Used for evaluating the time and cost needed to complete activities or DELIVERABLES at a low level of detail. (See also TOP-DOWN ESTIMATING.)
Budget	The amount of time or money set aside for the completion of a specified DELIVERABLE.

Budgeted cost of work performed (BCWP)	In EARNED VALUE ANALYSIS, the budgeted cost of work which has been completed in the period being measured.
Budgeted cost of work scheduled (BCWS)	In EARNED VALUE ANALYSIS, the budgeted cost of work which was planned in the time being measured.
Business as usual (BAU)	A term used to describe the regular, non-PROJECT work of an organisation.
Business case	A document which describes the financial justification for a PROJECT.
Business plan	A document which describes how an organisation intends to deliver its proposed BUSINESS AS USUAL and change agenda.
Capability maturity model (CMM)	A mechanism for describing the varying levels of an organisation's PROJECT MANAGEMENT effectiveness.
Change control	A process for managing the consequences of intended or unplanned variations in a PROJECT.
Change log	A document used to record and summarise the CHANGE REQUESTS which have been submitted during the life of a PROJECT.
Change request (CR)	A document which describes an application for a change to be made in a PROJECT.
Common data repository	A database or other storage mechanism which holds facts and figures about an organisation's PROJECTS so that management reports about them may be created.
Communications plan	A document which describes how specified stakeholders are to receive the messages which are essential to maintain their engagement in a PROJECT.
Configuration control	A discipline which allows for the management of a PROJECT'S DELIVERABLES.
Contingency	A planned budget of time or money set aside to fund the mitigation of identified RISKS or anticipated change.

Control	The taking of corrective action when something has varied from its plan.
Control cycle	The considered process of delegating work, monitoring and reporting progress, and exercising CONTROL, which leads to the effective maintenance of a plan.
Corporate dashboard	A form of report which provides a level and format of management information appropriate for senior managers in charge of a PORTFOLIO of PROJECTS.
Cost/benefit analysis	A form of numeric comparison between the costs and benefits of a PROJECT, planned or actual, to determine its financial viability.
Cost variation	In EARNED VALUE ANALYSIS, the BUDGETED COST OF WORK PERFORMED minus the ACTUAL COST OF WORK PERFORMED (that is, how much should have been spent to date based on what has been achieved, minus the amount actually spent to date).
Critical path	The sequence of dependent activities with the longest overall DURATION which therefore determines the shortest time possible to complete the PROJECT.
Customer	A PROJECT'S STAKEHOLDER(S) with an interest in the suitability of the DELIVERABLE to meet their needs as a user of it.
Delegation	The assigning of work to members of a project team.
Delegatee	A person or group assigned work by a manager in the PROJECT.
Delegator	A person who assigns work to a member of a PROJECT team.
Deliverable	The outcome of a process which is both definable and measurable in qualitative terms. Other terms used are milestone or product.

Delphi estimating technique	Used for developing a consensus about an estimate through meetings, questionnaires and surveys.
Developer	A PROJECT STAKEHOLDER(s) responsible for developing and implementing a DELIVERABLE which conforms to agreed standards and meets the needs of those who will use it.
Discounted cash flow	An approach to forecasting cash flow which takes into account the future value of money.
Discount factor	The amount by which the net difference between future costs and benefits must be multiplied in order to discount it by a specified amount.
Duration	The time between the start and end dates of an activity. In an ACTIVITY NETWORK, it is the number of days between the EARLIEST START TIME and the EARLIEST FINISH TIME, or the LATEST START TIME and the LATEST FINISH TIME.
Earliest finish time (EFT)	In an ACTIVITY NETWORK, the earliest point at which an activity can finish.
Earliest start time (EST)	In an ACTIVITY NETWORK, the earliest point at which an activity can start.
Earned value analysis (EVA)	A technique which objectively measures a project's performance against time, cost and quality targets.
Effort	The time it would take someone to complete an activity if they were able to work at 100% productivity all the time, unfettered by any other work or distraction. Effort is sometimes called "work".
Error list	A pro forma used in preparation for a QUALITY REVIEW on which are written the faults in a product identified by the reviewers of it.

Escalation conditions The terms defining when a forecast breach of targets must be made known to one's superiors, commonly when a PROJECT MANAGER must inform the PROJECT STEERING GROUP that a project is forecast to deliver off target by more than a certain amount.

Escalation management A management discipline which allows for the creation of certain conditions, the breaching of which enables superiors to take control of a PROJECT from their subordinates.

Estimate to complete (ETC) An estimate of the EFFORT or cost to complete an activity, product or PROJECT beyond what has already been spent.

Estimating sheet A pro forma used to record the data that is most relevant to the creation of a GANTT CHART and RESOURCE PLAN.

External audit Similar to an INTERNAL AUDIT, but conducted by an external party to specific terms of reference in order to identify and attend to any areas of concern within a defined timetable.

Financial dependency network A numeric tool which identifies the financial relationships between projects.

Fit for purpose A term used to describe the suitability of a product or service to meet the intended needs of its users; in other words, whether it is fit for their purposes.

Float In an ACTIVITY NETWORK, the difference between the EARLIEST START TIME and the LATEST START TIME, or the EARLIEST FINISH TIME and the LATEST FINISH TIME. This is the amount by which an activity may slip before it affects any successors. An activity with zero float is said to be on the CRITICAL PATH.

Forecast	An estimate or calculation of what is likely to happen in the future. The term is used in many ways in PROJECTS For example, in project reports the "forecast start date", "forecast end date" or "forecast benefits" describe what is currently considered to be the planned "start date", "end date" or "benefits", given what is known at the time.
Forecast at completion (FAC)	In project reporting, the total EFFORT or cost expected to have been invested by the time a task, PRODUCT or PROJECT has been completed.
Gantt chart	A diagrammatic tool used to illustrate some of the component parts of a plan, principally the time scale. It was originally developed by Henry L. Gantt in 1910.
Head of project management	The manager of a department or RESOURCE POOL within which the prime resources are PROJECT MANAGERS.
Health check	A means by which a PROJECT is reviewed (perhaps by invitation) by those involved in the project, often using buddies. The outcome will be a report identifying opportunities for improvement and areas of strength that could be promoted to others who work on projects. Those working on the project will be responsible for carrying out the actions arising from the health check and there may or may not be a requirement for an external party to check that they are carried out as agreed.
Highlights	Positive events (such as the starting or completion of activities on time and on BUDGET) often reported in the PROJECT FORECAST REPORT in a section of the same name. (See also LOWLIGHTS.)

Internal audit	A formal PROJECT review that takes place perhaps as a result of some evidence of a failing. It should be conducted by someone who is impartial and has the competence to identify opportunities for improvement and propose solutions. It will be the project management team's responsibility to implement these, with progress usually being tracked by the person who conducted the review.
Internal rate of return (IRR)	The discount factor that results when a net present value of zero is achieved in a discounted cash flow. This financial measure is commonly used to compare one project with another.
Issue	A term used in project management to refer to a problem or challenge which has arisen and therefore cannot be prevented, although its effects may still be mitigated to some degree.
Issue management	Identifying, recording, evaluating and controlling the adverse consequences of an ISSUE.
Latest finish time (LFT)	In an ACTIVITY NETWORK, the latest point at which an activity may be completed before it will start having an impact on other activities.
Latest start time (LST)	In an ACTIVITY NETWORK, the latest point at which an activity can commence before it will start having an impact on other activities.
Lessons learned report	A report produced as a result of a LESSONS LEARNED REVIEW after the closure of a project describing the management lessons which may be used to improve the execution of future projects.
Lessons learned review	A session to determine the extent to which a recently completed PROJECT was well managed. The product of this review is a LESSONS LEARNED REPORT.

Lowlights	Negative events (such as the failure to start or complete activities on time or on budget) often reported in the PROJECT FORECAST REPORT in a section of the same name. (See also HIGHLIGHTS.)
Management by objectives (MBO)	An incentive scheme used by many organisations to reward employees for meeting or exceeding specified objectives.
Margin	In the context of a PROJECT, the difference at a point in time between the actual or forecast financially quantified benefits arising and the actual or forecast total project investment plus operational costs.
Matrix management	The planning and controlling of human resources who are involved simultaneously in BUSINESS AS USUAL and PROJECTS.
Milestone	See DELIVERABLE.
Monitoring	Comparing actual progress with planned progress.
Net present value	A measurement in present values of the excess or shortfall of future cash flows.
Overspend	Describes where a planned budget has been, or is forecast to be, exceeded.
Person-day	A measurement of EFFORT.
Plan	A forecast of future events (see also PROJECT PLAN).
Portfolio	A list of PROJECTS characterised by a common BUDGET or department.
Portfolio management team (PMT)	The team charged with commissioning and delivering a value-adding mix of PROJECTS within a BUDGET, aligned with their organisation's strategic and commercial imperatives.
Product	See DELIVERABLE.

Product-based planning	A planning technique which provides for the definition of deliverables as a precursor to estimating the timescale and costs of the activities needed to develop and deliver them.
Product breakdown structure	In PRODUCT-BASED PLANNING, a technique by which a large or complex product is broken down into smaller component parts so that the PROJECT's scope may be more readily clarified.
Product description	In PRODUCT-BASED PLANNING, a technique whereby a product is defined in detail so that it may be more readily estimated, planned, developed, reviewed and approved.
Product flow diagram	In PRODUCT-BASED PLANNING, a technique whereby a project is expressed as a sequence of dependent products, providing the foundations for a time schedule.
Product outline	A table summarising the most important characteristics of a list of products.
Productivity	A measure of the efficiency of a resource to deliver a specified product within a defined budget and timescale.
Programme	A management vehicle for co-ordinating and implementing an organisation's strategy, specifically by linking together an often complex combination of BUSINESS-AS-USUAL activity and new PROJECTS, both of which are focused on the delivery of a defined business objective.
Programme office	A body responsible for providing support and/or assurance to those engaged in the management of a programme. (See also SUPPORT/ASSURANCE FUNCTION.)
Project	A temporary management environment, created to deliver a specified outcome according to a defined business justification.

Project closure	The final STAGE of a PROJECT. It is only when a project is deemed to have met the success criteria of the PROJECT STEERING GROUP that a project can be closed and its management environment dismantled.
Project closure meeting	The last formal meeting of a PROJECT at which the PROJECT STEERING GROUP considers the PROJECT CLOSURE REPORT as a foundation for its decision to close the project.
Project closure report	A document describing the condition of a PROJECT at the point at which closure is requested, thereby enabling the PROJECT STEERING GROUP to make an informed decision.
Project delivery	A STAGE during which the approved PROJECT PLAN is used as a guide to deliver the project's products to time, cost and quality expectations.
Project evaluation and review technique (PERT)	A technique that helps identify the CRITICAL PATH, DURATION and FLOATS of dependent PROJECT activities.
Project forecast report (PFR)	A report produced by a PROJECT MANAGER to communicate the present and intended status of a project to the PROJECT STEERING GROUP, so that corrective actions may be identified to address VARIANCES.
Project governance report (PGR)	A management document, developed by a PROJECT MANAGER during the PROJECT INITIATION stage, to describe how the targets expressed in the BUSINESS CASE may be met. It contains a description of the roles, responsibilities and reporting lines of those involved in the project management team, together with the project plan.
Project initiation	A STAGE during which the necessary preparations are made to justify and plan the PROJECT, and to put in place the management environment which will serve as its foundation.

Project initiation meeting
The first formal meeting of a PROJECT STEERING GROUP at which it considers the BUSINESS CASE, the PROJECT GOVERNANCE REPORT, the USER REQUIREMENTS DOCUMENT and the SOLUTION DESIGN DOCUMENT in order to formally take ownership of a project from the PORTFOLIO MANAGEMENT TEAM. If the project steering group is comfortable with the project governance report, it will also consider instructing the PROJECT MANAGER to commence the delivery stage.

Project life cycle
The series of STAGES which allows a PORTFOLIO MANAGEMENT TEAM and a PROJECT STEERING GROUP to control the progress of a PROJECT.

Project management
The principles and techniques used for the identification, initiation, delivery, closure and benefits realisation of a PROJECT.

Project management office
A body responsible for providing support and/or assurance to those engaged in the management of a PROJECT. It may be called the project office or project support office (see also SUPPORT/ASSURANCE FUNCTION).

Project manager (PM)
The person responsible for planning, monitoring and controlling a PROJECT, to meet expectations of timeliness, cost and quality.

Project office
See PROJECT MANAGEMENT OFFICE.

Project outline
A document recording the answers to the most important management questions before a project has been commissioned. It is used to seek sufficient investment to fund the PROJECT INITIATION stage.

Project plan
A management document produced by the PROJECT MANAGER as part of the PROJECT GOVERNANCE REPORT. It is used to show how expectations for time, cost and quality will be met.

Project register	A log of PROJECTS and some associated detail, used by the PORTFOLIO MANAGEMENT TEAM to assist in the planning, monitoring and control of the PORTFOLIO.
Project sponsor	The most senior individual involved in a PROJECT (and PROJECT STEERING GROUP), chiefly responsible for leading the project to a successful outcome, specifically ensuring that the intended benefits are delivered and that they sufficiently outweigh the total investment.
Project start date	The date acknowledged and approved by the PORTFOLIO MANAGEMENT TEAM as that at which the PROJECT INITIATION stage should or did commence.
Project steering group (PSG)	A project's most senior management authority, composed of experts from customer, developer and commercial backgrounds. The PSG serves as the point from which all original instructions derive, and to which any matters outside the authority of its subordinates can be referred.
Project support office	See PROJECT MANAGEMENT OFFICE.
Quality	The features and characteristics of a product which affect its ability to meet the defined needs of those who will use it.
Quality control	The process of identifying failures to meet quality expectations and taking the necessary action to correct them.
Quality criteria	Closed questions or quantifiable statements used to describe the extent to which a feature or characteristic of a product will meet the defined needs of those who will use it. For example: "Does this glossary explain every term used in this book?" Also called quality measures. (See also SUCCESS CRITERIA.)
Quality log	A table used to record the progress of a product through its development life cycle so that a failure of quality at any point may be identified and dealt with.

Quality measure	See QUALITY CRITERIA.
Quality method	The various means by which QUALITY CONTROL may be exercised.
Quality plan	A management document forming part of the PROJECT PLAN that describes how the project will deliver a product which meets the expectations of those who will use it.
Quality review	A QUALITY METHOD commonly used to determine by formal or informal means the extent to which a product may be considered fit for its intended purpose.
Revise and reschedule (RAR)	An outcome from a QUALITY REVIEW indicating that the product is not ready or needs significant change. Alternatively, this outcome may be because there were not enough reviewers or they were unprepared or unqualified.
Red, amber, green (RAG)	The colours commonly used to provide a graphical representation of ESCALATION CONDITIONS. Green indicates that a target is forecast to be met. Amber indicates that it is not, but that the authority to take corrective action remains with the person currently in charge. Red indicates that the escalation conditions have been breached and that the matter must be immediately passed to a higher level.
Resource	An asset used in the development and delivery of a PROJECT's outcome – people, capital, machinery, and so on.
Resource levelling	The process by which the over- and under-utilisation of project resources is minimised. Resource levelling is a function of many PROJECT MANAGEMENT software support tools.
Resource plan	A management document forming part of the PROJECT PLAN which describes what resources the PROJECT will require, when, and how they will be deployed.

Resource pool	A group of people falling within a single management structure, usually with a common skills profile. They might otherwise be called a department or a team from which people may be selected to participate in PROJECTS.
Resource pool manager	The head of a RESOURCE POOL, responsible for making the most effective use of the people in the manager's charge.
Risk	An exposure to the adverse consequences of future events.
Risk evaluation	The process of determining whether or not a RISK is worthy of the investment needed to mitigate it.
Risk factor	The result of multiplying together the likelihood and impact of a RISK. This is helpful in determining which level of management may authorise the necessary mitigation(s).
Risk identification	The process of uncovering RISKS to a project so that they may be evaluated and assigned for mitigation.
Risk impact	A numeric measure denoting the effect that a RISK may be thought to have on a PROJECT or the wider organisation.
Risk likelihood	A numeric measure denoting the probability that a RISK may become an ISSUE.
Risk management	The control of exposure to the adverse consequences of future events.
Risk matrix	A graphical way of showing the relative likelihood and impact of identified RISKS and ISSUES.
Risk mitigation	The process by which a RISK's impact, likelihood, or both are made less severe or less painful.
Risk owner	The person or body empowered to authorise the mitigation of a RISK.

Risk qualification The process of determining the likelihood and impact of a RISK so that its RISK FACTOR may be known.

Risk register A document used to record identified RISKS and ISSUES, together with other information necessary for their management, such as their impact, likelihood, factor and mitigation.

Schedule delay In EARNED VALUE ANALYSIS, when the BUDGETED COST OF WORK SCHEDULED is the same as the BUDGETED COST OF WORK PERFORMED minus the date when the data was captured, measured in days.

Schedule variation In EARNED VALUE ANALYSIS, the BUDGETED COST OF WORK PERFORMED minus the BUDGETED COST OF WORK SCHEDULED (how much should have been expended to date based upon what has been achieved minus the amount that was planned to have been spent to date).

Scribe The person assigned responsibility for recording the actions and decisions arising from a QUALITY REVIEW.

Single version of the truth (SVOT) A term used to emphasise the importance of a clear, current and commonly held interpretation of a PROJECT plan.

Solution design document (SDD) A document used to describe how the needs of the users or CUSTOMERS of the PROJECT are to be met.

Sponsor See PROJECT SPONSOR.

Stage A period within a PROJECT that has a clearly identified start date, end date, budget and DELIVERABLE(s), which can be used to facilitate estimating and provide the PROJECT STEERING GROUP with points at which the viability of the project may be reaffirmed.

Stage meeting	A meeting of a PROJECT STEERING GROUP which takes place just before the beginning of a STAGE (and just before the end of the closure stage) to allow the project steering group to formally confirm (or not) the completion of the previous stage, approve the plan for the next stage and reaffirm the project's viability.
Stakeholder	A person or group with an interest in the PROJECT, whether through their involvement with the change or because they will be affected by its outcome.
Stakeholder map	A graphical technique used to identify a PROJECT'S STAKEHOLDERS.
Stakeholder matrix	A graphical technique used to prioritise a PROJECT'S STAKEHOLDERS so that resources may be used efficiently to manage their respective interests.
Standard product/ project estimating technique	Used to identify a cost for a common product or PROJECT, based on knowledge of its size and complexity.
Success criteria	Closed questions or quantifiable statements used to describe the extent to which a feature or characteristic of a PROJECT will meet the defined needs of those who will use it. Success criteria are used to express how the completion of a project will be measured, whereas QUALITY CRITERIA are commonly applied to an individual product.
Support/assurance definition report	A document used to describe what products and services a SUPPORT/ASSURANCE FUNCTION may offer, and how it will do so.
Support/Assurance Function (SAF)	A body of support and/or assurance to those engaged in the management of a project or programme. (See also PROGRAMME OFFICE; PROJECT MANAGEMENT OFFICE.)
Systemised approach	The underlying method and discipline which articulates an organisation's approach to PROJECT MANAGEMENT.

Team leader	An individual charged with meeting a PROJECT MANAGER's expectations of time, cost and quality through the effective planning, monitoring and control of a team within a project.
Time schedule	A representation (often graphical) of a project's timescale.
Timesheets	Forms used to capture the effort invested by members of the PROJECT team on the development of products assigned to them, together with the actual and estimated start and end dates, so that the PROJECT PLAN may be updated with progress.
Top-down estimating	Used at the commencement of a project to obtain a high-level forecast of its entire timescale, cost and DELIVERABLES. This may be corroborated with the BOTTOM-UP ESTIMATE created at the commencement of each STAGE.
Training needs analysis (TNA)	A document used to identify the training needs of those involved in project work and how, for each individual, they should be met.
Underspend	A term used to describe where not all of a planned BUDGET has been spent, or is forecast to be spent.
User requirements document (URD)	A document used to describe the needs of the CUSTOMERS that the PROJECT's outcome must satisfy.
Variance	The difference between the BASELINE and the forecast at completion, be it a date or a monetary value.
Work	See EFFORT.
Work distribution estimating technique	Used to attribute proportionate values to PROJECT STAGES or resource types, based on knowledge of those values for previous projects.

INDEX

Page numbers in *italics* refer to Figures; those in **bold** type refer to Tables.